Fiddes Castle

CONTENTS

Maps and notes on other sites occur at the ends of the gazetteers

INTRODUCTION

The word castle came into use in Britain in the 11th century. It was recognised that the many privately owned defensible residences with which William, Duke of Normandy and his followers had filled England after their conquest of that country in 1066 represented something new both in function and appearance. Strategically positioned castles allowed the new Norman landowning class to establish their rule over the Saxon populace. Under a new system called feudalism the King gave units of land called manors to tenants-in-chief in return for specified annual periods of military service. The tenants then in turn gave land to their knights on the same basis.

Feudalism was introduced to Scotland in the time of David I. He ruled Strathclyde from 1107 to 1124 under his brother Alexander I, and then himself ruled the whole kingdom until 1153. David lived much of his early life in England under the capable rule of Henry I and became Earl of Huntingdon as a result of his marriage in 1113. David saw the advantages of feudalism over the system previously customary in Scotland when the King was little more than a noble with a special title, having little power outside his own domain. The imposition of the new system increased the King's power and provided him with a regular army, although many districts still remained semi-independent. During this period primogeniture, or automatic inheritance of a lord's estates and inheritable honours by his eldest surviving son took the place of older systems under which any adult male relative with recognised leadership qualities might claim to be his successor, which resulted all too often in family quarrels.

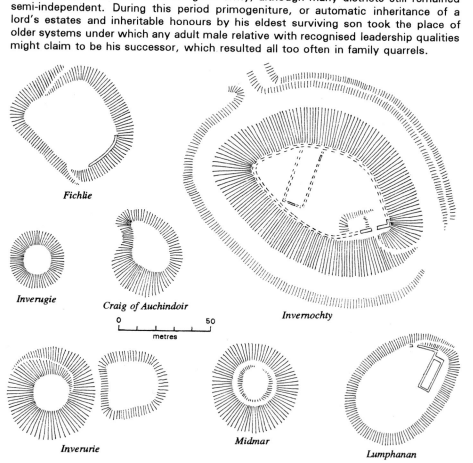

Fichlie

Inverugie

Craig of Auchindoir

Invernochty

0   50

metres

Inverurie

Midmar

Lumphanan

Plans of mottes in Aberdeenshire

With the possible exception of a long-lost castle of mortared stone at Invergowrie said to have been built by King Edgar in the early 1100s, the strongholds of rulers in Scotland before King David's time took the form of low unmortared stone ramparts or wooden stockades on either craggy hilltops or artificial islands called crannogs. Crude huts of timber, daub and wattle, or unmortared stone would be scattered around in the enclosure. Our knowledge of fortifications and life in general during the so-called Dark Ages between when the Romans gave up their occupation of the Scottish Lowlands and the reign of David I is still patchy but it is clear that the castles built by Norman knights brought to Scotland by David represented something radically new. These castles were partly residences, and partly refuges from the initially hostile native people of the land. They served as symbols of status and power and as home-farms from which the manors were administered and to which produce was brought.

The new castles generally did not at first have mortared stone walls for the construction of which years of security and peace would be needed plus far more masons than were then available in Scotland. Instead they were hastily erected structures of earth and wood. Commonly earth was dug from a circular ditch and piled within it to form a mound called a motte on which was erected a wooden house or tower forming the lord's residence within a small palisaded court. There might be on one side or around the motte a base-court or bailey defined by a ditch with a stockade on the inner side and containing a hall suitable for feasts and gatherings of the lord's followers, plus a kitchen, chapel, stables, barns, workshops, etc. Many Scottish mottes such as Inverugie lack baileys, but Inverurie and Duffus are good examples of the classic motte and bailey type more common in England and Wales, and a truncated motte lies beside a bailey now filled with later stone buildings at Huntly. Where possible mottes were created by scarping natural features such as spurs and mounds of glacial deposits. The mottes at Invernochty and Lumphanan formerly defended by water-filled ditches have summits large enough to contain all those buildings that might otherwise be within a bailey. The Lumphanan mound is quite low and could be regarded as a transitional type between comparatively high 12th century mounds and the 13th century type of homestead moat with a low platform, usually quadrangular, as at Fordoun and Caskieben (Keith Hall). These homestead moats are not castles, merely manor houses surrounded by wet ditches to help with drainage on marshy low lying sites, to provide a habitat for water-fowl, eels, and fish (all then an important part of the diet of the landed classes), and to help keep domestic animals in and wild ones out. The moats were also status symbols, a way of distinguishing between the homes of the upper class and otherwise similar houses of those lower down the social scale, for only a lord could command the labour force needed create a moat. The timber buildings of all these sites have perished long ago although occasionally traces of wooden posts on them are revealed by excavation.

The Bass Mound of Inverurie

Inverugie Motte

Grampian had more 13th century stone castles of enclosure, i.e, with curtain walls around courtyards, than any other part of Scotland. Most, if not all, of them were destroyed by Robert Bruce and his followers in the period 1308-13 to prevent them being used by the invading English during the Wars of Independence. Some, such as Aberdeen, which has vanished, and Cowie and Migvie of which little remain, were never rebuilt. Foundations survive of a 2m thick wall probably of c1200-20 around the mound summit at Invernochty, then the chief seat of the Earldom of Mar. It was superseded in this function by Kildrummy built on the orders of Alexander II in the 1220s. Parts of the 2.3m thick wall around a polygonal court remain plus the lower parts of a hall. A chapel raised over an undercroft was added in the 1240s and then Alexander III c1260-80 added a round tower keep with its rooms covered with dome-vaults, and three other flanking towers, one a full round, the others D-shaped. The Durward seat at Coull of c1250-75 had a similar layout with a more modestly sized round keep, at least one small flanking tower, a twin towered gatehouse facing the approach, and a domestic range on the opposite (and more secure) side of the court. Kildrummy also had a twin towered gatehouse, although there are reasons for thinking it was added in the 1290s on the orders of Edward I of England. The palace of the Bishops of Elgin at Spynie also had a polygonal court and a round tower similar in size to the keep at Coull but it has recently been ascribed to the 14th century.

A stone keep on a motte at Duffus

The lower parts of the walls around a square court remain of Kincardine, a royal castle also probably built for Alexander II c1220-40. The curtain wall at Fyvie may also have been of this period but the square corner towers were probably not added until the late 14th or early 15th century. The Comyns became powerful in NE Scotland after one of them in 1210 married the heiress of the last of the Celtic Earls of Buchan. They built several stone castles, their lands being vulnerable to Norse raids, and their seats at Balvenie and Lochindorb are among the best preserved of their period (c1270-90) in Scotland. Lochindorb lies on an island and has four round corner towers plus a plain outer court of c1300. Balvenie has been remodelled in the 15th and 16th centuries and has lost the round towers which stood at three corners. An apartment block projects from the fourth corner and there are remains of a hall block in the corner diagonally opposite. Of other Comyn castles there remain the northern half of a rectangular court at Banff, fragments of walls and what may represent a round keep and a twin-towered gatehouse at Kineddar, and parts of an outer wall and a rectangular keep at Dundarg. There are slight remains of another keep and a court at the royal castle of Elgin and of promontory castles at Rothes and Gauldwell.

Not enough remains of the keeps at Elgin and Dundarg for us to be sure of the internal arrangements. Dundarg appears to have only had two storeys with possibly a hall and private chamber side by side over a storage basement, as appears to have also been the case in the wide keep at Dunnideer. Elgin may have had a third storey, i.e. with a private chamber on top of a hall raised over a basement as is the arrangement in the tower at Drum thought to have been under construction for Alexander III as a hunting seat at the time of his death in 1286, and probably not completed until the 1320s. There each storey is vaulted, the corners are rounded, and there are plain battlements upon a single row of corbels. Only the basements now remain of other early towers at Hynd and Aucherhouse. It should be noted that in the medieval period towers were simply called such (occasionally the word donjon is also used) and the terms keep and tower house (i.e. a house with rooms stacked one above another) used to describe these buildings are of much more recent origin.

Chapel & Warden's Tower, Kildrummy

Drum Castle

Dunnottar: The Keep.

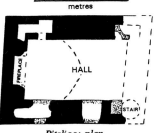

Roof at Darnaway

HALL

2nd STOREY

Cairnbulg: plan

HALL

2nd STOREY

Edzell: plan

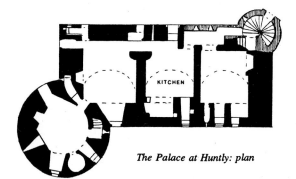

KITCHEN

The Palace at Huntly: plan

0 ———————————— 10
metres

FIREPLACE

HALL

STAIR

Pitsligo: plan

Thanks to a scarcity of contemporary records, a lack of accurately datable architectural features, and the limited amount of information from excavations, the dating of many early secular buildings in Scotland is still uncertain. Ascribed to the 14th century are the towers at Hallforest, Skene, Castle Maud, and Finavon. The last two are reduced to basement level but it appears that all four were entered at hall level as at Drum and Auchterhouse and access down to the basement was only by means of a hatch in a vault or wooden floor. Other 14th century keeps at Duffus and Dunnottar had their entrances at ground level. Duffus is a very wide building of just two storeys. At least part of the basement was used as an office or living room and above was a hall and chamber side by side. Of the same period is the plain wall around the bailey. Dunnottar is fairly securely dated to the 1390s and is a much smaller but loftier L-plan building with a projecting wing containing a tiny kitchen at hall level. The parapet at the top was carried on a corbel table and had tiny projecting angle rounds. What has now become a wing at Glamis is thought to be a much altered late 14th century block containing a hall over a kitchen. The block has a round tower at one corner, i.e. a similar plan to the hall block at Rait, near Nairn. Kindrochit has the lower part of a huge and massively walled hall block, probably of c1370-80, part of which was removed c1400 to make way for a large tower house.

The tower houses at Pitsligo, Tolquhon, Cairnbulg and Glamis are thought to be of c1425-40, and those of Drumin and Old Slains may be of the same period if not slightly earlier. Glamis is L-planned with private rooms in the wing and a main block long in proportion to its width. All these towers seem to have had their entrances at hall level although Pitsligo and Tolquhon also had entrances at ground level as well. The L-planned towers at Huntly and Inverquarity may also be of this period, but those at Auchindoun, Affleck, Ravenscraig, and Thornton are of c1475-1500. At Thornton and Affleck the wings are small and contain only staircases, plus in the case of Affleck a tiny but exquisite chapel above where the main staircase ends. Auchindoun had a rib-vault (possibly a later insertion) over the hall. Ravenscraig is an enormous and extremely massive building, one of the largest of its type in Europe, with a tier of private rooms at one end of the hall and another such tier in the wing. Castle Fraser, Guthrie, and Spynie have rectangular towers of the 1460s, the last having a tier of bedchambers in one side wall thought to be safe from bombardment and being built over the basement of the earlier round keep. The rectangular towers at Kinnairdy, Benholm and Broughty are probably all of the 1490s.

Huntly, Druminnor, Arbuthnott, and Findlater (principal seats respectively of the important families of Gordon, Forbes, Arbuthnott, and the Banffshire Ogilvies) all have mid 15th century buildings containing a hall and private chamber end to end on the upper storey. Such a building was known in 15th and 16th century Scotland as a palace. In each case the rooms below the hall and chamber were used as offices or living spaces rather than for storage and, except at Arbuthnott, the fall of the ground allows another storey for the storage and preparation of food and drink below courtyard level. There was once a fifth building of this class built by the Abernethys at Rothiemay, and Darnaway (where the only ancient feature now remaining is a magnificent open roof) seems to have been another. Duffus has a hall-block on one side of the bailey, to which the block now replaced by a later house at Airlie, seat of the main line of the Ogilvies, was similar. This building lay within a court on a promontory like that at Arbuthnott, except that both the natural and man-made defences were considerably stronger. In these cases the main block was safely hidden behind the defences but at Glenbervie there is a main block probably of the 1490s facing the approach and having on that side two round towers. Cortachy, another Ogilvie seat, is also thought to have been a courtyard castle from which two of the round towers survive, whilst the court had Lauriston had rectangular towers. Fyvie, an earlier courtyard castle, probably gained its square corner towers in this period.

Old postcard of Findlater Castle

Buildings datable to the first half of the 16th century are not common in Grampian and Angus. The L-plan tower at Edzell with a wing just big enough to contain a spiral stair takes pride of place. As in the late 15th century towers the basement is subdivided into more than one cellar, but a new feature is the series of wide mouthed gunports opening out of these rooms, firearms now being in vogue. Inverallochy has a tower, now very shattered, in one corner of a small court with domestic ranges on either side, probably all of c1510-40. The towers at Balquhain, Redcastle and Corgarff are also of this period, but the last has been remodelled. The Kinnaird's Head tower belongs typologically with these towers and has a parapet with angle rounds, although it is probably as late as the 1560s. Other early to mid 16th century buildings are the main block and a wing at Castle Grant, a much damaged tower and court at Inverallochy, and considerable parts of Spynie Palace.

Houses of the period 1560 to 1620 with castellated features are very numerous. Many were built as seats of members of minor branches of old established families. A further impetus for the building of new houses was the large number of former monastic and episcopal estates acquired by laymen at the Reformation. These buildings were not intended to withstand cannon-fire or sieges lasting more than a few hours but they were not easy to break into and thus gave some security from small parties of raiders. Feuds within and between families were common and raids by Highland brigands not unknown so security had to be borne in mind even if comfort normally took first place. There was usually just one entrance doorway commonly secured by a hinged gate of interwoven iron bars known as a yett. These existed by the end of the 14th century and one is mentioned in a mid 15th century licence for the building of the tower at Inverquarity. Usually there was an oak door secured by a drawbar just inside the yett. Storage and food preparation spaces at ground level are almost invariably barrel-vaulted and lighted only by small windows (often just slits) and horizontal splayed gunloops. Larger windows higher up were secured with iron stanchions or projecting grilles. They made the buildings death traps on the rare occasions when either maliciously (as at Corgarff and Frendraught) or accidentally they were set on fire and have usually been removed, although their marks often remain.

From the mid 16th century onwards stones carved with dates, initials, and arms commonly appear in niches over entrance doorways, on dormer window pediments, and occasionally on other features such as fireplaces and the brackets or skewputs supporting the stepped gables fashionable in Scotland during this period. Original furnishings and panelling where they survive may also have these features. The dates usually refer to new construction or additions or remodelling, although there a reasons for thinking that in some instances they refer to an inheritance, marriage or coming of age. Buildings accounts and other reliable contemporary documents indicating periods of construction rarely survive before the 18th century so these stones give much useful information.

1596 datestone, Crathes

1603 datestone & Royal Arms, Pitsligo

1581 datestone, Corse

In recent years there has been much debate about the provision of so-called defensive or castellated features in late 16th century Scottish buildings. It is now accepted that in many cases they were for visual effect as status symbols rather than for active defence. Splayed gunloops or small circular shot-holes are often grouped around the entrance. Shot-holes also sometimes appear under the sills of upper windows or even in the jambs (as at Knock) of these window embrasures. The multiple groups at Fordyce and Tolquhon can only be regarded as being for show and few of the buildings have sufficient loops for firearms provided in such a way as to allow an attacker at any range or angle to be fired upon by a concealed defender. Machicolation or slots allowing defenders to drop or fire missiles down from the upper parts without exposing themselves occurred occasionally, as over the entrances at Corgarff and Blairfindy. After 1550 continuous wall-walks and parapets went out of fashion elsewhere in Scotland although in the North-East they remained in use longer. A common compromise in this area c1600 is for a wing or tower to have a flat roof forming a look-out platform with a parapet or balcony and the remainder of the building to be roofed over down on to the outer edges of the walls but with gabled dormer windows providing light for a topmost storey partly in the roof. The angle rounds found on earlier parapets were retained in the form of conical roofed "pepperpot" turrets or bartizans providing closets opening off the topmost storey. These bartizans are often carried on finely moulded corbelled courses. Bartizans often contain shot-holes but they were basically provided for show rather than defence.

It has long been customary to refer to late 16th and early 17th century castellated houses in Scotland as castles, most of them being marked as such on Ordnance Survey maps. The word castle has connotations of a long-lost romantic age of knights and chivalry and has since the late 18th century made the buildings sound more appealing to tourists. However contemporaries mostly described them as houses, the word castle being normally reserved for older buildings of the courtyard type. The expression "tower and fortalice" was commonly used in the 15th and early 16th centuries to describe a tower with an accompanying court and outbuildings, but later buildings in Grampian and Angus are rarely described as towers, only a few such as Knock and Craigievar having a truly tower-like form with their height noticeably greater than their length. Recently some post-Reformation buildings have begun to be referred to as chateaux. Many of them, such as Dudhope, do resemble the post-medieval castle-like country houses of France, although it appears that inspiration for the planning and architectural detail of some buildings in the North-East, and also supplies of timber, came from the Baltic countries, with which there was considerable trade.

The "chateau" of Dudhope

Most buildings of this period have the lowest storey divided into at least two or three rooms connected by a passage to the entrance and main staircase. Usually there is a kitchen with a fireplace often extending the full width of the room. Ovens are not all that common (they were provided in outbuildings) but sometimes there is a slop drain or an inlet to allow water to be supplied through the wall. Wells either within the mansions or in their accompanying courtyards and outbuildings are surprisingly uncommon. Usually next to the kitchen is a room with a service stair used either for storing wine or as an additional space where food was prepared, and there is normally at least one other cellar for storing food. In the hall above the old pattern of having a fireplace in the end wall behind the laird's table with the main windows set close by in the side walls is discarded (except at Pitcur) in favour of a fireplace near the middle of a side wall and a more even distribution of windows, thus allowing the whole room to be heated and lighted better. The abandonment of wall-walks on the main block made the provision of chimney stacks on side walls easier. Usually there was a private room or withdrawing room leading off the hall into which the laird and chosen companions could withdraw after a public main meal at the end of the day with the whole household in the hall. Above the hall and private room would be one or two storeys of bedrooms for the laird, his immediate adult relations, and guests. Some servants would sleep in attic rooms often unheated and lighted only by tiny windows in the end gables. Other servants might sleep in the rooms of their masters who obtained a little privacy by means of four poster beds fitted with curtains.

Corbelling is used in almost every building of this era, not only to carry parapets and bartizans where they occur, but square caphouses upon round towers and turrets and to support turrets containing stairs to upper rooms. Glenbuchat and Midmar have rare instances of arches being used instead of corbelling to carry turret stairs. Round corners squared off just below either the eaves or where bartizans project occur at Balfluig, Craigievar, Crathes, Fedderate, Monymusk, Tillycairn, Tilquillie and Udny.

Craigievar Castle

A bartizan on ornamental corbelling at Brodie

North-East Scotland tended to be conservative in architectural fashion as well as in politics and religion. In a closely related group of buildings erected for Catholic lords in the 1570s and 80s at Craig, Gight, Towie Barclay, and Delgatie the walls are rather thicker than is normal for this period elsewhere in Scotland. Some of the upper rooms had rib-vaults of a medieval type, although actually rare in secular buildings of any period in Scotland. They are all L-planned with the wing containing the laird's private room over a kitchen. In each case a passage leads between the kitchen and two or three cellars in the main block to a wide spiral stair in the far end wall. Delgatie is lofty and tower-like, but Craig and Gight were more cubical in form with only three main storeys. Fedderate, now very fragmentary, seems to have been another building of this type. The feature of a passage between the wing and main block to a stair on the far side occurs in thinner walled buildings of more modest size at Colquhonnie, Crombie, Corse and Knockhall. The last two have a projecting turret containing the stair and Corse additionally has another round turret on the main block far corner.

Monymusk, Crathes and Balbegno are L-plans where the re-entrant angle between the main block and wing is partly filled in to provide space for staircases and extra chambers. There are vaulted halls in the last two and at Craigston, which has two wings on the same side, and Craigievar, which has a wing placed to flank two sides of the main block and a turret in the larger of the two re-entrant angles. Balfluig has a similar plan to Craigievar except for the turret. Forter, Flemington and Blairfindy also have single wings flanking two sides of the main block. In each case the wing contained a wide staircase from the entrance to the hall and then a turret stair corbelled out over the re-entrant angle rose up to serve bedrooms both in the main block and the upper part of the wing. This is a common arrangement in this period and is also found in the more conventional L-plans with only one re-entrant angle at Kellie, Braikie, Fordyce, Gardyne, and Inchdrewer as first built. Tillycairn and Braemar have round stair turrets in the re-entrant angle rising the full height of the building. Glamis, a remodelled older tower, also has one. A block added at Balvenie in the 1550s also has this plan with the added refinement of a round tower on the outermost angle.

Mansions of the period 1560-1620 in North-East Scotland commonly have the so-called Z-plan with round or square towers or wings set at diagonally opposite corners of a main block which could be anything from a square to a long rectangle in shape, and of either three or four storeys. This allows all-round flanking fire but only a few examples have enough gunports and shotholes to really exploit the plan-form to best advantage in this respect. At least as important was that this plan form allowed both the wings and main block to contain windows on all four sides. Terpersie, Claypotts, Powrie, Pitcaple, Colliston, and Careston all date from the 1560s and 70s and have two round towers, as do the rather later Cluny and Benholm's Lodging at Aberdeen. Hatton, Tilquillie, Glenbuchat, Keith Hall and Arnage all have two square wings. At Beldorney, Carnousie, Harthill, Park and Vayne a round tower contained the laird's suite whilst a square wing contained guest rooms over the main stair from the entrance to the hall. Generally there is both a main stair and a private stair serving the laird's suite. Castle Fraser, Cairnbulg and Huntly are older buildings rebuilt or extended into Z-plans whilst Brodie seems to have been designed as an L-plan building but soon extended into a Z by the addition of a square tower. Ballindalloch is Z-planned with an extra round tower containing the main stair in the middle of one side.

Abergairn, Abergeldie, Ballinshoe, Clova and Pitfichie have a single round tower at a corner of the main block. Aboyne has a round corner tower and a square wing on an adjacent corner, whilst Inverugie had two round towers on one side and a round turret on the other side towards a large court. Melgund is a very interesting instance of a house of the 1560s made to look like an embattled tower of c1500 with a later hall-block added to it. Fiddes is L-planned with several corner turrets, whilst Balbithan is a sprawling L-plan of more than one period and Pitcur and Kilmaichlie are T-plans.

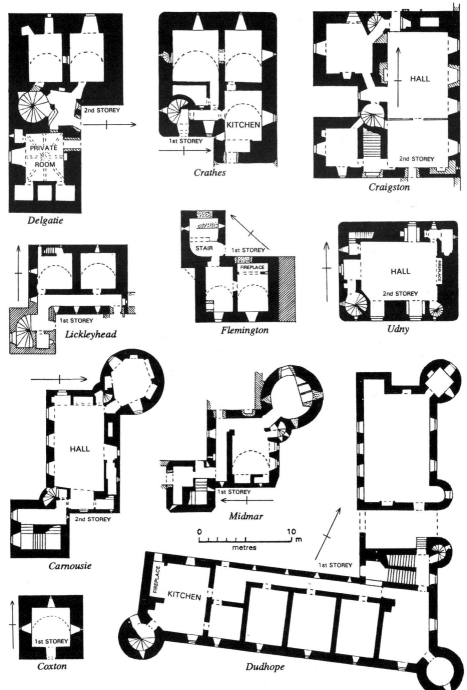

Plans of late 16th century castellated houses

Boyne and Dudhope are both courtyard castles with round corners and a twin towered gatehouse in the middle of one side. In each case the hall and main apartments lay in a long range on the left hand side of the court as you entered. The older castle at Fyvie with square corner towers was also rebuilt into a mansion with the same layout. Craig (Angus) had a square court with ranges on all sides and non-projecting square corner towers. Boddam was also built around a court, but lacks towers and was altogether lower and less impressive. Mains, Barra, and Muchalls all had three ranges with a screen wall on the fourth side. At the last two the screen was hardly high enough to be defensive, but that at Mains, which is a generation earlier, had bartizans, including one over the gate with machicolations. Mains is also noted for its lofty caphouse over a stair turret projecting into the court from one range. Barra has a number of round towers on the outer corners. The domestic ranges at Dunnottar are also built a round a court. One range contains a row of private rooms with a gallery along, another the hall, a third a suite for the Countess, and the fourth an earlier chapel. The Earl Marischall's suite, built as late as 1640, projects awkwardly from the junction of the hall and the Countess's suite. Also of note at Dunnottar are two other detached ranges and a third range overlooking an entrance impressively commanded by huge gunports. Of courts attached to more tower-like structures we have a fragment of walling with a neat little gatehouse at Harthill and one long wall with a simple gateway and a round corner turret at Craigievar, plus single corner turrets in which were dovecots at Pitlurg and Knockhall. It would appear that these houses usually had an outbuilding, "the laigh biggin", which was basically a multi-purpose barn, but no examples survive. Auchendoun, Edzell, Pitsligo, and Tolquhon are instances of late 16th century courts containing new lodgings being added to earlier towers. Each has a single round flanking tower, and Tolquhon also has a square tower at the corner diagonally opposite and a twin round turrets flanking the gateway. At both Pitsligo and Tolquhon the old tower rooms were relegated to secondary use and a new set of chambers were provided for the laird. Both have a long gallery in which pictures could be displayed and indoor exercise taken, positioned in the upper storey of a range adjoining a wide new staircase up to the laird's suite.

Old postcard of Inverugie Castle

Long galleries also occur at Craigievar, Craigston, and Crathes where they are positioned in the way that was customary in Elizabethan houses in England, on the top-most storey. The Bell family of masons worked on these three houses, and at Castle Fraser, Cluny, Midmar, and Muchalls, and Pitfichie, although in several instances they seem to have been mostly employed to graft fantastically picturesque upperworks onto plain structures begun under other craftsmen some years before. The provision of label-shaped mouldings and flat-roofed lookout points with balustrades are characteristic of work designed by the Bells in the period 1595 to 1625. Each building managed to end up looking distinctively different, Cluny for instance having had a unique multi-sided caphouse, now destroyed, upon one of its round towers.

Rough rubble external wall faces were usually harled, leaving only the dressed stone surrounds of windows and doorways and corbelling uncovered. Entire wall faces of finely cut ashlar blocks rarely survive in these later buildings. Ashlar was sometimes used for the uppermost parts of staircase turrets and for thinly walled bartizans and was normally left unharled. Cut stones prepared by highly skilled craftsmen have always been expensive and retain their value. There is evidence of ashlar-faced upper portions of some buildings having been dismantled, as on the stair turret at Pitsligo.

Innes House

Craig Castle

Castle Fraser

Ceiling at Crathes

The internal wall faces of castles and houses of all periods were plastered and either painted with Biblical or heroic scenes or covered with hangings with similar themes. Wainscoting only really came into fashion in the 17th century, and carpets were rare until the 16th century. Hall floors might be of polished slabs laid on top of the vaults of cellars below but other floors were normally of planks laid on heavy beams resting either on a beam called a wall-plate set on a row of corbels, or on an offset in the wall-thickness or in holes in the walls. Floors were often covered with straw or rushes. Both ceiling beams and the plaster or boards between them might be painted, again with biblical or heroic scenes, simple patterns, or heraldry and other allusions to family history. Windows in the medieval period were often closed with wooden shutters but by the 16th century glass was more common. Windows at Benholm's Lodging at Aberdeen and the tower house at Spynie have been restored in recent years to their original form with leaded glass in the upper part and pairs of wooden shutters below. The sash windows usually found in the larger openings of still inhabited towers and houses are insertions of the 18th and 19th centuries. Latrines with shoots descending to a pit or outlet at the foot of the walls are uncommon in buildings of the post-Reformation period when chamber pots were in use. Fireplaces sometimes have impressive hoods supported on moulded jambs. Others have lintels of many stones which are joggled (cut to a dog-leg shape) as at Powrie.

By the 16th century even the most modest tower house would have beside it a walled garden, a dovecot, an orchard, and various outbuildings providing storage and workshop space. These adjuncts are frequently mentioned in 16th century documents and were essential both from a practical point of view and as status symbols of the rank and wealth of the owners. Edzell has a particularly fine walled garden of the turn of the 16th and 17th centuries with an assortment of interesting statues. In some cases garden enclosures or dovecots have survived the destruction of the main house.

In the 17th century there was a tendency to make walls thinner and for the windows to be arranged in tiers, as at Bognie, a simple rectangle without vaulting. Pittulie of the 1630s has a lofty wing with diagonally set oriels on the outer corners, whilst the main block is long and low and without vaulting. The mansion at Drum lies on one side of a court and has boldly projecting square towers on the outer corners. Innes and Leslie are identically planned buildings of the 1640s and 1660s respectively with a square turret containing a scale-and-platt staircase and surmounted by a flat roof and balustrade set within the re-entrant angle of an L-plan. Leslie still has bartizans, as does the original rectangular block of the same period at Leith Hall, an unusually late survival of this motif. Leslie even has shot-holes around the entrance, yet it is advanced enough to have a form of central heating for the staircase. A similarly planned house at Cluny Crichton also has shotholes around the entrance. The small tower dated 1644 at Coxton seems well equipped to withstand an attack, having an upper floor entrance plus vaults at each level making the building fire-proof. It has shot-holes in its three bartizans, one of which is a square open platform with machicolations. By the late 17th century, lairds' houses were mostly plain and simple structures lacking even mock defensive features, which only returned with the early 19th century Romantic Revival. An exception was the huge mansion with square corner towers of c1670 at Panmure. During the 18th century it was not uncommon for conical roofed turrets to be cut down and the main roofs swept over the stumps because of difficulty of maintenance or because a building had been downgraded in function and no longer needed to pretend to be a castle. Inchdrewer has an example whilst these at Inglismaldie have now been restored to their original form.

Fireplace at Powrie

Park Castle

Ornamental entrance at Huntly

Several castles in Grampian and Angus played a part in the Covenant Wars of the 1630s and 40s, and they were involved in the struggles between the exiled Stuarts and the regimes of William III and the Hanovarian monarchs more than other buildings elsewhere in Scotland. Many estates were confiscated after the 1715 and 1746 rebellions and were subsequently acquired either by neighbours already having adequate nearby houses or absentee lords by which they were ruthlessly exploited. Consequently houses on transferred estates were sometimes allowed to decay, used only as tenanted farm houses, or dismantled for the value of their timber, lead, and dressed stone. Rough rubble was not worth much and was usually left standing. Braemar and Corgarff were adapted as garrison posts for Hanovarian troops to keep the Highlands in check after the 1745 rebellion, the towers being surrounded by star-shaped walls loopholed for musketry. Corgarff still held a garrison in the 1820s because of local unrest after the passing of the Distilleries Act. Broughty lay in decay in the 18th century but was refortified as a coastal battery in the 19th century, remaining in use until after World War Two.

In Angus quite a number of castles and castellated houses have vanished but in Grampian the survival rate is quite high with more than a third of all known castles and houses of c1200-1660 still roofed, although many are heavily altered. Inverugie was blown up in 1899, most of Castle Newe and Lauriston have been removed since World War Two, and Aldbar, Gartly, Rothiemay, Towie and Wester Elchies have gone since 1960. However, restoration and preservation is now the order of the day, a trend started with the rebuilding of ruined Birse and Cairnbulg in the 1890s and the remodelling of Tillyfour in the 1880s and Shivas in the 1930s. Benholm tragically collapsed before restoration could begin but still-roofed buildings at Arnage, Balfluig, Balbithan, Beldorney, Carnousie, Davidston, Druminnor, Dudhope, Easter Elchies, Fiddes, Gordon, Hallgreen, Inverquarity, Mains, Mayen, Monboddo, Murroes, Tilquillie, Towie Barclay, Udny and the later range at Powrie have since 1960 been rescued from various states of decay, whilst Fetteresso, Forter, Harthill, Hatton, Pitfichie, Terpersie and Tillycairn have all been restored from a state of total ruin, mostly for use a private houses. Inchdrewer has been structurally restored but never fitted out or lived in. Later extensions have been stripped away at Aboyne and Benholm's Lodging has been removed from a site in central Aberdeen and rebuilt on the outskirts. The National Trust for Scotland has taken over Brodie, Castle Fraser, Craigievar, Crathes, Drum, and Leith Hall. A second attempt to restore derelict Castle Grant will hopefully begin soon and work is about to start upon rebuilding ruined Melgund.

Old postcard of Boyne Castle

Hatton before restoration

FURTHER READING

Grampian, The Castle Country, Cuthbert Graham, Aberdeen, 1982.
Medieval Archaeology (published annually).
Pamphlet guides for Braemar, Broughty, Dunnottar, Glamis and Kellie.
Queen's Scotland series by Nigel Tranter: The Eastern Counties, 1972, The North East, 1974, Hodder and Stoughton, London.
Portrait of Aberdeen and Deeside, Cuthbert Graham, London.
Proceedings of The Society of Antiquaries of Scotland. The volumes for 1923, 1928, 1929, and many from 1931 to 1954 have accounts of various castles in Grampian by W. Douglas Simpson; volumes for 1966-7 and the 1970s & 80s contain similar articles by H. Gordon Slade. See also Charles McKean's account of Pitsligo in the 1991 volume, & Edward Meldrum's account of Benholm's Lodging in that for 1961.
The Castellated and Domestic Architecture of Scotland, 5 vols, David MacGibbon & Thomas Ross, David Douglas, 1883-92. Facsimile reprint by James Thin 1977.
The Fortified House in Scotland, Nigel Tranter, Vol 4, 1966, Vol 5.
The National Trust for Scotland has produced guides for Brodie, Castle Fraser, Craigievar, Crathes, Drum, Fyvie, and Leith Hall.
The Province of Mar, W. Douglas Simpson, Aberdeen 1949.
The Royal Incorporation of Architects in Scotland (Rutland Press) has new architectural guides for Aberdeen, Banff & Buchan, Dundee, Gordon, and The District of Moray.
The Scottish Castle, Stewart Cruden, Nelson, 1960.
The Scottish Office and Historic Scotland have produced guides for Balvenie, Claypotts, Duffus, Huntly, Glenbuchat, Kildrummy, and Tolquhon.
The Statistical Account of Scotland, 1st, 2nd, 3rd editions, each in several volumes.

PUBLIC ACCESS TO THE CASTLES AND MANSIONS

In the gazetteers the names of the buildings are followed by the Ordnance Survey grid references and codes as below indicating availability of access.

A	Buildings now in use as hotels, restaurants, etc.
G	Grounds or gardens only open to public (A fee may be payable).
F	Ruins freely accessible at any reasonable time.
HS	Maintained by Historic Scotland (Fee payable at some sites).
NTS	Administered by The National Trust for Scotland (Fee usually payable)
OP	Opened to the public by private owners and local councils (Fee payable).
V	Not open but visible at close range from a public open space or right of way.

CASTLES OF ABERDEENSHIRE

ABERDEEN   NJ 944063

The first recorded Provost or civic head of the burgh is Richard Cementarius (Mason) in 1272. He had been commissioned by Alexander III in 1264 to repair the royal castle of Aberdeen which must then have been a stone building. It stood on the site of a 12th century castle of wood and probably had round corner towers and a twin towered gateway. After the fall of John Balliol in 1296 the castle was held by the English, although in 1298 its custodian, Sir Henry de Lathan was described as a rebel and an adherent of the Scots. Edward I paid a visit in 1303. The castle was stormed by the townsfolk in the interest of Robert Bruce in 1308 and demolished. It was replaced by a chapel of St Ninian. In the 1650s Cromwell built a fort in the same position of which a small fragment remains on the east side. The site, which is south of Castle Street between Marischal College and Regent Quay, was later occupied by a barracks and now bears two lofty blocks of flats, Virginia Court and Marischal Court.

ABERGAIRN   NO 358974

East of the farm track to Balmenach NE of Bridge of Gairn is the stump of a small tower positioned to command the junction of the valleys of the Dee and Gairn. It was built c1600 by the Farquharsons and is 6.7m square over walls 1.7m thick. One corner has a round turret 4m in diameter containing the entrance and spiral stair. This turret was probably covered with a gabled caphouse reached by a turret stair over the entrance but nothing now remains of the upper parts. The castle has alternative names of Glencairn Castle or Whitehouse which presumably referred to white harling.

0   5
metres

Abergairn Castle

Aboyne Castle

Abergeldie Castle

ABERGELDIE NO 287953

In 1481 Abergeldie passed to Sir Alexander Gordon of Midmar, second son of the 1st Earl of Huntly. The castle was built by the 4th laird of this line, Alexander, better known as Black Alister. He supported is kinsman the Earl of Huntly at Corrichie in 1562 and was subsequently imprisoned by Queen Mary at St Andrews. He took a leading part in Gordon-Forbes feud and in 1594 his son was killed fighting the Campbells and Forbes at Glenlivet. In 1592 the castle successfully resisted a raid by the Mackintoshes and other western clans known as the Great Spulzie. When the Covenanters finally took control of Deeside in the 1640s the castle was ordered to be destroyed because Alexander, 7th laird, was an ardent Royalist, but for some reason the instruction was not executed. In 1689 Abergeldie Castle was used as a mustering point by John Graham of Claverhouse, Viscount Dundee, when he was raising a Highland army against William III. The castle was captured and garrisoned by General Mackay but it was soon blockaded by the Farquharsons and in 1690 Mackay had to come to its relief. He reported that it would have had to surrender within three more days if the garrison had not been "timely succoured".

When Victoria and Albert began to develop neighbouring Balmoral as a holiday home they rented Abergeldie Castle, it being used by the then Queen Mother, the Duchess of Kent. It was later inhabited by the Princess Eugenie, widow of Napoleon III, and then became the Deeside home of the Prince of Wales and his family. More recently it has been used to accommodate guests of the royal family when they were residing at Balmoral. It has now, however, reverted to the Gordons.

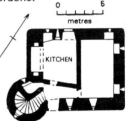

The late 16th century tower house lies to the east of substantial 19th century extensions. It consists of a block of four storeys including one mostly in the roof, and a substantial round tower at the SW corner. The tower contains the main stair and is corbelled out to a square balustraded top now bearing a modern clock and cupola. The three other corners are rounded but are squared off just below the eaves. That diagonally opposite the round tower carries a round conical roofed bartizan.

Plan of Abergeldie Castle

ABOYNE NO 526995

The Bissetts occupied a 12th century motte in this vicinity until they fell from power in 1242. Alexander III then used it as a hunting seat but there is no evidence it was rebuilt in stone and references to Coull during the Wars of Independence are thought to refer to Coull 3km to the NW. Aboyne was later held by the Knights Templars, the Frasers, and the Keiths, and in 1449 passed by marriage to the 1st Earl of Huntly, being subsequently used by younger sons of the chiefs. Now restored and with late 18th century and late 19th century additions stripped away, the tall building close to the Dee north of the village comprises a main block of four storeys and an attic with a square wing with a balustraded top at the NE corner and a round turret with a square caphouse at the NW corner. It probably mostly dates from c1600 but on the lintel of the entrance in the wing is the date 1671 and the initials of Charles Gordon and Elizabeth Lyon. Charles was the fourth son of the 2nd Marquess of Gordon and had recently been created Earl of Aboyne as belated thanks for helping to persuade General Monck to support the Restoration of Charles II in 1660. In 1836 George, 5th Earl of Aboyne, succeeded as Marquis of Huntly after the death of the 5th Duke of Gordon. It was held by Sir William Cunliffe Brooks in the late 19th century but now forms again a seat for the Earl of Aboyne, son of the Marquis of Huntly.

ARDIHERAULD   NJ 839224

The farm of Old Kendal lies on the site of a castle of the Burnetts. From it came Gilbert Burnett, historian, author, Professor of Divinity, Bishop of Salisbury under Charles II.

ARNAGE   NJ 936370

On the edge of a ring of woods above the Ebrie Burn is a Z plan castle built by the Cheynes, who acquired the estate by marriage in the late 14th century and held it until 1643. John Ross, then Baillie, later Provost, of Aberdeen purchased the estate in 1702 for 40,000 merks and his descendants held Arnage until 1927. The dilapidated building was saved from demolition when it was purchased by the Aberdeen building contractor Donald Stewart. He restored the castle, stripped off the harling, and located and brought back into use a well lying in the small court to the east. The main block is 12m long by 7m wide and has a wing 4.5m square containing the main stair up to the hall at the SW corner and a larger square wing at the NE corner. The entrance lies in the south wall near the foot of the stair and is covered by a shot-hole. It gives onto two vaulted cellars. The hall has three small windows in the south end wall and it is likely that a service lobby was screened off at this end. The third storey has two bedrooms over the hall and one in each wing, these being reached by stairs in conical roofed turrets corbelled out over the NE re-entrant angles.

ASLOUN   NJ 542149

In the grounds of a house are remains of a Z-plan castle in which Montrose stayed the night before his victory over General Baillie's Covenant army in 1645. Asloun was then held by the Forbes family (who were on the Covenant side) but was formerly a possession of the Calders. The castle may have been built around the time of an exchange of lands between John Cowdell (or Calder) and John Forbes in 1563. Most of it was dismantled in the 18th century to provide materials for the present house and the remaining fragment was probably left as a garden ornament. The castle consisted of a main block about 12m long by 7.5m wide over walls about 1m thick. There were round towers 5.8m in diameter at the NE and SW corners. The remains comprise the NE tower and the lower part of the main block north wall with evidence of vaults over two cellars. The tower has gunports but the entrance doorway, now lacking one jamb and the former heraldic stone above it, is placed in a rather indefensible position facing nearly east. From it a wide spiral stair led up to a dome vaulted lobby at hall level with a cable moulded sandstone pendant. A turret stair corbelled out over the NW re-entrant angle then served upper rooms in the main block and at least two private rooms in the tower.

ASWANLEY   NJ 445397

Aswanley originally belonged to the Cruikshanks family, one of whom, Elizabeth, was the mother of the celebrated pair of Gordon lairds, Jock (John) o' Scurdargue and Tam (Tom) o' Ruthven. In 1440 Hugh Calder obtained Aswanley from the Gordons. After the last Calder laird died in debt in 1768 Aswanley passed to his creditors, the Duffs, later Earls (and subsequently Dukes) of Fife. The house is a long, low yellow harled L-plan building with a round stair turret on the north side with a later ogival roof. The building has been much altered and may have once been higher. There are shot-holes but no vaults or any other features of interest apart from the arch of the kitchen fireplace. To the south is a court dated 1692 over the round-arched entrance with the initials of one of the Calders and his wife, one of the Skenes.

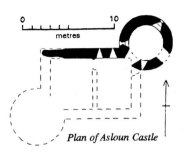

Plan of Asloun Castle

Auchanachie

AUCHANACHIE NJ 498469

Above the Burn of Cairnie lies a small, almost square, tower which formed the seat of the eldest sons of the Gordons of Avochie. Over the entrance is the inscription "From Ovr Enemies Defende Vsochrist 1594" and the basement vault is carved with the arms of the Gordons, Frasers, and Campbells. There are two upper storeys served by a round stair turret at the NE corner. The series of square openings below the eaves of the roof of the stair turret may be crenels of a former open parapet although it is possible that at one time the whole building rose a storey higher. Extending north from this turret is a long low two storey 17th century wing with a projecting chimney breast on the east side.

AUCHENHOVE NJ 555024

The Duguids held this estate from the 15th century until 1746 when after Culloden the Jacobite laird is said to have watched from a vantage point on Corse Hill the burning of his house by Cumberland's troops. Only the overgrown bases of thin walls of late date survive on a low lying site perhaps once protected by marshland. No main house or tower is recognisable.

AUCHLOSSAN NJ 571021

Auchlossan was long held by the Ross or Rose family, a younger son of Sir William Rose of Kilravock having obtained the estate in 1363. The 8th laird was killed at the battle of Malplaquet in France in 1709, and the Provost Ross who has left his name to a 16th century house in Aberdeen was his contemporary and kinsman. The 17th century house here has been much altered but its doorway, now obscured by a modern porch, is covered by shot-holes and is surmounted by a panel with the Rose arms. The roof has been lowered and the crow-stepped gables have gone but there remain at eaves level a row of eight corbels for either a parapet or gallery.

AUCHRY NJ 788507

Built into the gable of the farmhouse above the Burn of Monquitter is a dormer window pediment from the castle. It bears a quartered Comyn shield with the initials P.C. and M.C. and the motto "Constant and Kynd". The estate was held by the Comyns (also corrupted to Cummings or Cumines as in Cuminestown, 1.5km to the east) until it was sold in 1830.

AVOCHIE   NJ 536466

The unimpressive ruins of this 17th century Gordon house lie high above the east bank of the Deveron close to a modern mansion. It was a thinly walled block 13.7m long by 6.8m of three storeys, the topmost being mostly within the roof and having had a closet in a bartizan on the SE corner over the stair.

BALBITHAN   NJ 812189

A metal sundial on the SW bartizan bears the year 1679 and initials of James Chalmers but it seems that much of the house lying in a secluded dell SE of Inverurie is earlier. Charters of 1600 and 1635 indicate a then newly built structure replacing an older house further west. The oldest part is the south wing with a rectangular tower at its NW corner containing the entrance over which is a stair turret carried on a high cone and corbelling bearing a head with a moustache. The east wing was later added to make an extended L-plan with the high tower in the re-entrant angle. Both wings are of three storeys plus attics and have a pair of bartizans on the end gable. Now owned by a Mrs McMurtrie, the house has been extensively restored recently and the main hall made into a library and sitting room.

BALFLUIG   NJ 593153

The castle was built in the late 16th century by a younger son of Forbes of Corsindae. The estate was erected into the barony of Alford in 1650 and in 1753 was sold to the Farquharsons of Haughton. The castle has a lofty rectangular wing engaging the SE corner of a three storey main block 11m long by 7,3m wide. Both parts have round corners, squared off just below the eaves on the main block but further down on the wing which then has two extra storeys. The SW re-entrant angle is filled by a round turret containing a prison tucked under a stair serving all the rooms. The entrance in the other re-entrant angle is covered by gun-ports in a guard room in the base of the wing. From the lobby are reached two vaulted rooms under the hall. That at the north end is a kitchen with its fireplace in the end wall whilst the other was a cellar with a service stair. At hall level there is a vaulted private room in the wing. The squat turret on the NW corner has been re-instated by Mark Tennant who has made what had become a dilapidated farm store into a fine home again.

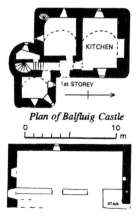

KITCHEN

1st STOREY

Plan of Balfluig Castle

0   10
|_|_|_|_|_|_| m

STAIR

Plan of Avochie

Balbithan House

BALMORAL NO 255952

The architecture and historical memorabilia of the famous house built for Queen Victoria and Prince Albert and still the holiday home of Queen Elizabeth II and the Duke of Edinburgh are adequately discussed elsewhere and need not concern us here. However, there was here a genuine late 16th century castle built by the Gordons. It is known from old illustrations to have had a large round tower at one corner of a main block like neighbouring Abergeldie Castle. The building was extended in 1835 for Sir Robert Gordon and in 1848 was leased to Queen Victoria. The last relics of it were cleared away in 1855, the year that the present building was completed.

BALQUHAIN NJ 732236

The Aberdeenshire Leslies had their chief seat here from 1340, when Sir Andrew married the heiress Mary Abernethy, until the castle was burnt in 1746 by the Duke of Cumberland on his way to Culloden because of the family's Jacobite sympathies. Queen Mary was entertained at the castle in 1562. It stands on level ground above the small ravine of a tributary of the Urie. On the edge of the ravine is a tower 14.1m long by 9.1m wide over walls 1.9m thick. It is assumed to have been built by Sir William Leslie shortly after the original castle was destroyed in 1526 during the course of a feud with the Forbes family. The NW wall containing the entrance has been destroyed and the interior has been badly damaged, whilst the lower openings have been blocked on the outside. The basement was divided into two cellars. Probably a straight mural stair led to the hall and then a spiral stair in the north corner led to the upper levels. On the landward side are fragments and foundations of a court with buildings on all sides. The SW range touching the tower by just one corner is probably of c1590-1610. It is 15.6m long by 8.2m wide and has a square turret which probably contained a scale-and-platt staircase in the angle between it and the tower whilst the west corner had a round turret about 3m in diameter. The other ranges are probably somewhat later.

Balquhain Castle　　　　*Balfluig Castle*

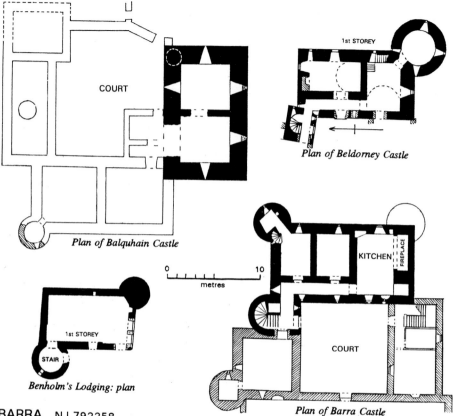

Plan of Balquhain Castle

Plan of Beldorney Castle

1st STOREY

Benholm's Lodging: plan

1st STOREY

STAIR

KITCHEN

FIREPLACE

COURT

0 _____ 10
metres

Plan of Barra Castle

BARRA NJ 792258

The King family held Barra from the mid 13th century with the Lords of the Garioch as overlords. In 1598 the estate passed to their neighbours the Setons of Meldrum with who they had a long and bitter feud. In 1615 Elizabeth Seton pursued at law James King "sumtyme of Barra" for the slaughter of her father "with schottis of hagbuttis and muskattis, committed upon the landis of Barra....". The castle was later held by the Reids, the Ramseys, and then passed via an heiress to the present owners, a junior branch of the Irvines of Drum. The castle has three ranges around a small court with on the fourth side a wall pierced by a gateway and surmounted by three vases. The oldest part is the west range which has a small wing at the SE corner with a rounded southern end which forms a stair turret with a square caphouse. The square part of the wing contains the entrance and a lobby off which there is access to a passage along the east or courtyard side of the main block. This connects with a wine cellar at the south end with a service stair and a small adjoining cellar in the foot of a second round turret at the SW corner, a food store in the middle, and a kitchen at the north end with its fireplace in the end gable. The upper parts of this range are dated 1614 and 1618 so it was evidently added by the Setons. About the same time the square block forming the south wing was added. This in turn has a round SE turret so that there are three south facing turrets in all, with those at the ends covered with conical roofs. The more thinly walled north wing containing a scale-and-platt staircase was added by the Ramseys in 1755.

BELDORNEY NJ 424369

The Ogilvies held Beldorney from the late 15th century until it was granted in 1545 to George Gordon and Janet Rose. He was the eldest of three illegitimate sons of Adam Gordon, Dean of Caithness, the third son of Alexander, 1st Earl of Huntly. It is likely that the castle was built between 1552, when the Crown confirmed the transfer, and 1562 when the estate was confiscated for three years after the battle of Corrichie. In the mid 17th century the Gordons of Beldorney got into financial difficulties. A relative named John Lyon obtained the superiority but was hated by the tenants and was murdered by them in the Braes of Abernethie in 1667. John Gordon, 5th laird, spent a year confined in Edinburgh Tollbooth before he was cleared of complicity in the crime. He and his wife Anne have left their initials and the date 1679 on the courtyard entrance, so somehow they must have found the funds to built this court with low ranges on either side. In 1689 Beldoney was pillaged by Highland Jacobites during their pursuit of the Williamite forces under General Mackay. In the 1790s the estate was sold to Thomas Buchan of Auchmacoy who in turn sold it to Sir William Grant. After the Grant male line failed in 1919 the estate was sold to Sir Thomas Birkett for whom alterations were made. Further works were carried out for Commander Vivian Robinson, who purchased the castle after Sir Thomas died in 1959.

The castle consists of a block 13m long by 7.5m with a round tower 6.3m diameter at the SE corner and a 3.6m square stair turret at the NW corner. From the original entrance in the stair turret leads a passage running past the kitchen to a cellar at the north end. The cellar has a service stair and access to another cellar in the round tower. The hall has two windows in each of the east and west walls and a mural chamber in the NE corner. The round tower contains at this level the main private chamber and has a turret stair corbelled out in the SW re-entrant angle. This stair forms the only access to two bedrooms on the third storey of the main block, the round third and fourth storey rooms in the tower, and two small square rooms in the stair turret. The south range of the courtyard has just one storey with two big rooms, whilst the north range has two storeys. All the ground level rooms only have south facing windows. At about the time when these were added a new doorway was made into the main block, being symmetrically positioned with regard to the court, and opening onto the passage. The kitchen fireplace was reduced in size and the hall was divided into two rooms with a connecting lobby. One of the rooms has a low ceiling above which is secret room where John Gordon, 10th laird, an ardent Jacobite, was concealed after Culloden. The private room was remodelled as an irregular heptagon.

Barra Castle

Beldorney Castle

Benholm's Lodging

Birse Castle

Plan of Bognie Castle

BENHOLM'S LODGING, ABERDEEN   NJ 936089 (formerly 943063)

This building, also known as Wallace Tower, was a town house built by Sir Robert Benholm in the last few years before he died in 1616. It originally stood just outside Netherkirkgate in Aberdeen but in 1963 was removed stone by stone to a new site 3km to the north to make room for offices. The first tenant of the reconstructed building was the eminent castle expert the late Dr W. Douglas Simpson. Sir Robert was a younger brother of George, 5th Earl Marischal. There were a number of family squabbles involving these two and other Keiths in the 1590s during which Deer Abbey was seized and garrisoned by Sir Robert, and he stormed his brother's castle of Ackergill in Caithness. Eventually Robert got what he wanted, some of the Keith possessions, and in particular the barony of Benholm from which he subsequently took his title. The house reverted to the Earl in 1616 and was occupied by Dr Patrick Dun, principal of the new Marischal College. It was subsequently acquired by William Hay of Balbithan and then was owned in turn by various merchants. The lower parts formed a public house prior to being taken over by the city council in 1918, by whom it was neglected. The house has a main block 12m long by 6.2m wide and has three storeys. Round towers lie at diagonally opposite corners. One contained the entrance and principal staircase. The other originally lay in the angle of a Y-shaped junction of streets and has on the outermost face, above corbelling making the upper part slightly bigger, a niche containing a quaint statue of Sir Robert holding his sword with a dog at his feet. This tower has an additional fourth storey reached by a stair in a rounded projection carried on corbelling. See plan on page 28.

BIRSE   NO 520905

In the late 16th century William Gordon, Bishop of Aberdeen, built a remotely sited castle here as a hunting seat. It was occupied by Gordon lairds until left to decay in the 18th century. Highland brigands took to using it as a lair. About a hundred years ago the castle was restored from ruin and given a new NE wing with bartizans. The old part comprises a modest rectangular tower of three storeys with a fourth in the roof. It has a round stair turret at one corner and round bartizans carried on label mouldings at the others. Most of the tall square caphouse containing two bedrooms over the main stair is modern repair work.

Boddam Castle

Bognie Castle

Plan of Boddam Castle

GATEWAY

BODDAM NK 124419

On a level promontory between two deep vertical sided sea inlets south of the village are remains of a castle built by the Keiths of Ludquharn in the late 16th or early 17th century. Although strongly sited, the building lacked serious defensive arrangements although a tower here is shown on an engraving of 1784. The remains comprise a court about 31m long by 28m wide containing ranges to the north, west and south. The only part standing higher than the base of the walls is a projection in the middle of the west side containing the entrance passage with a room above it and an attic in the roof. Loops on either side of the passage allow flanking fire along the west wall which is the only side open to attack. However, defence of this side would have been jeopardised by the cover afforded to attackers by a large, perhaps later, stable block situated close by.

BOGNIE NJ 595450

The east and north walls of a block 22.4m long by 6.9m wide stand four storeys high with large windows in tiers. There are no signs of vaulting nor are there indications of how the interior was divided, but there seem to have once been bartizans on the corners. The house was built by the Morrisons, probably c1660-70.

Bognie Castle

Plan of Braemar Castle

BRAEMAR NO 156924 OP

John Erskine, Earl of Mar, began the L-planned tower here in 1628 as a hunting seat and to keep in check the belligerent Farquharsons. In 1689 John Farquharson, the celebrated Black Colonel, defeated Williamite troops in a skirmish here and then burnt the castle to prevent it being garrisoned against him. The Deeside Mar estates were forfeited after the then Earl led the 1715 Jacobite rebellion but in 1724 they were purchased by two Eskine kinsmen, Lord Grange and Lord Dun. They in turn sold the lands to John Farquharson, 9th laird of Invercauld, in 1732. Having been coerced into taking part in the 1715 rebellion and imprisoned after capture at Preston, he declined to participate in the 1745 rebellion. The Jacobites plundered his estates and in 1748 this prompted him to lease the ruined castle to the government for 99 years for restoration as a garrison post to help maintain law and order in the Highlands. The garrison was withdrawn in 1797, and some years later the castle was restored to the Farquharsons. Their direct male line had failed with James, 10th laird, but James Ross of Balnagown who married the heiress Catherine adopted the Farquharson name to continue the line. It was their son, the 12th laird, who finally took up residence in the castle. He entertained Queen Victoria here when she attended the Braemar Gatherings.

The castle originally consisted of an L-plan tower of fairly low profile yet containing four full storeys plus a fifth in the roof. The main block measures 14m by 8.6m and the wing is 7.5m wide and projects 6.4. In the re-entrant angle is a round stair turret rising above the rest. It contains the entrance, which still has an original yett. From the base of the stair there is direct access to one cellar and a passage leads to a second cellar and the kitchen. In the passage floor is a hatch to a pit prison sunk in the ground. At the restoration of 1748 the bartizans were heightened and the building surrounded by a small court in the shape of a eight pointed stair. The court walls is pierced by musket loops and four entrances, two of which are covered by baffle walls. The other two are probably later insertions. The battlements on the bartizans, the stair turret and the court wall are of the period when the Farquharsons took up residence.

Cairnbulg Castle

Braemar Castle

BRUX NJ 500169

This Forbes stronghold is first mentioned in 1546. Reset stones from it including lintels, jambs with chamfers and roll-mouldings, and a few corbels, lie in the derelict farmhouse on the site and the nearby mill. One lintel has a quirked roll and hollow moulding not likely to be earlier than the late 17th century. There is a monument to Alexander, 4th laird, at Kildrummy, and Alexander, 9th laird, and his wife Elizabeth Murray have left their monogram on a burial enclosure not far from the castle site.

CAIRNBULG NK 016640

Sir Alexander Fraser obtained the estate of Philorth in 1375 by marrying a daughter of the Earl of Ross. The 8th laird founded the town of Fraserburgh in 1569 and the 10th laird succeeded through his mother Margaret Abernethy to the title of Lord Saltoun, first assumed by Sir Laurence Abernethy in 1445. This laird got into debt to his kinsman at Castle Fraser and in the 1630s the latter took over Cairnbulg. Lord Saltoun built himself a new house at Philorth in 1666. Lord Fraser took refuge from Montrose at Cairnbulg in 1645 and his descendants held the castle until 1703 when it was sold to Colonel John Buchan of Auchmacoy. The castle was dismantled in 1782, sold to the Earl of Aberdeen, and was further damaged by a gale in 1806. The estate was sold to the ship-owner William Duthie in 1862 and in 1896-7 the ruins were restored to make a residence for John Duthie. Lord Saltoun's seat at Philorth was accidentally burnt in 1915 and since their purchase of the castle in 1934 his descendants have been back at Cairnbulg.

The tower house was probably begun c1390 although its upper storeys may be 15th century whilst the battlements with small angle rounds carried on ornamental corbelling are early to mid 16th century. The tower measures 12.5m by 9m and is 18m high to the top of the merlons of the parapet. It contained a vaulted cellar, a lofty vaulted hall, and suites of two rooms on each of the third and fourth storeys. The original entrance was placed in a recess close to the SE corner. This is now masked by a tall gabled stair turret added in the 16th century to join the tower to a long new block with a round tower on the far corner. The tower has a sub-basement containing gunports and has at the summit a thinly walled top storey within a corbelled parapet and wall-walk. The top stage is itself also embattled. Most of the block itself is of the period of the restoration, still part having been very ruined previously.

CASTLE FRASER NJ 723126 NTS

During a general dispersal by James II in 1454 of estates formerly belonging to the Earldom of Mar this estate, then called Muchall, plus Stoneywood were granted as a barony to Thomas Fraser of Cornton in Stirlingshire who built the original tower which measured 11.7m by 9.7m over walls 2.2m thick. Michael Fraser, laird from 1565 to 1589 added the 9.4m square tower named after him at the NW corner and a round tower 8.4m in diameter at the SE corner. The master mason is thought to have been Thomas Leiper, who later worked at Tolquhon. Andrew Fraser, laird from 1589 to 1636 added two new upper storeys over the vault of the lofty 15th century hall, lengthened the main block to the west, built three new storeys on top of the existing three of the Michael Tower, and put no less than four more storeys on the round tower to create one of the more remarkable buildings in Scotland. In the 1630s, during which time he was created a peer and also took over possession of Cairnbulg Castle, he added the low building on the north side of the court.

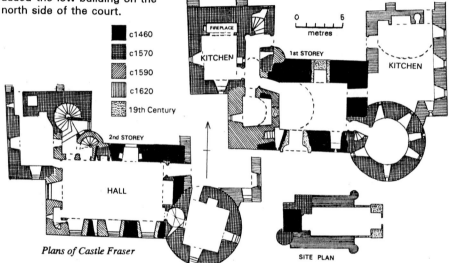

- c1460
- c1570
- c1590
- c1620
- 19th Century

Plans of Castle Fraser

SITE PLAN

Castle Fraser

The 2nd Lord Fraser supported the Covenanters and in 1638, whilst he was absent, the Royalist Lord Aboyne sacked the barns and policies at Castle Fraser, although the castle itself was not captured. During Montrose's campaign of 1645 Lord Fraser took refuge at Cairnbulg whilst the Castle Fraser estate was again ravaged. Under the 3rd Lord the estate was allowed to decay and after the 4th Lord fell over a cliff whilst a fugitive following the 1715 rebellion Muchall, or Castle Fraser as it was now generally called, passed to the Frasers of Inverallochy. The castle later passed through other branches of the family and in 1922 was sold to Lord Cowdray. It was restored for use as a home by his son Clive Pearson. After the Second World War 19th century additions in the courtyard were demolished and during the 1960s further restoration was carried out. The harling was stripped off and only then did the building's complex architectural history become clear after a century and a half of debate. The main block has now been left without harling. Since 1976 the castle has been in the custody of the National Trust for Scotland.

The original tower had separate entrances to each of the cellar and hall in the north wall. Communication between these levels was only by means of a hatch in the lower vault. The Michael Tower contains a new main entrance onto a passage connecting a wide new stair to the hall, a kitchen and the cellar in the main block. The steps up to the original hall doorway (now blocked) had to be removed to make way for the new entrance to the Michael Tower. The old and new towers just touched by one corner and until the older part was lengthened 3.3m westwards twenty years later it appears that there was no communication between them at any level. A window on the north side of the hall was utilised during that period as a doorway to the hall. The added section of the main block has a service stair in the SW corner and a staircase to the upper levels is projected out over the NE re-entrant angle. This interfered with the entrance to what is thought to have been an oratory on the third storey of the Michael Tower, and a new doorway new cuts through where the altar is thought to have been. In the SW corner of the main block at the level of the hall vault is a small chamber once thought to be some sort of device allowing the laird to listen to conversation in the hall without being present, but now considered to be a prison cell.

The round tower contains a round cellar with six loops and six upper rooms, all approximately square. An inserted stair within the original corner of the main block serves the four lower levels and then another stair over the southern re-entrant angle carried on to serve the three upper levels and the balustraded roof platform. These upper parts are carried on decorative corbelling which carried right round the whole building, supporting round bartizans at the corners and dormer windows light the top storey, plus on the north side a heraldic frontispiece with the Fraser arms. There is also a small tablet with the date 1617 and IBEL MM referring to master mason John Bell, designer of these masterful top-works.

The courtyard ranges are of two storeys with dormer windows lighting the uppermost. On the outermost northern corners are conical roofed bartizans with turret stairs corbelled out in the southern re-entrant angles. The west wing is dated 1631 with initials of Michael Fraser, his first wife Elizabeth Douglas, his second wife Anne Drummond, and his daughter-in-law Margaret Elphinstone. The east wing has the initials of Andrew and the last two ladies. Extra initials indicate a date of construction around 1633 when Andrew became a Lord and the two ladies thus became Dames. The southern part of the east wing is wider and was built in the 1620s to contain a large new kitchen at ground level with a dining room above. Most later additions and alterations have now been removed. Apart from a northerly extension to the court the chief post-17th century feature is a south doorway at ground level into the main block.

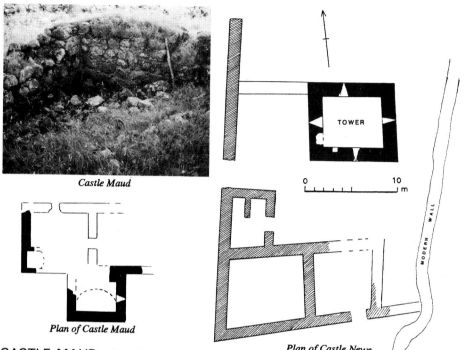

Castle Maud

Plan of Castle Maud

TOWER

MODERN WALL

0   10
              m

Plan of Castle Newe

CASTLE MAUD   NO 624995

Hidden in a clump of trees on a flat low-lying site originally probably protected by marshland are ruins about 1m high of the seat of the barony of Onele held by the Durwards in the 13th century. The irregularly laid out tower 9.6m by 8.3m over walls 1.5m thick may perhaps be late 13th or early 14th century. It has a single loop in each wall. There is no staircase, vaulting, or doorway, so the entrance must have been at hall level with just a hatch giving access to the basement. The tower lies in the remains of a court of uncertain date. The L-plan building in the SW corner looks like a house of c1600 with a wide, possibly scale-and-platt type staircase, in the wing.

CASTLE NEWE   NJ 380124

Scanty remains of this building lie hidden in an estate which belonged to the Forbes family until recently. They built the castle in 1604. It was engulfed in a large granite mansion in 1831 and the whole structure was demolished a few decades ago leaving only fragments and foundations. The old part appears to have been T-planned with a main block 7.2m wide from which a wing 6.6m wide projected 5m. Part of the vault remains over the cellar in the wing. The thick south wall of the main block contained a mural room or blind passage like that at neighbouring Colquhonnie Castle.

CLACKRIACH   NJ 933471

Hidden in trees on the north side of a farm road at Mains of Clackriach is a fragment of a late 16th or early 17th century house of the Keiths. It consists just of one corner standing two storeys high with at the upper level the jambs of windows and a circular recess in the corner itself. The walling is about 1m thick.

CLUNY NJ 688128

The barony of Cluny was held by Sir Andrew Fraser in the early 14th century. In 1345 David II granted it to his sister Margaret and her husband William, 5th Earl of Sutherland. By 1437 it had passed to Alexander Gordon, later 1st Earl of Huntly, and his descendants still own it. In 1604 the mason John Bell designed an extremely picturesque new Z-plan castle for Thomas Gordon, probably setting it on the site of a 12th century motte with a water filled ditch. Sketches of this masterpiece survive from before 1836-40 when a great neo-Gothic mansion was raised on the site and the surrounding grounds landscaped. It was not until the building was investigated after a fire in 1926 that it was realised that the SW corner of the mansion was in fact the castle of 1604 shorn of its turrets, refaced in granite, and remodelled inside.

The castle consisted of a central block 14.6m by 9m with round towers 7.5m and 7.2m in diameter respectively at the SE and NW corners. The central block and NW tower had four storeys, the SE tower had five, and there were attics above. The main stair at the junction of the main block and NW tower was surmounted by a small square tower. The NW tower is increased in girth by means of a corbelled moulding at the level of the third storey. There is a similar moulding at the level of the present summit. Old sketches show a conical roof on this tower but it is likely that the upper moulding was intended to support a balustrade with a flat roof as at Midmar, Castle Fraser, Craigston, and Craigievar. Until rebuilt in the 1930s the other tower was crowned by a caphouse which was basically a square set diagonally to the main block but with the outermost side actually two faces meeting at a shallow angle on which was a tiny false oriel window with a small secret room behind it. Square gabled turrets projecting diagonally from the remaining two corners of the main block and an array of chimneys and stair turrets completed a spectacular skyline.

The entrance (from which has probably come the yett in the walled garden gateway) leads into a passage on the west side of the main block close to the foot of the main stair. From the passage there is access to the kitchen and a cellar in the main block, and square and round cellars in the NW and SE towers. Above was the hall with a polygonal private room in the SE tower. On top were pairs of bedrooms with further rectangular rooms in the NE tower, and irregularly polygonally rooms in the SE tower.

Old postcard of Cluny Castle

COLQUHONNIE NJ 365126 A

Beside the hotel are remains of a late 16th century castle of the Forbes of Towie. A wing 6.5m wide projects 5.8m from a main block 12m long by 7.6m wide. A gap representing the former entrance leads into a passage between a cellar in the wing and a kitchen in the main block. There is a spiral stair in the north wall at the end of the passage. The kitchen fireplace back wall has fallen. The rest of the main block contains another cellar with its vault at a different axis and a vaulted room or blind passage in the thick east wall. Little remains above the vaults.

CORGARFF NJ 255086 HS

The bleak forest of Corgarff in upper Strathdon formed part of the Earldom of Mar until 1507 when James IV granted it to Alexander, later 1st Lord Elphinstone. The tower was built about twenty years later when the 2nd Lord Elphinstone gave Corgarff to his eldest son as a marriage gift. The tower was subsequently occupied by the Forbes of Towie as vassals of Lord Elphinstone. In 1571 it was the scene of a celebrated outrage when the Gordons set the tower (probably then roofed with thatch) on fire. Among 27 people burnt alive were Margaret Campbell, wife of Forbes of Towie. The castle was repaired and taken back by the Elphinstones but the Forbes family still regarded it as theirs and in 1607 Alexander Forbes and some highland caterans captured the "fortalice of Torgarffa" by breaking in the door with "grete geistis, foir hammers", etc, and subsequently "fortified it as a house of war".

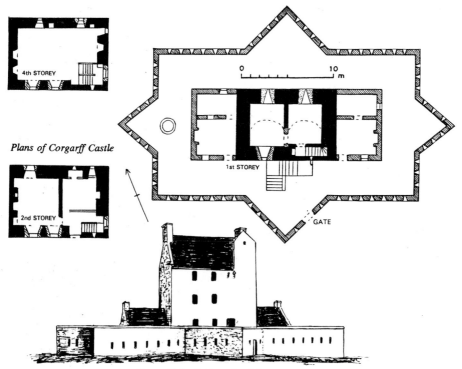

Plans of Corgarff Castle

Corgarff Castle from the SW.

In 1626 Corgarff was recovered from Lord Elphinstone by the Erskines when after nearly two centuries of dispute, they finally obtained the estates of the Earldom of Mar which were rightfully theirs. They can only have used it as an occasional hunting seat. In 1645 the castle was used as a headquarters by Montrose before the campaign which led to his victory at Alford, although it is said to have then been in a dismantled condition. In 1689 the castle was burnt by Jacobites to prevent it containing a Williamite garrison. It was reported to the government that repairs would cost £300 sterling. During the 1715 rebellion led by the Earl of Mar the castle was used as a muster point for his forces. After his forfeiture and exile abroad Corgarff was occupied by Forbes of Skellater who himself fled abroad after taking part in the 1745 rebellion. The castle was used by the Jacobite to store munitions although they hastily abandoned it when a party of dragoons marched over the snowy moors from Aberdeen in March 1746. In 1748 the Hanovarian government repaired the old tower and built a chemise wall around it to hold a garrison to maintain the peace in this area. The crisis soon passed, the garrison in 1794 being only "two or three invalids", and by 1802 Forbes of Skellater was back in residence. There was trouble and smuggling in Strathdon after the Distillery Act was passed in 1824, a distillery close to the castle being destroyed by arson in 1826. The castle was then re-garrisoned with a captain, a subaltern and 56 men. Peace was soon restored and in the 1890s the only occupants of the castle were two old women. The building is now in state care as an ancient monument, having been restored from decay in the 1960s.

The tower house measures 10.9m by 7.6m and now has four storeys and an attic. Old drawings made before conversion work started in 1748 show that above the pair of little-altered cellars there was originally just a lofty vaulted hall and a private room on top. The entrance at hall level is reached by external steps and communication both up and down from there was by a spiral stair in a square well. Adjoining the stair at hall level was a low barrel-vaulted kitchen with another vaulted entresol room above it. In the alterations of 1748 the hall vault was taken down and the kitchen and room above ripped out, allowing space for two full storeys, the lowest of which was divided into a suite of two rooms for an officer. The upper levels then formed barrack rooms while extra barrack rooms were provided in single storey wings added against each end wall of the tower. At the summit there is a gabled caphouse over the stair, adjoining which are corbels for a former machicolated projection defending the entrance. A square bartizan on the NE corner has now gone. The tower and its new wings were surrounded in 1748 by a rectangular wall with salients in the middle of each side, that on the south having the entrance. Musket loops are provided all round. On the west side of the court is a well, now filled in.

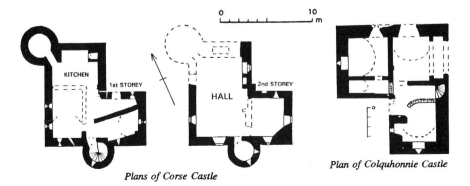

Plans of Corse Castle

Plan of Colquhonnie Castle

Corse Castle

Corse Castle

CORSE NJ 548074

In the early 15th century Corse went to Patrick, brother of the 1st Lord Forbes. The ruin has above its entrance a stone with the year 1581 and the initials of William Forbes and Elizabeth Skene. After a previous house here was plundered by Highland caterans William is said to have vowed "If God spares my life I shall build a house at which thieves will knock ere they enter". His son Patrick became Bishop of Aberdeen and Chancellor of King's College and was the brother of the builder of Craigievar Castle. The castle has a main block 11.2m long by 6.8m wide with a wing 5.7m wide projecting 4.4m from the east side. There is a round tower 4.2m in diameter (now reduced to within a metre of the ground) at the NW corner and a round stair turret projects at the meeting of the main block and wing on the south side. The entrance in the re-entrant angle gives onto a peculiarly shaped lobby from which could be reached the stair, a small cellar in the wing, a cellar in the southern part of the main block, and a kitchen with its fireplace in the broken down north end wall. All these spaces except the kitchen have doubled splayed gunports. There are shot-holes in the bartizans containing closets at fourth storey level and the lozenge-shaped holes at the third storey may also have been intended as shot-holes. The wing probably contained a private room at hall level. Above were three rooms on each of the third and fourth storeys with smaller rooms in the NW tower so there was plenty of accommodation.

CORSINDAE NJ 686088

A small slender whitewashed late 16th century L-plan tower lies in the middle of a row of trees. At the end furthest from the original wing is a modern extension in the same style but with larger windows. The entrance lies between two round turrets set in the re-entrant angles created by the wings and the main block. Only the turret to the left, containing the staircase, is old. A branch of the Forbes family descended from the 2nd Lord Forbes (a charter was granted in 1486) lived here. James VI's government described John Forbes of Corsindae as one of "the insolent society of boyis denounced for slaughter and other enormities". In 1605 he was arrested by Irvine of Drum and a strong guard had to escort him to Edinburgh for trial for fear of a rescue attempt or reprisals by his kinsmen.

COULL NJ 513023

Coull was the chief Aberdeenshire seat of the Durward family, who also held estates in Fife and Inverness-shire. They were originally called de Lundin but adopted a new name from their hereditary post of Door Ward to the Scottish Kings. After they unsuccessfully claimed the Earldom of Mar in the 1220s Alexander II detached part of it for them as the barony of Onele. Lumphanan may have been the original seat of the barony and the new seat at Coull was probably begun in the 1250s when Alan Durward, Regent for the young Alexander III, and husband of the King's illegitimate sister, was ruling Scotland. In 1299 Coull was held by Sir John de Hastings as tenant of Joan de Clare, widowed Countess of Fife. It then probably held an English garrison as the contemporary references to the castle of Aboyne must surely refer to Coull, then the only castle of importance in the area. It is last heard of in 1307 when Edward I ordered the Chamberlain of Scotland to repair and garrison it in response to the rebellion and crowning of Robert Bruce. Excavations in 1923 found evidence of the building having been dismantled, restored, and then finally destroyed by fire. Probably this means that it was damaged during the Aberdeenshire rebellion of 1297, was patched up by John de Strathbogie, Earl of Atholl (who was responsible to Edward I for in 1304), and then finally destroyed during Bruce's expedition of 1307-8 against the Comyns. Perhaps Castle Maud was built as a successor.

Coull Castle

Keep, Coull Castle

The remains of Coull Castle lie above a bend of a tributary of the Tarland Burn SE of Coull Kirk. Walls up to 2.3m thick enclosed a pentagon with maximum dimensions of 45m by 35m. Of a gateway with twin round towers at the north corner just one curved fragment of wall and the drawbridge pit remain. A fragment remains of a tower about 7m in diameter at the west corner and the SW side of the court was filled with a range 10m wide containing a hall and chamber probably set over mess-rooms or stores. The principal survival is the round keep 9m in diameter still partly 5m high on the SE side of the court. It has a latrine shaft on the NE and a broadly splayed plinth which is thought to have been added after the tower was wrecked in the 1297 rebellion. A postern pierces the curtain between the keep and the hall-block.

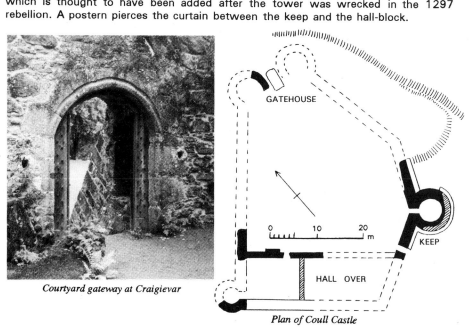

Courtyard gateway at Craigievar

Plan of Coull Castle

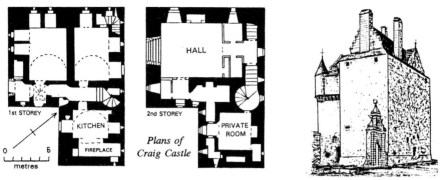

HALL

1st STOREY

KITCHEN

FIREPLACE

0   5
metres

2nd STOREY

PRIVATE ROOM

Plans of Craig Castle

Craig Castle

CRAIG OF AUCHINDOIR NJ 477245 & 472248

On a strong site between the ruined church of c1200 and the burn is a tree-clad motte with a summit 30m long by 20m rising 5m above the ditch to the east. The west side is somewhat eroded. This site may have remained in use until the stone castle was built further up the Den of Craig. The earliest recorded laird is John of the Craig, Captain of Kildrummy Castle in 1335 and hero of battle fought that year at Culblean. Patrick Gordon, grandson of Jock o' Scurdargue, obtained Craig in 1510. Although it bears the initials of Patrick and his wife Rachel Barclay of Towie plus those of his son William (d1559) and his wife Elizabeth Stewart of Laithers in addition to the Royal Arms, the existing L-plan building is now considered to have been built in the 1570s by William, 3rd laird. He was involved in the murder of the Earl of Moray at Donibristle in 1592 and took part in the rebellion of the Catholic lords in 1594. His successors sold the estate in 1892.

The stone castle is strongly sited on a ledge above a sheer drop to the burn. It is harled and presents a forbidding appearance with few windows towards the approach on the north. A wing 7.2m wide projects about 6m from a main block 13m long by 10.4m wide. There are so many passages and mural chambers that there is little solid masonry of the great thickness which appears in the window embrasures. The arms referred to above lie over the segmental-headed and roll-moulded entrance. There is a wide mouthed gunport between the shield and the window above and there are similar gunports elsewhere in the building. The entrance leads to a rib-vaulted lobby with a doorway to a cellar opposite, a porter or guard's lodge on the left in the corner of the building, and a passage running northwards between a second cellar in the main block and a kitchen in the base of the wing to the main stair in the north wall. The hall has a service stair down to the northern cellar. A mural room in the east wall communicates both with a window embrasure of the hall and with the vaulted private room for the laird over the kitchen. The hall has a fireplace in the west wall and high up in the north wall is a gallery, perhaps for musicians, reached off the main stair.

The third storey, now subdivided, is poorly lighted and without any latrines or original fireplaces so it can only have been used for those of menial rank. There are also at this level two more mural chambers and a second private room in the wing. Above are attics surrounded by a loopholed walkway which is now covered by roofs although perhaps originally intended to be open to the sky. Gables are provided on the thin inner walls and the sections of roof over the walkway are hipped. The part above the entrance projects slightly on ornamental corbelling and there is a conical roofed bartizan on the SE corner of the main block. East of the main building is a fine rusticated gateway leading to a small court. The gateway and the range on the east date from 1726, whilst the south range is of 1832 and the SW block is of 1908.

CRAIGIEVAR NJ 566095 NTS

Craigievar belonged to the Mortimers at least as early as 1457 and they are thought to have begun the present castle in the 1590s. They got into debt and in 1610 sold the estate and unfinished castle to William Forbes of Corse, a successful merchant with a particular trade connection to the Baltic city of Danzig. Forbes employed the Bell family of masons to complete the castle, which was achieved both structurally and decoratively by 1626. His son William succeeded in 1630 and was created a baronet of Nova Scotia the same year. It was at this time that a number of Highland rustlers and crop stealers were arrested and executed for their depredations on the Forbes' estates of Corse and Craigievar. Sir William supported the Covenant and in 1640 captured Harthill Castle but the Leith owners had revenge when a part of Craigievar's men were captured at Inverurie. Sir William himself was captured at Aberdeen in 1644 but escaped by breaking parole. In 1884 the 8th baronet, Sir William Forbes, became the 17th Lord Sempill on the death of his cousin Baroness Maria Janet. After the 19th Lord Sempill died in 1965 Craigievar was taken over by the National Trust for Scotland. They re-harled the building in 1973, numerous shot-holes in the bartizans being discovered for the first time when the old harling came off.

The tower house stood in the NE corner of a court 26.6m by 24.5m enclosed by a wall mostly 0.7m thick. Of this there survive only the conical roofed SW turret 3.3m in diameter and the west wall which for most of its length is thickened to 1.6m to support a parapet and wall walk over a centrally placed entrance. This wall, perhaps older than the rest, leans inward upon modern buttressing. The gateway has a recess on either side each with a shot-hole commanding the approach and from it steps lead down into the court, the ground on this side being at a higher level. The south side of the court was filled with a range called the "laigh biggin" or low building.

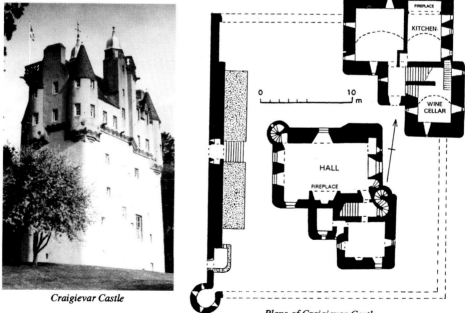

Craigievar Castle

Plans of Craigievar Castle

The tower house represents a climax in the design of such buildings in Scotland in which thanks to sheer height and clever use of space a substantial number of comfortable rooms are squeezed into a building of comparatively modest dimensions. The tower has a main block 11.7m long by 8.3m wide over walls 1.3m thick. A wing 6.4m wide is attached to the SE corner so as to make a deep re-entrant angle on the west which contains a square turret, and a shallow re-entrant angle on the east. The rounded corners give a soft outline to the lower part of the building. The round-headed entrance doorway retains its yett. It leads into a lobby in the base of the turret from which there is access into a cellar and kitchen in the main block, a wine cellar in the wing, and a straight stair running up between the latter two. Passing over a straight service stair from the wine cellar to the hall, the main stair leads up to the foot of a spiral stair in a slight projection corbelled out above the eastern re-entrant angle. Thus the square turret in the other re-entrant angle, a favourite position elsewhere for a staircase, is here free to contain numerous small rooms.

The hall is a noble apartment equivalent in height to two stages in the wing and has a magnificent display of the Royal Arms over the fireplace, an elaborate plaster ceiling with ornate pendants, and a gallery for musicians placed over the screens passage at the east end. On the plasterwork and woodwork appear the arms of William Forbes and Marjory Woodward. The extra initial M is for the style of Master which William was entitled to use as an arts graduate of Edinburgh University. The hall ceiling is adorned with medallion portraits of ancient personalities such including Joshua, David, Hector of Troy, Tarquin, Lucretia and Alexander the Great. The Ladies' Withdrawing Room at this level in the wing is panelled with Memel pine from NE Europe (evidence of the trade with Danzig) and has another ornate ceiling with medallions of St Margaret of Scotland, Lucretia, Roma, and Tarquin.

In addition to the main stair the upper rooms can be reached by a second stair in a round turret corbelled out at the NW corner. At the summit this turret has a square gabled caphouse containing a room reached by a tiny stair in a round turret. This secondary turret does not have a separate roof like the other turrets. Instead the crowsteps of the main turret roof are carried across its outer face. The fourth storey contains the Queen's Room on the west, a small room on the east, Landy Sempill's Room in the wing, and a small room in the re-entrant angle turret. Above are the Nursery and Tank Room in the main block and the Blue Room in the wing. These rooms and those above have round closets in the bartizans. Ornamental corbelling is carried round the entire building to carry the bartizans and allow an increase in the width of the top parts. Above this level the main stair is surmounted by a rectangular turret with a flat roof and balustrade. A smaller stair leads up in an adjoining turret which is covered with a ribbed ogival dome. A similarly roofed turret serves the another flat roof with a balustrade on the square turret in the west re-entrant angle. In the roof are a bedroom in the west part of the main block and a long gallery extending across the remainder into the wing, this being the longest room in the castle.

Delgatie Castle

CRAIGSTON NJ 762550

Craigston is still occupied by the Urquharts, who acquired the estate in the mid 16th century. An inscription on the castle tells us that "This Wark Foundit Ye Fourtene of March Ane Thousand Sex Hounder Four Yeiris And Endit Ye 8 Of December 1607". It was built by John Urquhart, styled Tutor of Cromarty because he had custody of the affairs of his great nephew Thomas until the latter came of age. The house was probably built by the Bell family of masons who are thought to have been given a more precise brief than was usual, thus the unusual plan and restraint in the elevations reflects the laird's personal taste. Two wings on the west side facing the approach. are united by an arch carrying a gallery at fifth storey level. This arrangement is disguised by the use of a dummy balustraded parapet over the arch. A genuine balustraded turret lies on the west wall of the main block above and behind the gallery. Otherwise the roofline is fairly plain, without dormer windows, stair turrets, or bartizans, although there are on the outer corners mouldings for square bartizans never built, whilst there are label mouldings across the top gables on the wings.

The main block measures 17.6m by 11m externally and the wings project 4.6m. They are of unequal width, that to the NW being wider to contain a private suite for the laird. The entrance lies within the recess between the wings and is covered by a modern porch. From it there is access to the foot of a straight stair leading to a lobby at the SW corner of the hall and to passages connecting with a back door on the south, a kitchen on the NE and five vaulted cellars. The hall now forms a drawing room and has an ante room of some size partitioned off at the south end. A spiral stair in the west wall by the SW wing then forms the principal stair leading upwards. A second stair in the north wall at the junction of the main block and wing connects the kitchen with the hall and continues up to serve the laird's private suite. On the fourth storey (the hall is equivalent to the second and third storeys in the wings) the main block contains a corridor linking three bedrooms, the largest of which are called the Brown Room and Red Room respectively. Above are three more rooms, that in the middle being a library, whilst a study and a vaulted muniment chamber are squeezed in on the south side between them and the gallery.

The 4th successive John Urquhart of Craigston succeeded to the barony of Cromarty held until then by a senior line. His own line failed with his son John and Craigston then went to the Urquharts of Meldrum and Lethendry. In 1746-53 they added the long narrow two storey wings and courts to the north and south. A new dining room is contained on the upper floor of the south wing.

Craigston

CUSHNIE NJ 535111

The Old Place of Cushnie is a boarded-up and deserted late 17th century L-plan laird's house incorporating older masonry on the west and having many 19th century windows. The roll-moulded doorway in the re-entrant angle is 16th century work later heightened rather crudely. Two panels bear the arms of the Lumsdens, who acquired Cushnie from the Leslies in the early 15th century.

DAVIDSTON NJ 429451

This 16th and 17th century house built by the Gordons on a shelf above the Davidston Burn is thought to take its name from David de Strathbogie, Earl of Atholl in the time of Robert Bruce. Under the NE bartizan is a grinning mask and the date 1678 with the inscription I.G. (John Gordon?) and T.A. Builded This House. The house is an L-plan of a long and low profile standing at the SE corner of a court retaining an original west facing entrance flanked by shot-holes. The north range is modern. The house has three storeys but the wing, probably the oldest part, and the adjacent part of the main block also have an attic. There are conical roofed bartizans on the NE and SW corners. The big windows facing south at all three levels are not old. In the 1970s Davidston was restored by Keith Shellenberg, an upper floor entrance then being found.

DELGATIE NJ 755506

A motte is thought to have stood here and the plan form of the present lofty L-plan tower built by George Hay, 7th Earl of Erroll, in the 1570s suggests that the main block may incorporate masonry from an early tower. Part of the west wall was battered down when the castle was besieged for six weeks by James VI during the Catholic rebellion of 1594. Sir William Hay of Delgatie was Chief of Staff to Montrose during his last campaign in the far north in 1650. He was executed along with Montrose in Edinburgh by the Covenant authorities. Delgatie was later held by the Duffs and in the late 19th century was occupied by the Ainslies. It is now a Hay possession again and is the seat of the Commissioner of the Earldom of Erroll.

The tower has a main block 12.4m long by 9.8m from which a wing 8m wide projects 10.4m. The wing is thus large compared with the main block. The wing is surmounted by a plain parapet supported on ornamental corbelling with open rounds whilst the much rebuilt upper part of the main block has a sloping roof with attic windows in the gables. The entrance in the re-entrant angle leads into a rib-vaulted lobby which has access either directly or by a dog-legged passage to two cellars in the main block, a much altered kitchen in the wing, and a wide spiral stair in the south wall. Above the kitchen is the laird's room which is rib-vaulted with a central boss having the Hay arms. The ridge ribs rest on four carved human masks, three male and the other female. The last has wings and probably represents the Earl's deceased spouse Margaret Robertson. The fireplace has the sacred monogram IHS and the motto "My Hope Is In Ye Lord" and the date 1570. The room has a latrine and two mural chambers flanking the kitchen fireplace flue in the east wall. The hall in the main block is at a higher level and has no old features of interest, the three round-headed west windows and the high bay window on the south being 19th century. Above the hall are two storeys of private rooms, several of which have old painted ceilings. One was called the Tulip Room, having a tulip motif painted on the walls until the 19th century. When in 1950 the lath and plaster were stripped from its ceiling beams dated 1592 bearing old Scottish proverbs were revealed. On the level above is the Painted Room, with more proverbs on the beams and gaily painted designs in between. Faces on this ceiling are thought to be caricatures of members of the household. See p 45.

DRUM NJ 796005 NTS

The theory that the mason Richard Cementarius was building the tower for Alexander III at the time of the King's death in 1286 is now generally accepted. The tower served as a hunting seat in the royal forest of Drum first mentioned in 1247. Robert Bruce in 1323 granted the tower and most of the forest to his armour bearer and secretary William de Irvine of Woodhouse in Dumfries-shire. William was succeeded in 1332 by his son Thomas and then there were twelve successive lairds all called Alexander, the first of them being the hero of the battle of Harlaw in 1411 when he was mortally wounded in slaying Maclean of Duart. The second Alexander married Elizabeth de Keith, thus ending a feud between the two families. In 1439-40, during unrest after James I's murder, this laird was chosen as Captain and Governor of the city of Aberdeen, an office unknown before and not used since.

The 9th laird, who died in 1630, and was highly regarded by contemporaries for his charitable work and decent living, replaced late medieval outbuildings beside the tower with a fine new mansion probably created by the Bell family of masons. In 1640, after a brief resistance, the wife of the 10th laird surrendered the castle to a force of Aberdonians led by Major General Robert Munro and the Earl Marischall. She was allowed to remain in residence with her ladies while Munro garrisoned the place. In 1644 the Marquis of Argyll was welcomed by Lady Irvine and her daughter-in-law Mary, who was Argyll's niece. In spite of this Argyll "shortly removed the two ladies and set them out of the gate perforce, with two grey plaids about their heads. The whole of the servants were also turned out. The ladies came, in pitiful manner to Aberdeen, mounted on two work-nags. Then the renegade Irish soldiers fell to and plundered the place of Drum, wherein was abundance of all necessary and rich furniture and every kind of provision. They left nothing that was portable, and broke down the stately beds, tables, and timber work. They killed the cattle, sheep and cows, and broke up the granaries, in which was abundance of meal and malt. They found yerdit (buried) in the courtyard of Drum a trunk full of silver plate, goldsmith work, jewels, chains, rings, and other ornaments of great value estimated about twenty thousand pounds.....Thus is this ancient house of Drum oppressed and pitifully plundered". The castle was handed over to the National Trust for Scotland after the death in 1975 of the 24th laird, Henry Quentin Forbes Irvine.

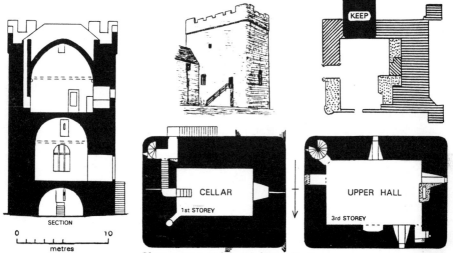

Plans, section, and sketch of Drum Castle

Drum Castle

The tower house measures 15.5m by 11.8m over walls 3.5m thick at ground level. It contains three vaults, the lower two semi-circular, and the uppermost slightly pointed. This upper vault is remarkably close in shape and dimensions to the Bridge of Balgownie at Aberdeen built for Bishop Cheyne or Chein, in office from 1285 to 1328 and it has been suggested that the same wooden shuttering was used for both constructions. Perhaps the tower at Drum was left incomplete after the middle vault over the hall was finished about the time of Alexander's sudden death in 1286, and the topmost vault, under which were two storeys divided by a timber floor, was added by the Irvines 40 years later. The tower is now covered by a gently sloping roof of 1960 with a flat apex resting directly on the top vault, but at one time there must have been a gabled attic room for use by soldiers within the high plain parapet carried on a single row of corbels. The corners are raised slightly on short sections of a continuous moulded course and one of them has a latrine.

The original entrance lies in the south wall at the level of the hall. The original stockaded court and outbuildings would have been placed on this side to catch the sun instead of being in the shadow of the 21m high tower. The entrance once led through to the main hall, altered into a library in 1845, when a new means of access from the mansion was provided at the SW corner and a large round-headed window inserted in the east wall. This level, which at one time seems to have been subdivided by a timber floor, thus does not now retain original features or communicate with the rest of the tower. From the original entrance a spiral stair leads up in the SE corner whilst a straight stair in the east wall leads down to a cellar dimly lighted only by two very narrow slits and having a well in a recess in the NE corner.

The spiral stair now terminates at the level of the laird's room above, although it seems to have been intended to continue to the battlements, which are now reached by an awkward arrangement of a ladder and low hatch. The laird's room has a fireplace in the north wall, windows with seats to the north, west, and south, and a latrine in the NW corner. Another opening to the east is blocked and the west embrasure has been altered to accommodate the flue of a fireplace inserted in the library below. The loft above this room was poorly lighted with two slits between which is a fireplace, probably inserted later and now blocked.

The low building forming the NE corner of the court north of the tower is a 15th century brew-house. Next to it is a modern gateway and NW range, while on the west is the 17th century courtyard entrance. A short distance to the west is a small 16th century chapel restored in 1857. The 17th century mansion occupies the whole of the south side of the court and has boldly projecting square towers at the SE and SW corners. Secondary staircases are fitted in where these join the main block, that on the west rising up as a conical roofed turret. The mansion has a narrow wing extending from the principal private rooms in the slightly higher SE corner to the old tower. This wing contains another staircase. A projection at the NW corner contains the original entrance leading onto the foot of a straight stair to the hall. It also has access to a passage running the full length of the building connecting the kitchen, cellars, and other service rooms. From the hall in the western part at second storey level a fourth spiral stair leads up above the entrance. At a later period a passage was created between the hall and the drawing room east of it to connect an inserted south door to the lawn to an added square tower towards the court. There are numerous bedrooms on the third storey with dormers in the roof dated 1619 on the pediments with initials of Alexander Irvine and his wife. The numerous stairs allowed independent access to these rooms and 19th century additions have allowed the provision of a corridor at this level facing the court plus another spacious stair to replace one which has been ripped out of the added turret.

DRUMINNOR NJ 513264

The Forbes family, probably original natives of this area, had their chief seat in this area from an early date, Duncan Forbes having obtained a charter from Alexander III in 1272. North of Castlehill Farm, 2km north of Druminnor are slight traces of what is probably a 12th century motte. A later Sir Alexander was created Lord Forbes c1445 and the holder of this title is now Scotland's premier baron, no higher title ever having been granted later as so often happened. Extra lands were obtained by the family about that time from the Erskines, whose claim to the Earldom of Mar they supported. Two documents help date the existing building. The first records payment in 1440 to the masons John Kenlock and William Inverkip for work at Druminnor, whilst the second is a licence granted by James II in 1456 to James, 2nd Lord Forbes for the construction of the "tower or fortalice of Druminnor, commonly called Forbes, and the fortification of the same with walls, ditches, and doors of iron and the construction of a decorative and defensive superstructure". The castle was sacked by Adam Gordon in October 1571 when the Forbes feud with the Gordons was at its height. In November the Master of Forbes was captured at the battle of Crabstanes and taken off to at Spynie to be kept in the care of Bishop Hepburn. On release two years later the Master divorced his wife on the grounds of her infidelity at Druminnor with the Bishop's illegitimate son Patrick Hepburn.

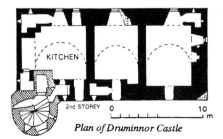

Plan of Druminnor Castle

Druminnor Castle

The three armorial panels on the staircase tower commemorate a remodelling c1660. They recall the then Master of Forbes and his wife Jean Campbell and William, 7th Lord Forbes, and his wife Elizabeth Keith with the date 1577. General Mackay was at Druminnor in 1689, and received provisions for his troops there. James, 17th Lord Forbes, got into debt in 1770 and sold the castle to his kinsman John Forbes of Newe. The latter sold it to Robert Grant of Rothiemaise, whose family held it until 1954. The estate was then broken up and the dilapidated castle sold to the Hon Margaret Forbes-Sempill who died just before a restoration of it was completed.

The castle has a block of two main storeys with bedrooms in the roof and is built palace-wise, i.e. with the hall and main private room to end on the upper storey. It has a low profile when seen from the site of the former court but is rather higher on the NE, where there is a drop to a burn, allowing height for three cellars and a connecting passage below courtyard level. The building is 22m long by 10m wide and has a round stair turret at the west end of the SW side. At the southern end of this wall there was originally a substantial tower-like wing apparently of the same period. This part was demolished in 1800 and replaced by a Gothic villa in 1815, which was in turn pulled down in 1960. At courtyard level the main block contains three vaulted rooms each having their own doorway from the court secured by drawbars. Two of these now serve as windows. This multiplicity of entrances suggests that it was not intended that for the building to be defended independently of the courtyard defences which may have been substantial but have now vanished. All three rooms have latrines. That at the north end was a kitchen with a large fireplace, and that at the south end was a living room called The Happy Room, having an ancient inscription calling it such. The stair turret appears to be original but the gunports are probably of c1570 and the doorway with a five-sided head and yett has probably been transferred here from Lesmoir. The stair leads to the hall and a secondary stair then rises to the bedrooms and a room in a caphouse over the main stair.

DUDWICK NJ 976371

Dudwick was a barony which was purchased from the Mitchel or St Michael family by General James King, one of the Kings of Barra, and a veteran of the Swedish Wars. He built a new house here in 1636 and was created Lord Eythan by Charles I as a reward for his services. The building was demolished in 1865.

DUMBRECK NJ 897288

A castle was probably built after the Meldrums succeeded the Dumbrecks of that Ilk here in 1564. All that remains is an unusual shaped shot-hole built into the farm steading wall and a decorated stone nearby.

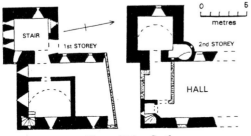

Plans of Eden Castle

Plan of Dundarg Castle

Dundarg Castle

Plan of Dunnideer Castle

Eden Castle

DUNDARG NJ 895649

The name means Red Fort in Gaelic, referring to the sandstone ramparts. There was an Iron Age stronghold on this narrow coastal promontory probably in use until the 4th century. The castle is thought to have been built in the late 13th century by the Comyn Earls of Buchan to help defend the NE coast against Viking raids. An inner court lay on the promontory and there was an outer enclosure on the mainland with a long SW wall with two lines of ditches in front, a gatehouse near the middle, and a substantial rectangular tower or keep at the west end. Like the other Comyn castles it would have been demolished by the Bruces in 1308. Alice, heiress of the last Comyn Earl, married the English baron Henry de Beaumont to whom Robert Bruce in 1328 agreed to restore many of the honours and estates. After the King died in 1329 the Regent Randolph refused to acknowledge de Beaumont's rights. De Beaumont thus supported Edward Balliol as the puppet King of Scots installed by the English, but after a quarrel between them in 1334 de Beaumont retired to Buchan where he took control of the Earldom and hastily refortified Dundarg Castle. There late that year he was besieged by the Regent, the castle being eventually surrendered and destroyed.

Dundarg lay derelict until refortified in the 1550s by John, 6th Lord Borthwick. The barony of Aberdour including Dundarg was sold by the 7th Lord Borthwick in 1571 to Patrick Cheyne of Esslemont. A charter transferring the lands to his son Patrick in 1600 mentions the "tower and fortalice of Dundarg". The fortalice is mentioned again in 1630 when Alexander Fraser of Philorth granted Dundarg to Alexander, Lord Forbes of Pitsligo, but it may by then have been derelict and it is uncertain as to how much use it saw throughout this period. However the site is now back in use for in 1938 Air Vice-Marshal Carnegie built a house in the southern corner of the outer ward.

Much of our knowledge of the scanty remains at Dundarg derives from excavations by Dr Simpson in the 1930s. The inner court occupied a vertical sided promontory 80m long with a greatest width of 16m. Along the east side is an enclosing wall of stone and earth whilst the west side is bounded by a series of crudely built rectangular structures of uncertain date. One near the south end is roughly orientated east-west and may have been a chapel, whilst the next two were perhaps a modest hall and chamber. Near the point of the promontory is a well. Closing off the only access is a gatehouse still standing up to 5m high. No back wall survives, while the narrower front has rounded corners. The passage was flanked by recesses. The gun-ports date the superstructure to the 16th century rebuilding (the only work on the site definately of that period) but the base may be older. The groove in the rock in front may be the site of the original 13th century inner gate. The outer ward is D-shaped with the straight side facing to landward. The inner parts of the keep are missing but it seems to have been composed of two bodies, one wider than the other with an arch between them. The maximum internal dimensions were 10m by 9m inside walls 2m thick. The timber tower battered by the Regent's catapults in 1334 was probably a hasty construction built upon what was left of the stone walls on the tower. A new gateway with two square turrets then was built over an older base whilst a breach made in 1308 in the thick curtain between the keep and gateway was quickly patched up with earth sods.

DUNNIDEER   NJ 613282   F

The castle which Sir Jocelyn de Balliol is recorded as having here in 1260 may be the existing ruin 200m up on a commanding hill west of Insch. Around the building are remains of a Pictish fort with ramparts of vitrified (fused by heat) unmortared stone enclosing an area 66m by 27m with a well and outworks. The medieval castle comprised a block 15.5m long by 12.6m wide over walls 1.9m thick above a plinth. There were probably just two storeys which are likely to have been subdivided partly because of the difficulty of spanning a width of 8.8m and partly because of a need to provide both a public hall and a private room for the lord on the upper storey, with presumably just dark storage spaces below. Probably the entrance was at hall level. The only surviving features are single basement loops in each of the east and west walls, a jamb of third facing south, and one second storey window in the west wall, the only part to survive to that level. The Tyrie family are said to have remained in residence here until 1724 although there are no signs of extensions or alterations.

EDEN   NJ 698588   V

This castle was built by the Meldrums in 1577, that year appearing on a lintel. It was sold to the Leslies in the mid 17th century, modifications being reportedly carried out for George Leslie in the 1670s. The estate was sold in 1711 to Sir Francis Grant and to William Duff in 1712. A wing 6m square engages the SW corner of a main block 8m wide and probably about 12m long. The north end wall now entirely gone is shown standing by Macgibbon and Ross. It had a roof mark of a later, lower extension perhaps of the 1670s and the base of a round stair turret rising from the ground at the NW corner also then survived. Originally it seems there was a bartizan on that corner. The entrance lies in the largest of the two re-entrant angles and gave onto the foot of a scale-and-platt staircase up to the hall. Tucked under the stair was a room with gunports commanding the approaches in all directions. Under the hall were a cellar with a service stair leading up and a larger room which was probably a kitchen. Both have gunports. Little remains of the features of the hall and the two storeys of bedrooms above it which were reached by a stair in a turret corbelled out over the re-entrant angle. The small lobby created at the south end of the hall is not ancient.

ELLON NJ 956305 & 960307

A public convenience and bus shelter lie on the Moot Hill in Market Street which is the site of an early castle of the Comyns. The ruin lying in an estate once known as Kermucks NE of the town bears arms of 1635 with the names of James Kennedy and Isobel Cheyne, although the building may actually be partly 16th century. After a violent incident called the Slaughter of Westertown in 1652 when a neighbouring Forbes laird was killed, this branch of the Kennedies was outlawed from the mainland of Scotland and was obliged to sell Ellon in 1657. James Gordon, Baillie of Edinburgh, bought the property in 1706 and it was he who landscaped the gardens and created the terrace. After his death his two eldest sons were murdered by their Tutor (guardian) and in 1752 their mother sold the estate to a kinsman, George, 3rd Earl of Aberdeen. In the 1780s the Earl had the old castle greatly extended by adding two wings. In it he installed his mistress Penelope Dering. The succession was disputed on his death as he had two other mansions also furnished with mistresses and their offspring, but eventually Penelope's son Alexander Gordon became laird of Ellon. The house was then in a decayed state and he built a new residence to the west. Explosives were used to destroy most of the old building but the surviving fragment was left as a garden ornament. The new house was itself destroyed in the 1920s when another mansion was created out of a former stable block and servants' quarters. The remains of the old castle comprise the south wall with a lofty round tower at the SE corner. The part adjacent to it had three upper storeys over a cellar vaulted from south to north. The portion to the west may be later and has evidence of two vaults arched from east to west. At the SW corner are traces of a later stair.

ESSLEMONT NJ 932298

Esslemont passed in the 14th century from a family called Mareschal to the Cheynes of Straloch. A castle here was destroyed during a feud between the Cheynes and the Hays of Ardendracht, William Hay being ordered by James IV to compensate Henry Cheyne and his son John. Soon afterwards, in 1500, John Cheyne was licensed "to big apoun his landis of Essilmond a tour and fortalice quhair he or thai thinkis mayst expedient, and to raise the samyn to quhat hicht thai empleissis, and thai-uppon to mak bertasing, battaling, machevling, iron yettis, portculais, draubriggis, fowssis, and all other defens and strenchtis as thai think mayst ganyng and conueinent thairto; and for the keeping thairof to haue watchmen, garitouris, portaris, jevillours and all vthir officiaris neidful". The Cheynes lost Esslemont during the Reformation period and it passed to the Earls of Errol. A party of Covenanters occupied the castle in 1646 but Captain Blackwater attacked them from Fyvie, driving them out and killing 36 of them. Esslemont was sold to James Gordon of Ellon who in 1728 sold it to Robert Gordon of Hallhead. His descendants in 1799 built a new house nearer the Ythan.

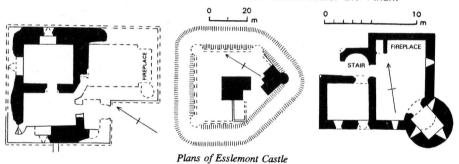

Plans of Esslemont Castle

A shallow ditch remains of a former wet moat around a pentagonal court up to 50m long. Little remains of a curtain wall about a metre thick which seems to have had round towers at the corners. One tower 5.2m in diameter at the south corner is incorporated in a 17th century L-plan house. The fact that the tower projects awkwardly within main block and is the only part to have a vaulted basement is indicative of its earlier origin. The house has a main block 10.2m long by 7.2m wide over walls 1m thick and has on the west side a wing 5.7m wide projecting 5.4m, the end wall of which is broken down. In the re-entrant angle is a square stair turret, now gutted, with the entrance at its foot. The main block basement formed a large kitchen with a fireplace at the north end. In the NW corner beside the kitchen fireplace and its now destroyed flue is a small closet for a chamber pot at each of the three storeys. The main private room lay in the wing at hall level, and there were probably three bedrooms on the third storey and presumably attics within the now destroyed gables. The round tower would probably only have had two storeys and perhaps a parapet as originally built but was heightened and given a square caphouse at third storey level when the house was added.

It was only when trees filling the court were cut down in 1937 that other exciting remains were discovered and were excavated by Dr Simpson the following year. The base of a substantial tower house was revealed, possibly that which the Cheynes were licensed to build in 1500 although its plan form has similarities with neighbouring buildings of the immediate post-Reformation period, so it was probably built or rebuilt by the Earl of Errol c1575. It had a main block 12.3m long by 11m wide over walls 1.9m thick above a plinth. A wing 7.8m wide projected 6.6m from the south side. This wing contained a kitchen with a fireplace and oven in the end wall, although this part of the building had been extensively robbed of materials, presumably for the construction of the new house just beyond it. The main block had an entrance lobby on the south side from which a stair rose in the SW corner. A service stair in the NW corner connected the hall with one of the two cellars which had arched recesses containing slit windows. Presumably the private room lay over the kitchen. It is likely that this building was destroyed during one of James VI's expeditions against the Catholic Earls of Errol and Huntly. Thus it may only have been in use for a few years between completion and destruction.

Esslemont Castle   *Ellon Castle*

FEDDERATE NJ 897498

Two high fragments remain of a castle said to have been blown up either in 1689 after being captured by Williamite troops, or more recently. Fedderate originally belonged to the Crawfords, and later passed to the Irvines of Drum, but the existing building seems to have been built by the Gordons in the 1570s, and had affinities of plan form with Gight and Craig. A wing 8.6m wide containing the laird's room over a kitchen projected 8.3m southwards from a main block 13.3m long by 10m wide over walls 2m thick. The staircase lay on the west side at the junction of the wing and main block. The fragments rise four storeys high and are the SE corner of the wing, with a latrine at second storey level in the corner beside the kitchen fireplace flue, and most of the north and east walls of the main block with remains at hall level of two windows with seats looking north and a fireplace and mural room on the east. All the external corners were rounded and there was an external offset all around the building at the level of the hall vault. The basement is filled with fallen rubble which if removed would probably reveal the bases of the fallen walls. A moat once surrounded the castle.

FETTERNEAR NJ 723171

Randolph, Bishop of Aberdeen built himself a house here which was altered and completed in the 1330s by Bishop Kyninmund, but the "auld founds" representing what appear to be the last traces of an L-plan tower house with walls 2m thick close to the existing ruin must be late 14th or early 15th century. In 1549 Bishop William Gordon leased the barony of Fetternear to his kinsman the Earl of Huntly, but later it was taken back and granted to John Leslie, 8th Baron of Balquhain. William Leslie, 9th Baron, Sheriff of Aberdeenshire, protected the Bishop and his cathedral from the band of fanatics called The Congregation who swept into Aberdeen in 1559. In return the Bishop converted a lease into a direct grant in 1566. A modest house was then built out of the materials of the long-neglected older building. From 1627 to 1690 Fetternear was held by the Abercrombies, although they temporarily fled in 1640 when a Covenant force under the Earl Marischal attacked the house. After the house was returned to the Leslies it was greatly extended by a long range built on the same axis by Patrick Leslie. Further extensions were made in 1818-9 and 1841-4 but the family now live in a new house close by to the north of the ruin.

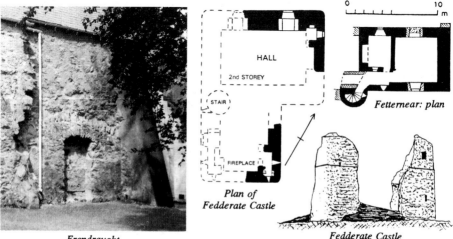

HALL

2nd STOREY

STAIR

FIREPLACE

Fetternear: plan

Plan of Fedderate Castle

Frendraught

Fedderate Castle

Fetternear House

Fetternear House has a long facade facing SW with two round crenellated turrets set in from the ends. Much of this dates from the 1690s but most of the southern turret and that end of the building represent the house of c1566-70. It measures 10.5m long by 5.7m wide and contains a kitchen and cellar at ground level, a hall over, and bedrooms above, all connected by a spiral stair in the round turret. The building has plain gables and lacks dormer windows or bartizans, although such may have been shorn off. The work of the 1690s contains a gallery linking the hall in the house and a dining room over a kitchen at the NW end. Projecting from the NE side is a square tower which contained a scale-and-platt staircase. Above the front door is a fine coat of arms with the initials of Patrick Leslie and his wife Mary Irvine and the date 1693. The arms have a form of coronet not known in English and Scottish heraldry, referring to the rank of Count of the Holy Roman Empire given to Patrick for service there. His Catholic sympathies are demonstrated by a small stone with the sacred initials IHS and MRA for Jesus and the Virgin Mary. Later additions are the large apsidal extension with another kitchen, a dining room or ballroom added to the square tower, and other ranges on the north with a corridor connecting these parts.

FICHLIE   NJ 459149

A roughly rectangular motte has been carved out of a natural spur north of the Don 2.5km SSE of Kildrummy Castle. It rises 7m above the ground to the NE but less than that to the SW where there are indications of an outer enclosure. The summit is roughly quadrangular, measuring 45m by 38m, and having foundations of thin walling of uncertain date on the SE side.

FOVERAN   NJ 992243

Foveran House lies on the site of an early castle of the Turing family. The tower whose fall was prophesied by Thomas the Rhymer in the 13th century was probably of wood, although a stone tower here did indeed collapse in 1720. By then the estate was held by Sir Samuel Forbes, author of "A Description of Aberdeenshire".

FRENDRAUGHT   NJ 620418

The existing mansion is said to incorporate old cellars and other parts, and what is probably a much altered 17th century wing is visible on the SE. After Frendraught Castle was burnt in 1630 under obscure circumstances with several Gordons inside it, including the laird of Rothiemay and Lord Aboyne, the Crichton owner was tried for their murder but acquitted and a feud between the families got even more bitter. Crichton's son was created Viscount Frendraught in 1642 in spite of having Covenant sympathies. He fought beside Montrose at Carbisdale in 1650. After the 4th Viscount died in 1698 Frendaught passed to his wife's family the Morrisons of Bognie.

FYVIE   NJ 764393   NTS

Fyvie was an early royal castle used by William the Lion and Alexander II, and visited by Edward I of England in 1296. Robert II granted it to his son John, Earl of Carrick (later Robert III) who in 1380 granted Fyvie to his cousin Sir James Lindsay, Lord Crawford. His wife Margaret Keith was besieged there in 1395 by her nephew Robert and there is a record of masons being employed on repairs afterwards. The lands of Fyvie had been re-granted in 1390 to Sir Henry Preston in exchange for the ransom of the English knight Ralph Percy captured at Otterburn two years before but it seems that he only obtained the castle in 1402. One tower is named after him and another is named after Alexander Meldrum who obtained the castle in 1433, having married Sir Henry's younger daughter. In 1596 the Meldrums sold the castle and barony to Alexander Seton, fourth son of George, 5th Lord Seton. Alexander served as a privy councillor and was in 1597 given custody of James VI's younger son Prince Charles. He was created Chancellor in 1601 and in 1604 was made Earl of Dunfermline. He commissioned the Bell family of masons to add the ornamental superstructures. In 1644 the castle was occupied by Montrose and close by are traces of entrenchments of his encamped army which Argyll tried unsuccessfully to attack. The castle was still being held for King Charles in 1646 but later held a Cromwellian garrison.

The 4th Earl died in exile in 1694 with his possessions forfeit after taking part in the rebellion of 1689. In 1733 the Crown sold Fyvie to William Gordon, 2nd Earl of Aberdeen who required another seat for his third wife Anne and her children because Haddo House was due to be inherited by his son by his second wife. Anne's son William built the Gordon Tower at the NW corner in the 1790s. The next laird, another William, built a new entrance hall on the east side of the west range. In 1847 Fyvie passed to a cousin, Charles Gordon. After being held in turn by his sons Cosmo and Alexander the estate again passed to a cousin Sir Maurice Duff-Gordon, a notorious spendthrift who was in 1889 obliged to sell the castle and its contents for £175,000 to the American steel magnate Alexander Leith, a descendant of Sir Henry Preston's elder daughter Mariota, who married Sir John Forbes of Tolquhoun. This new laird then styled himself Forbes-Leith and built a new block called the Leith Tower to the NW. In 1905 he was created Lord Leith of Fyvie. His daughter's grandson Sir Andrew Forbes-Leith sold the castle to the National Trust for Scotland in 1984.

Fyvie Castle

The south front of Fyvie is one of the most splendid facades in Scotland. It is almost symmetrical with a former gatehouse called the Seton Tower in the middle and the square Preston and Meldrum towers at either end. Each tower has five storeys, the highest of which are partly in the roofs and have closets in conical roofed bartizans. These towers could be late 14th or early 15th century whilst the curtain walls, now much pierced with openings and heightened, are probably 13th century. Excavations have revealed traces of the 2.5m thick walls on the east and north sides of the former court which had vanished by the late 18th century. The Seton Tower was originally a narrow rectangular structure to which a pair of D-shaped towers with gunloops were added, perhaps as part of a general remodelling c1600. The towers have squared tops united by an arch surmounted by a gable, and with diminutive bartizans on the outer corners. All these projections are carried on ornate mouldings. In spite of its splendid external show the south range was quite narrow after the remodelling, much of its width being taken up with the thickness of the older outer wall in the lower levels. Thus it was subservient in purpose to the west range in which a new suite of apartments were provided. Over several vaulted cellars lay a hall, now divided into two drawing rooms. At the north end of the range is a particularly fine staircase which has arches thrown across it every few steps carrying vaulting. Below the brackets carrying the arches are the Seton arms and those of his first wife Lilias Drummond, who died on 1601, and his second wife Grissel Leslie. Near the top of the stair is an oak inscription dated 1603 with the names Alexander Seton, Lord Fyvie, and Dame Grissel Leslie. The Gordon tower beyond this stair contained a dining room over a kitchen. The tower is said to have replaced a chapel.

GARTLY   NJ 534335

Gartly was the seat of the Barclays, hereditary Sheriffs of Banffshire from the 12th until the 16th century, and originally lay in that county. The district was called The Barony to distinguish it from the rest of Strathbogie held by the Gordons. The remains of the castle, in which Queen Mary stayed during her expedition of 1562, have been cleared away.

Fyvie Castle

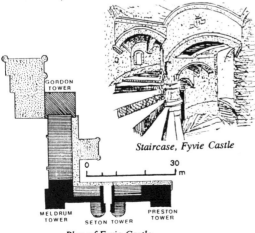

Staircase, Fyvie Castle

Plan of Fyvie Castle

GIGHT   NJ 827392   V

This ruin lies above a bend of the Ythan some distance from any house or road. The estate belonged to the Maitlands until in 1479 it passed to William Gordon, 3rd son of the 2nd Earl of Huntly. Many of this branch of the family suffered violent deaths. William himself was killed at Flodden in 1513, a son was killed at Pinkie in 1547, three of his grandsons including the 3rd laird of Gight and a son-in-law were murdered, a fourth grandson was executed by the Crown, a fifth drowned, and a sixth and seventh were killed fighting in Holland and Flanders respectively. The 13th laird was Catherine Gordon who married the Hon John Byron. Their son George was the celebrated Lord Byron, although he never owned Gight which had been sold off to the Earl of Aberdeen in 1787 to pay off his father's debts. By then the castle was probably long abandoned.

Gight is the largest of a series of similar L-plan buildings of the 1560s and 70s. It is the only one where the main block has three cellars below the hall instead of just two. It measures 16.2m long by 11.2m wide over walls mostly 2.1m thick. The wing is 8.7m square and contained the laird's private room with a latrine and what was perhaps a muniment room tucked in the corners either side of the flue of a huge fireplace across the east end of the kitchen below. The entrance lies in the main block east wall and has draw-bar slots and covering gunloops of an uncommon rectangular shape. It leads into a lobby with a ribbed vault on the central boss of which are the symbols of The Passion: The Five Wounds of Christ, The Crown of Thorns, The Hammer, The Ladder, The Nails, The Reed, and The Spear, an indication of the Catholic sympathies of the then laird. North of the lobby is a small room for a guard or porter whilst to the south leads off a passage with a kink in it which give access to the southern cellars, the kitchen, and to a spiral stair on the south side. The northern cellar is reached direct from the lobby and has an inserted fireplace. It seems to have been used as a forge, probably after the castle ceased to be a residence.

The hall is much ruined with only a featureless fragment remaining of the west wall and no surviving indications of a fireplace. In the thickness of the south wall was a passage connecting with both the main stair in the SE corner and a secondary stair in the SW corner extending down to the wine cellar and up to the bedrooms. A vaulted chamber is squeezed in between the hall and the private room. Off it was a mural chamber, perhaps a latrine with a dumbbell shaped loop. Probably there was another room over the laird's room, the two corresponding in height to the hall if it was vaulted, as is likely, and there would have been another storey above, but nothing now remains of these assumed upper parts. East of the main building are thinly walled outbuildings of late date without features of interest.

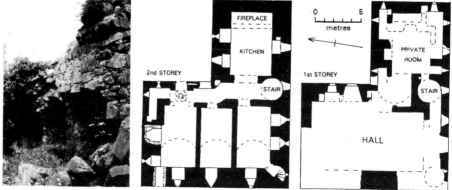

Gight Castle   *Plans of Gight Castle*

Gight Castle

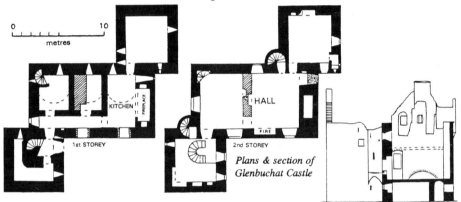

0 ____ 10
metres

KITCHEN FIREPLACE

1st STOREY

HALL

FIRE

2nd STOREY

*Plans & section of
Glenbuchat Castle*

GLENBUCHAT NJ 397149 HS

Over the entrance doorway in the SW wing of this Z-plan castle, built to replace an older house at Badenyon 7km further up the Water of Buchat, is an inscription now illegible but recorded as reading "Iohrn Gordone Helen Carnege 1590 Nothing On Earth Remainis Bot Faime". John Gordon of Cairnborrow was involved in the murder of the "Bonny Earl o' Moray" at Donbristle in 1592 and his house of Glenbuchat was taken over and garrisoned by the royal forces during the rebellion of 1594. His sons Adam and John fell out over the inheritance in 1623, and Adam was later in dispute with his mother on the same matter, resulting in her being imprisoned at Glenbuchat for a month. The estate passed in 1701 to John Gordon of Knockespoch, imprisoned after the 1715 rebellion during which he held the line of the Spey against the Duke of Sutherland until after the Earl of Mar and The Pretender fled abroad. He later became baillie to the Duke of Gordon and in 1738 sold Glenbuchat to Lord Braco. He died in exile in 1750 after taking part in the 1745 rebellion. After Culloden Glenbuchat was garrisoned by a detachment of dragoons. Lord Braco was created Earl of Fife in 1759 and his successors became Dukes. The castle was probably let to tenants but was ruined by the early 19th century. It was sold in 1883, and again in 1901 to the Barclays, who carried out some repairs. The castle was placed in State guardianship in 1946 and was extensively repaired in the late 1970s.

Glenbuchat has wings about 6.6m square at the NE and SW corners of a main block 13.8m long by 7.8m wide over walls mostly 1.1m thick. The entrance leads into a lobby from which rises a stair to the hall, an L-shaped guard room, and a passage leading to two cellars and a kitchen with a fireplace in the far east end wall. One cellar has a service stair. The other is half filled with masonry to carry the weight of a late 17th century cross-wall dividing the hall into what were then regarded as two more conveniently sized rooms. The cross-wall continues up to the third storey which was previously only divided with a timber partition. The hall had a fireplace on the south side between two large windows with the mark of former protective grilles. The NE wing contained the laird's private room with a latrine in the SE corner. The upper rooms at this end are reached from the hall by a stair carried on a squinch over the NW re-entrant angle. The other wing also has an upper stair over its NW re-entrant angle. There are shot-holes commanding the entrance and others are provided in round bartizans on the wings, and a square bartizan on the main block SE corner. There is a square bell-turret on the SW wing outermost corner.

HADDO NJ 868347

The estate has been a Gordon possession since at least the time of Patrick Gordon of Haddo, slain at the battle of Arbroath in 1446. Their seat here was called the Place of Kelly and stood beside a loch some way from the present house built in 1732 to a design by William Adam for the 2nd Earl of Aberdeen. The Marquess of Argyll captured the castle in 1644 after a three day siege and the Covenant authorities then had it destroyed. Sir John Gordon, 1st Baronet of Haddo, was taken to Edinburgh, being the first of a number of Royalist lairds executed there. His successor, Sir George, was Lord Chancellor under Charles II and was created Earl of Aberdeen in 1682. The 4th Earl was Prime Minister under George III. The present laird is bears the title Marquess of Aberdeen.

Glenbuchat Castle   *Glenbuchat Castle*

HALLFOREST NJ 777154 V

In 1326 Robert Bruce gave these lands, part of his inherited lordship of the Garioch, to Sir Robert de Keith, Marischal of Scotland. The Keiths built the existing tower soon afterwards and it remained an occasional residence of the Earls Marischal until it passed in the 17th century to a junior branch of the family, the Earls of Kintore. The five storey tower measures 14.5m by 9.3m over walls 2.1m thick. Much of the vaults over the second and fourth storeys still exist despite the loss of the upper parts of the east end wall. The lowest room was a cellar dimly lighted by meagre slits. Above was a kitchen-cum-servants hall with a fireplace in the east wall and a single narrow window in each other wall. Only hatches and ladders connected these rooms with each other and the hall on the third storey. From that level a spiral stair in the NE corner let up to a sleeping loft and the suite of two rooms for the laird on the fifth storey. The hall has large windows, perhaps enlarged later, facing south. There were entrances in the east wall at second and third storey levels. A breach has been made in the wall below to allow the basement to be used as a byre in later years. A drawing of 1840 shows the tower more or less as it is now plus a small portion of what was probably the wall of a court. The site was originally protected by marshland.

0   10
metres

2nd STOREY

1st STOREY

*Plans of
Hallforest Tower*

Hallforest Tower

Harthill Castle as restored

Squinch arch, Glenbuchat

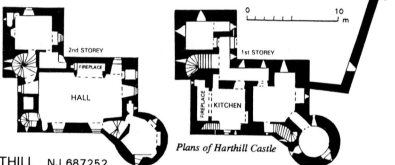

2nd STOREY

FIREPLACE

HALL

1st STOREY

FIREPLACE | KITCHEN

0   10 m

Plans of Harthill Castle

HARTHILL   NJ 687252

One of the Leiths was granted a charter of Harthill in 1531 but the castle was built somewhat later, being dated 1601 on a former dormer pediment. The Covenanters executed a younger son of the laird in 1647 for supporting Montrose. His brother quarrelled with and wounded the Provost of Aberdeen and when put in prison managed to set it on fire. Four generations later the last laird, heavily in debt and at loggerheads with his neighbours, set the castle on fire and went off to London where he died a pauper. In the 1970s the ruined castle was restored by the Remp family.

The castle is a pink-harled Z-plan building also retaining part of the south wall of the court with a round arched gateway over which decorative corbelling carries the remains of an upper storey with recesses for shields either side of a central window. The four storey main block is 13m long by 8m wide and has a round tower 5.8m in diameter at the SW corner containing a polygonal room for the laird over a cellar and three bedrooms. A wing 7.5m by 6.7m at the NE corner contains the entrance, a staircase rising the full height of the building, and four rooms over a cellar. The stair starts from an L-shaped passage off which are reached a kitchen with a stair to the service end of the hall and the wine cellar with a stair up to the laird's end of the hall. The hall has a fine fireplace and a buffet recess. High above the entrance is a short section of open walk-way with a parapet. Shot holes are provided in the lowest rooms and also in conical roofed bartizans on the main block and square wing.

Hatton

HATTON NJ 758469

Originally called Balquhollie, this estate belonged to the Monte Alto (or Mowat) family from the 13th century until 1723 when Alexander Duff bought it and renamed it Hatton. The castle is still inhabited by his descendants. The building was drastically remodelled in 1820 and its full original layout is unknown. The four corner towers, however, seem to be original as they have vaulted cellars containing gunloops. These seem rather close together to be the corners of an open court, yet the building would have been unusually large if the whole internal space was roofed. Perhaps there were two tenements on either side of a narrow open court as at Lachlan in Argyll.

Old postcard of Huntly Castle showing the Old Tower on the right.

HUNTLY   NJ 532407   HS

In the late 12th century William The Lion granted the district of Strathbogie to Duncan, Earl of Fife. He built a motte and bailey castle above a ford on the Deveron. Here in 1307 Robert Bruce convalesced when he fell sick during his campaign against the Comyns. David de Strathbogie turned against Bruce just before Bannockburn and was forfeited, and the estate granted to Sir Adam Gordon of Huntly in Berwickshire. However it was not until 1376 that the Gordons came north to take control of this lordship. The last of this line was Sir John Gordon who left illegitimate sons to succeed to other estates while Strathbogie went to his daughter Elizabeth who married Sir Alexander Seton. He adopted the Gordon surname and in 1436 was created Lord Gordon, whilst in the 1440s his son was created Earl of Huntly. During this period the old timber defences and outbuildings were supplemented by an L-plan tower. In 1452 Strathbogie Castle was destroyed by the Earl of Moray during the power struggle between the Douglases and James II. The Earl was absent at the time, having just held the Earl of Crawford (a Douglas adherent) in check at the battle of Brechin.

By the end of the 15th century the Gordons had built a splendid new block on the "palace plan" and were reaching towards the zenith of their power. Their castle of Strathbogie was frequently visited by royalty and there in 1496 a marriage was celebrated in the presence of James IV between Lady Catherine Gordon and Perkin Warbeck, a Pretender to the English throne. In 1506 the 3rd Earl, Alexander, obtained a charter confirming his possessions and officially changing the name of the castle from Strathbogie to Huntly. However the old name remained in use for some years.

George, 4th Earl, after visiting the sumptuous chateaux of France, had the palace-block rebuilt in a like manner from the basement upward in 1551-4. His initials, those of Elizabeth Keith, and the date 1553 appear on the base of one gable. The Queen Regent, Mary of Guise, visited Huntly in 1556 and the furnishings and entertainment so impressed the French ambassador that he advised the Queen Regent that the Earl, known as "The Cock O' The North", was too powerful and needed bringing down a peg or two. In 1562 Queen Mary did just that, the castle being pillaged and wrecked by her troops after their victory over the Gordons at Corrichie. Repairs continued slowly until 1594 when the Gordons sustained another defeat during the Catholic rebellion against James VI. In spite of the King's reluctance to damage the handsome building, gunpowder provided by the Provost and Magistrates of Aberdeen was used by the royal engineers to demolish the NE corner of the palace-block.

The Earl returned from exile in 1597, made his peace with the King, and by 1599 was in such favour at court that he was created 1st Marquess of Huntly. The missing corner was replaced by a stair turret embellished with a very fine heraldic achievement, whilst a new series of oriel windows were added on the south side with above them an inscription "George Gordovn First Marquis Of Huntlie Henriette Stewart Marquesse Of Huntlie 1602". Work, probably on the eastern wing of the courtyard buildings, was still in progress when the Wars of The Covenant broke out. The castle was then described as untenable because of these works. A Covenant army under Major General Munro occupied the place and no damage was done bar the hacking off of a few "popish" emblems on the palace stair turret. Montrose briefly held the castle against Argyll in 1644 and in 1647 it was starved until surrender when Lord Charles Gordon defied General Leslie. The garrison were hanged and their officers beheaded. The Marquis of Huntly was himself captured in the same year and was briefly detained in his own home while in transit to Edinburgh for execution. Charles II paid a brief visit in 1650. The Gordons were later elevated to a Dukedom but they developed residences elsewhere and Huntly saw no further use, becoming a source of materials for construction work in the town. However, the Palace was probably still roofed when Government troops occupied the castle in 1746.

The palace-block occupies the SW corner of the court. Below courtyard level it has a basement surviving of the building of c1470-90. It has doorways with half hexagonal heads and inverted keyhole type gunloops. Four cellars are connected by a passage which at the east end gives onto a flight of steps up to the entrance and main stair in the small round tower of c1600. An external offset and string course mark the level above which everything is of the 1550s and later. The lowest of these new storeys contains a kitchen in the middle with living rooms on either side, and a further living room in the round tower measuring 10.4m in diameter at the SW corner. Tiers of latrines are provided in the main block west wall. It is uncertain whether the next storey originally formed one huge hall 19m long by 7m wide or was always divided into a hall with a private room at the west end. The present thin dividing wall of c1600 partly blocks a window embrasure on the north side. Both parts have a fireplace in the north wall and wide window embrasures. A spiral stair is provided from this level upwards in the junction of the main block and round tower. The top storey has a fine series of three southward facing oriel windows and the inscription already quoted runs across the top and bottom of these. The round tower has a fifth storey with an oriel facing SE and an attic in the conical roof. There were also attic rooms in the main block plus two rooms in a destroyed square caphouse over the main stair.

Oriel at Huntly

0   5
metres

PRIVATE ROOM

HALL

Huntly, Plan of Palace　　　*The Palace, Huntly Castle*

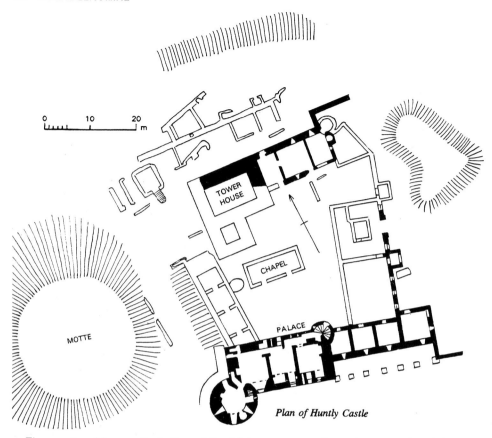

Plan of Huntly Castle

The courtyard lies on the bailey of the 12th century castle to the west of which is the motte, now truncated to a height scarcely above that of the court. On the east is a ravelin built in the 1644 to help protect the fragile new east wall. On the north side of the court are foundation of an L-plan tower with parts of the east and north walls standing 3m high without any features. It measured 16.4m by 11.7m and has a wing 8.6m wide projecting 6.4m, the walls being from 2.6m to 2.9m thick. This was probably the "Old or Cummingstower" demolished for its materials in 1731. Next to the tower was a room with north facing gateway and beyond to the east are vaulted rooms with ovens which were a bakehouse and brewhouse built in the 16th century. Excavations have uncovered the lower parts of several crudely built structures perhaps of 15th or early 16th century date. See the picture on page 65.

Extending north from the palace are foundations of a 16th century range with a round base for a stair turret towards the court. Freestanding in the court immediately east of this is the base of a building thought to be a chapel since it is orientated east-west. The main axis of the palace is continued to the east by a 16th century range with apartments set over three cellars. Outside it to the south are bases of a 17th century piazza. Originally there was probably a gatehouse on the east side of the court, traces of an ancient cobbled causeway being visible here. In the 1630s whatever was then here was replaced by a very wide range of which only the east wall stands above the foundations. In it was a new entrance flanked by a pair of square turrets and leading into the foot of a large and grand scale-and-platt staircase.

INVERALLOCHY NK 041629

Walls varying from 1.3m to 1.6m thick enclose an irregularly shaped quadrangular court with maximum dimensions of about 23m by 18m. There was a range of buildings on the SW side and another range on the NE which contained rooms supplementing those in a five storey tower measuring about 10m by 8m in the north corner. The gateway lies on the NW side. Most of the internal walls of the ranges and tower have collapsed, choking the courtyard and basements with debris. Half of the NE end wall of the tower collapsed a few years ago leaving the north end as a jagged fang. The sharply pointed east corner of the courtyard wall has also gone. Old plans show the tower as having a staircase turret in the angle between it and the adjoining range. The castle was probably built by Sir William Cumming, a descendant of the Comyns, later Lyon King of Arms, and his wife Margaret Hay, lands here being granted to them in 1504. The castle later passed to a branch of the Frasers of Lovat.

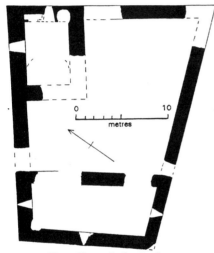

Plan of Inverallochy Castle

Inverallochy Castle

Inverallochy Castle

INVERNOCHTY NJ 352129 F

A huge, mostly natural, mound rising 15m to an elliptally shaped flat summit 80m by 45m stands near the confluence of the Nochty and Don. The Water of Bardoch filled a wet moat around the base and an artificial pool on the NW. Around the summit edge are traces of a wall 2m thick best preserved by the entrance at the SE corner where there are signs of an adjoining guard-room. The wall probably dates from c1200-20 as by the mid 13th century Kildrummy had superceded the Bass Mound at Invernochty as the chief fortress of the Earldom of Mar. On the north the wall had a broad unmortared base and on the west slight evidence was found during excavations of a thinner earlier wall. The other stone structure revealed was the base of a building 9m wide and nearly 28m long with walls just 0.8m thick. A fragment of a Norman stoup or piscina suggested that the building might have been a church, perhaps of much later date. However it could have been a foundation for a 12th century timber hall.

INVERUGIE NK 102487 & 102484 V

On a hill above the lowest crossing point of the Ugie is a motte rising 3m high to a summit 15m in diameter. The estate passed from the Cheynes to the Keiths in the mid 14th century. The castle above the east bank of the river south of the motte was begun c1550-60 by the 4th Earl Marischal as a new chief seat of the Earldom, superseding Dunnottar. It comprised a massively built main block with two round towers on the east and a court extending westward from it to the edge of a slope to the river. There are extensive remains of the courtyard walls and outbuildings although they are much overgrown and lack features of interest. The court was entered by a gateway on the south side once dated 1670 with arms and initials of William, 7th Earl Marischal, Lord Privy Seal under Charles II, and his wife Anna, daughter of the Earl of Morton. MacGibbon and Ross report a shield, initials, and the date 1660 on a piece of oak preserved in a nearby cottage. In their day the ruined main block stood four storeys high but it was blown up in 1899, and little of interest now survives above the basement, which is half buried with debris and in a dangerous condition.

The main block measured 19m by 9.1m although the south half is wider on the west side where the wall was thickened to contain passages and there was a half-round stair turret near the SW corner. The boldly projecting round towers 8.6m in diameter contained rectangular cellars with gunloops. The main block contained a kitchen at the south end with a now-blocked fireplace on the east side, and two cellars both of which have inverted keyhole-shaped loops in the east wall with the marks of former grilles over them. The southern cellar has a service stair leading up to the southern of two very large and high window embrasures in the hall east wall. These windows had grilles and there are also marks of former grilles on the narrow loops below. The hall had a fireplace at the north end and there were private rooms in the towers. There were two storeys of bedrooms above.

INVERURIE NJ 782206 V

The motte and bailey castle built by David of Huntingdon in the 12th century and used by Robert Bruce in 1307-8 lies in a graveyard on the south bank of the Urie just above its confluence with the Don, SE of Inverurie. The Bass Mound or motte rises 12m to a summit 18m across whilst the Little Bass or D-shaped bailey platform measuring 27m by 23m lies on the east.

Keith Hall, formerly Caskieben

Inverugie Castle

Plan of
Inverugie Castle

KEITH HALL   NJ 787212

Keith Hall lies east of the Urie opposite Inverurie. Immediately north of the
house is the site of the 13th century manor house of Caskieben, an enclosure 69m
across rising slightly above the surrounding land, having around it a ditch 13m wide
and 3m deep once full of water. The manor was originally held by the Gavioch or de
Garioch family but passed via an heiress in the 14th century to Stephen de Johnston,
clerk to the last of the old line of the Earls of Mar. In c1590 this family began building
a Z-plan house with two square wings. In 1662 it was sold to Sir John Keith, 3rd son
of the 6th Earl Marischal, and it was he who had the name changed to Keith Hall. Sir
John played a part in the saving of the Crown Jewels from being captured by
Cromwell at Dunnottar in 1652 and he was eventually created Earl of Kintore. He built
a substantial new block with a symmetrical face on the south side of the old house
facing the approach. After the 4th Earl died in 1761 Keith Hall passed to George Keith,
originally the 10th Earl Marischal, but forfeited as a young man for his part in the 1715
rebellion, but whom had found favour with George II after returning from exile. After
he died in Potsdam in 1778 descendants of the 4th Earl's sister succeeded to the
Earldom. Now surnamed Keith-Falconer, they still live at Keith Hall.

The Z-plan house has a main block 12m long by 8m wide and has a NE wing about
6.3m square and a SW wing 11.2m long by 6.3m wide. There are turret stairs in the
northern re-entrant angles serving all the upper rooms whilst the main stair from the
entrance to the hall occupies part of the SW wing. At ground level the main block
contains a cellar by the entrance, a kitchen on the east with its fireplace in the east
end wall. The principal private room in the NE wing is vaulted with a carved granite
keystone pendant. A dormer window in the wing dated 1665 indicates Sir John Keith
made minor additions to the existing house before building the new mansion. The
wings added to the north of the house are 19th century.

KEMNAY   NJ 733154

The Douglases of Glenbervie acquired Kemnay from the church at the Reformation. It
passed to Sir Thomas Crombie who in the early 17th century built an L-plan house
with a three storey main block and a four storey wing, a turret stair being corbelled out
high above the entrance in the re-entrant angle. There are two vaulted cellars in the
main block. Each arm of the L has been extended later, the north wing probably being
the work of Thomas Burnett of Leys, to whom Kemnay was sold in 1688.

Kildrummy Castle

KILDRUMMY   NJ 471169 & 454164   HS

The original 12th century castle at Kildrummy was a small motte created out of the top of a glacial mound not far from the parish church. The stone castle further west was built under the direction of Gilbert de Moravia, Bishop of Caithness, for Alexander II with the intention of commanding the roads between the provinces of Moray and Mar. Work on the castle continued during Alexander III's reign when the Earls of Mar had custody of it. Edward I of England was at Kildrummy in 1296 and 1303, and in 1305 he ordered Robert Bruce, Earl of Carrick, custodian by right of his wife, a daughter of an Earl of Mar, to "place the Chastle de Kindromyn in the keeping of a person for whom he shall answer". Bruce rebelled the next year and was crowned King of Scots. The end of 1306 saw Prince Edward besieging Sir Nigel Bruce and the ladies of Bruce's court at Kildrummy. They put up a good defence but were compelled to submit after Osborne the blacksmith treacherously set the castle on fire. The garrison were slaughtered and ladies, who had escaped beforehand, were caught, sent to Edward I and mistreated. At some point about this time the castle is said to have been made untenable by the destruction of the west wall but it is more likely that this was done by the Bruces themselves during their harrying of the Comyns in 1308.

The castle had been restored by 1333 when it formed the prison of Duncan, Earl of Fife. In 1335 Kildrummy was defended by Dame Christian Bruce and John of the Craig against the Earl of Atholl. On the expulsion of Edward Balliol and the restoration of David II the castle was returned to the custody of the Earls of Mar. David II visited the castle several times, and, after falling out with the Earl, besieged and captured it in 1361, retaining it under other governors until 1368. In 1404 Isabella, Countess of Mar, was seized at Kildrummy by Sir Alexander Stewart, who obtained the Earldom after forcing her to marry him. On his death in 1435 the castle and Earldom were retained by James I in spite of the clear right to them of Sir Robert Erskine who was descended from the old Celtic line of Earls. The Erskine claim was only recognised by Queen Mary in 1565 and it was not until 1626 that his descendant got legal possession of Kildrummy. Sir Robert himself stormed the castle in 1442 but was soon forced to yield it up. During this period the Crown carried out considerable work on the castle, and it was briefly held in turn by various royal kin and favourites.

In 1507 Kildrummy was granted to Alexander, 1st Lord Elphinstone whose family retained it until 1626. They remodelled the solar block as a high gable structure now called the Elphinstone Tower. In 1531 the castle was stormed and plundered by the freebooter John Strachan of Lynturk, although the full circumstances of this episode are unknown. The castle was captured from Royalist rebels in 1654 by Colonel Morgan and then garrisoned for Cromwell. In 1690 Graham of Claverhouse, Viscount Dundee, burnt the castle rather than allow it to be occupied by Williamite troops. It was presumably repaired, for in 1715 the last Earl of Mar was able to use the castle as a headquarters for planning and mustering for the rebellion he led that year. The castle was subsequently dismantled by the government and became a quarry for the district. Repairs were executed by Colonel Ogston, owner of the estate from 1898 to 1931, and in 1931 custody of the castle was vested in the state.

At one time it was thought that the whole of the defences of the D-shaped court about 55m across were of c1228-40. Investigations and excavations carried under Dr Simpson in the 1930s have led to a general acceptance that only the hall and parts of the 2.6m thick curtain wall of roughly coursed rubble are of that period. The chapel is a slightly later addition of about the time of Alexander II's sudden death in 1249, whilst the circular Warden's Tower at the NE corner, the keep or Snow Tower at the NW corner, and the two D-shaped towers facing east and west are of c1260-80, or possibly c1296-1300. The four towers are ashlar faced and have plinths. The two D-shaped towers forming the outer part of a gatehouse on the south side have a battered bases rather than proper plinths. The plan of the gatehouse as a whole is strikingly similar to others at Edward I's castles of Harlech, Beaumaris, and Aberystwyth in Wales except that they have staircase turrets on the inner corners. It is likely that this gatehouse was indeed built on the orders of Edward after his visit of 1296, although that begs the question of what it replaced, especially if the earlier date is accepted for the other towers. Both the gatehouse and the other towers had passages leading to latrines in the adjacent sections of curtain walling. The provision of these must have meant a lot of rebuilding of the original wall and with that plus repairs after repeated sieges it is doubtful if much original stonework of the 1230s actually now remains.

Hall and Elphinstone Tower, Kildrummy Castle

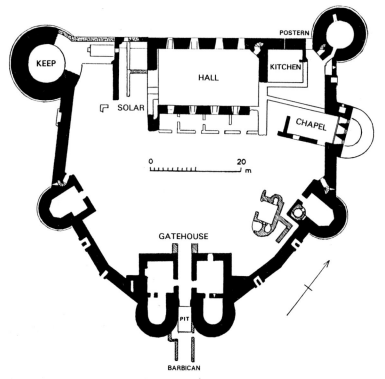

Plan of Kildrummy Castle

The gatehouse is 20.4m wide across the inner part, the rounded outer parts being slightly wider, exactly as at Harlech. The D-shaped rooms in the drum towers were later given dome-vaults. The more thinly walled inner part contained two large guard rooms, one of which has a typically Edwardian fireplace. The entrance passage was closed by a drawbridge over a still-surviving pit, a portcullis, and at least two pairs of doors. In the 15th century a barbican was added in front of the passage and walling was added at the inner end, perhaps to help support a timber outside stair. Nothing remains of the upper parts but analogy with the Welsh examples suggest two upper storeys having halls across the inner part with private rooms in the drum towers.

The two D-shaped intermediate towers contain rooms with polygonal outer ends. Each tower has a staircase which has a separate entrance from the court, being hidden on the furthest side from the gateway. Only the lowest courses remain of the Snow Tower although part of it stood to the full height until it collapsed in 1805. The tower was 16m in diameter over walls 3.5m thick and contained a series of dome-vaulted rooms with a well, now filled in, centrally placed in the basement. The Warden's Tower is 11.8m in diameter and still partly stands 19m high although the inner parts are mostly missing. The lowest room with a latrine but no windows was a prison. The room above was a military post with four shooting loops set in embrasures with shouldered arches. Above were two more rooms with noble twin lancet windows and from the name of the tower it can be surmised that these formed a suite for the captain of the garrison. Next to the Warden's Tower is a postern from which a passage led down to a cistern chamber and means of escape beside the stream below.

The great hall at Kildrummy was one of the largest and finest chambers in medieval Scotland. It measured 22m by 12m internally and had four large windows on each side with seats in the embrasures. The windows themselves have gone but were presumably twinned lancets possibly with transoms. The staircase in the NE corner led to a gallery over a screened service passage at that end. A kitchen lies beyond here, although without visible access to the hall. The gallery could have used by musicians but probably its main purpose was to give access through a lobby to the chapel, which was raised over a basement. In order to obtain a true orientation and sufficient length for the chapel the east curtain wall built only a few years before was breached and a projecting gable added on with three beautiful but vulnerable lancet windows with a single lancet above. It is incredible that the strength of such a great castle could be jeopardised in this way. Edward I of England probably thought so too, and in front of the gable are foundations of a D-shaped tower assumed to have been begun after his visit of 1296 but probably never raised above the lowest courses.

Embrasure in the Warden's Tower   *Back view of Kildrummy Castle*

There is another stair in the hall SW corner which led to the lord's private apartments in a solar block, now called the Elphinstone Tower, beyond. This part was remodelled in the 16th century, the internal crosswall dividing a passage from two vaulted cellars being of that period. Much of the north end wall is late 13th century, having a twin lancet window of that period set in a recess with a square head. However the wall stands on an earlier base, and has a 16th century crowstepped gable, now the highest part of the castle, whilst in the middle below the window is a huge area of modern patching. The window lighted the lord's principal private room. From it there appears to have been access via a drawbridge over a pit into the Snow Tower. The south wall of the solar block is entirely destroyed but it seems that the building was as much as 16m long internally, large enough for a suite of two rooms at each level. A low series of offices, each with their own entrances from the court, but interconnecting with each other, was built in front of the hall in the 15th century.

KINDROCHIT   NO 152913   F

Overlooking the gorge of the Clunie Water in the middle of the village of Braemar are remains of a 14th century palace built either by David II or Robert II. Both frequently came here and the latter dated several charters from Kindrochit. He came during the hunting season athough his age and informity must have precluded much participation in the sport by the King himself. His son John was probably unable to hunt either after being permanantly crippled by a kick from a horse in 1388. After that royal summers were spent elsewhere and after John succeeded to the throne (styling himself Robert III as the name John was considered unlucky for kings) in 1390 the palace was granted to his brother-in-law Sir Malcolm Drummond. He was granted a licence for the building of a "tower or fortalice on the lands of Kyndroch with their pertinents in the Earldom of Mar". In 1402, whilst Sir Malcolm was directing work on the new building, he was carried off by Highland caterans and treated so badly that he died. His widow married Sir Alexander Stewart who presumably completed the tower. It reverted to the Crown when he died in 1435 and was retained as a royal castle with short term custody of it being granted periodically to a series of royal kin and favourites. In the 16th century the castle was allowed to decay and in 1618 was described as a ruin. Probably it was plundered for material for building Braemar Castle in 1628.

Kindrochit Castle

Kindrochit Castle

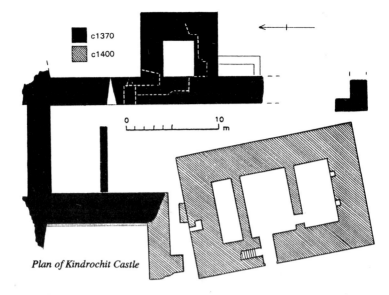

c1370

c1400

0   10
           m

Plan of Kindrochit Castle

It was only when a great pile of earth and debris was removed in the 1920s that architectural details of the building became known. The palace was a remarkable building, without a parallel in Scotland. Unfortunately all that remains of it is the north half of its basement now standing to a maximum height of 3m. Walls 3m thick enclosed a space 9m wide and probably about 30m long. As part of the original design there were boldly projecting square towers at the north corners, and presumably others at the southern corners. The tower 8.3m wide projecting 6.8m from the east wall was a later addition. It has some remains of an upper storey room with windows in each outer wall, being reached by a passage from the sole surviving embrasure now remaining in the main block. There are no traces of any vaults but it is possible that there were two levels under a vault with the hall above, probably with private chambers at one or both ends. There is a thin later wall dividing off the northern part of basement beyond the solitary loop remaining at this level in the east wall.

It is a mystery why Sir Malcolm Drummond considered it necessary to build a new tower for which the southern half of the palace had to be cleared away. One would have thought he could have raised a tower cheaply and easily by adapting and heightening one end of the palace. Instead he started afresh at an awkward angle to what remained of the old building which was probably retained in the form of a small open court with new parapets grafted onto the massive walls and the northern end roofed over as an outbuilding. The new tower was itself no mean structure, being one of the largest of its type in Scotland. It measured 19.5m long by 13.2m wide over walls 3.3m thick. The basement was divided into two cellars with a door between them and a narrow prison at the north end which could only have been reached by a trap-door from above. The middle room has a doorway facing the ravine from the north jamb of which a stair rises toward the NW corner which presumably contained a spiral stair to the upper levels. It is likely that the second storey was a kitchen-cum-mess-room covered by a vault supporting the paved floor of a third storey hall, with probably a suite of two rooms for the laird on the fourth storey and perhaps a fifth storey above. Another entrance at either second or third storey level in the north wall is likely. There are here remains of some sort of forebuilding, probably a later addition as a latrine shute in the tower north wall drained into what became its basement.

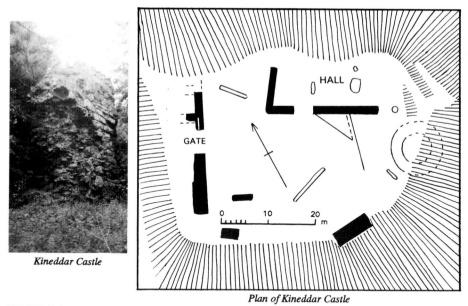

Kineddar Castle

Plan of Kineddar Castle

KINEDDAR NJ 722562

Kineddar or King Edward Castle (there is no evidence for a connection between the castle and the English kings of that name) was built in the late 13th century by the Comyns and like their other strongholds in Buchan is assumed to have been destroyed by the Bruces in 1308. The lands were later held by Sir John Ross and then in the early 15th century by Alexander Stewart, the notorious "Wolf of Badenoch", younger brother of Robert III. It was later held as part of the Earldom of Ross by the Lord of the Isles, and after their forfeiture by James IV the castle was retained by the Crown, although the lands were granted away in 1495. The castle hill and steading were in 1509 conferred on Lord Forbes "with stones and lime and the pertinents of the same, upon which he himself intends to build". He was also licensed to build "a castle tower or fortalice, with defences.....barmkin, and le machcolin with moveable bridges.....le drawbriggis, iron gates and other necessaries". This suggests the building was then ruinous, and had perhaps never been restored since 1308, and was now to be rebuilt. However, the meagre remains could all be fragments of the original building, and there is no certain evidence of 16th century work without excavation and clearance.

The castle is strongly sited on a promontory with steep drops to ravines. A road now runs along the south side of the site but the alignment of an earlier bridge of 1771 shows the old road skirted the north side of the castle. The site is much overgrown and covered in debris. Most of the curtain walls up to 3m thick have fallen down the steep slopes, probably because of inadequate foundations, but fragments remain on the west and south sides. They enclosed a court about 45m long by 35m wide. The west side was that least well defended by nature and has a deep ditch. Here there was a gateway with a draw-bar slot. On the north side of the gate are indications of a tower which was probably D-shaped, although its outer part is entirely missing, and it is likely there was a similar tower on the other side of the gate. At the east end of the court are traces of the base of what appears to have been a round keep 11m in diameter, and on the north side are remains of the 1.3m thick west and south walls of a hall block about 8m wide by 25m long.

KINNAIRD'S HEAD NK 999677 V

The lighthouse on the north side of Fraserburgh is built up upon one corner of a tower probably built by Sir Alexander Fraser of Philorth about the time of his founding of the burgh in 1569. The tower measures 12m by 8.4m and rises four storeys to the present flat roof and plain parapet with round bartizans at the corners and rectangular projections in the middle of the sides. Rebuilding to accommodate the lighthouse has cause considerable internal alteration although vaulting survives in the basement and the hall above still has some sort of identity as such. A wide new stair in the NE corner has replaced the former narrower stair in the SE corner.

On the rocky shore about 50m to the east is a second tower of about the same date measuring 8.1m by 6.4m. It seems to have served to command the harbour and act as a warehouse, hence the name of Wine Tower. A new outside stair provided in a recent restoration leads up to the topmost room, which has a fireplace, several windows, and a vault with three pendants with the arms of the Frasers, Erskines, and Douglases and the inscription "The Glory Of The Honorable Is To Feir God". From here a stair leads to the flat roof now lacking a parapet. Access down to two vaulted cellars below was only by means of hatches and ladders. These levels have a few gunloops and the basement has a door towards the sea. Below it is a cave.

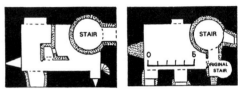

Wine Tower   *Plans of Kinnaird's Head Castle*

Kinnaird's Head Castle   *The Wine Tower*

2nd STOREY

1st STOREY

Knock: plans

Knock Castle

Knock Castle

KNOCK NJ 352952 HS

The Gordon laird of Knock was killed in 1592 by a party of Mackintoshes who were his guests. His successor Alexander, who is thought to have built the tower on a ridge high above the Dee soon afterwards is said to have fallen to his death down his own staircase after being overcome with grief when his servant reported that a party of Forbes's had killed his seven sons while they were out cutting peats and impaled the heads on their spades. The tower measures just 8.2m by 6.5m and contained a hall over a low vaulted cellar and two upper rooms. The uppermost room has closets in round bartizans supported on label-corbelling. The entrance leads directly into the cellar beside the foot of a now-destroyed staircase. The cellar has a loop on each wall and a service stair leading up. The hall has a fireplace opposite the stair and a window in each wall with shot-holes in the jambs. Other shot-holes are provided in the bartizans and in a square gabled caphouse raised high over the top of the staircase. By the entrance is just one jamb of a gateway into a now-vanished courtyard.

KNOCKESPOCH NJ 544241

The house is a large building of various periods standing on a shelf with a pool in front of it. At the back or south side a 16th century gabled tower with a stair turret and blocked gunloops can be seen. The Gordons, now Fellowes-Gordons, have been here since the 15th century.

KNOCKHALL NJ 992265 V

This house was built by the 3rd Lord Sinclair of Newburgh, who played a leading part in the Reformation movement, and is dated 1565 over the entrance. The estate was sold in 1633 to a son of Udny of that Ilk and was long owned by that family. In 1639 the Earl Marischal captured and plundered Knockhall, although Lady Udny was left in possession and suffered another visit by Covenant troops the following year. The building has been a ruin since it accidentally caught fire in 1734, the family being saved by their fool Jamie Fleeman or Fleming.

A wing 7.1m wide projects 6.6m from a main block 10.8m long by 7.7m wide over walls 1.2m thick. The entrance in the wing leads onto a passage leading between the kitchen in the rest of the wing and a single large cellar in the main block to a wide spiral stair in a square turret projecting from the far end wall where the wing and main block join. Over the entrance is a recess for a heraldic stone. Above the now destroyed kitchen vault was the private room with a fireplace in the wall between it and the hall and a small room for a chamber pot or muniments in one corner. The hall has its fireplace in the end wall furthest from the stair and a square recess in the a near corner. Above were three bedrooms on the third storey and attics in the roof. There are no projecting turrets, bartizans, or battlements, but the lowest rooms have double-splayed gunloops. Of the courtyard there still remains one corner tower which served as a dovecot.

Plans of Knockhall Castle

Gunloop at Knockhall

Knockhall Castle

Leith Hall

LEITH HALL NJ 541298 NTS

The north wing is the four storey rectangular block with four conical roofed bartizans on the corners built by James Leith in 1650 on the estate of Kennethmont purchased by his father John, the family having come from Lothian. The entrance was on the south side and had a gable high above to contain another room level with the attics. This gable and the dormers were removed in the 19th century and there are now modern skylights in the roof. A small court to the south had a two storey range on the east side, a thatched stable in the SW corner and a gateway facing west. A century later his great-grandson, another John, added a two storey NW block, heightened the east block, and built a new block on the south with symmetrically projecting end wings, the stables being removed away from the house. General Sir Alexander Leith-Hay, who raised the Aberdeenshire Regiment and fought in the Napoleonic Wars, built up the central part of the south range as a high block with bartizans as a copy of the original north block. The east range was also widened and heightened again. He took the additional name Hay from his uncle Andrew Hay of Rannes, who had rescued the Leiths from financial difficulties and eventually left his estate to Alexander. Charles O'Neill Leith-Hay, the last of the male line, was killed in the services in 1939 and in 1945 Leith Hall was presented to the National Trust for Scotland.

LESLIE NJ 599248 A

The Leslie family held this estate from the 12th century and probably once had a timber house within the moated platform 48m long by 44m wide still partly visible. The last Leslie of that Ilk died in debt and his widow married the creditor William Forbes of Monymusk whose son William built the existing building in 1661. A small gatehouse which once stood on the edge of the moat was dated 1663. The house was later sold to John Leith of Leith Hall and was allowed by his descendants to fall into ruin. It was restored by David Wood in the 1980s and is now used as an hotel.

Lickleyhead Castle

Leslie Castle under restoration

The house formed part of a group of buildings around a court in the western half of the moat, whilst the east half was used as a garden. It is L-planned with similarities of layout to Innes House in Moray. But whilst the earliest Innes House has a classical air about it Leslie was built in the older style with conical roofed bartizans, shot-holes around the entrance, and barred windows. William Forbes evidently fancied himself as an old style feudal baron and wanted a house to fit with that image although some features, such as the sloped instead of stepped gables and the diagonally set chimney stacks, betray its real period. The house measures 17.2m by 14.6m over its longest sides, both parts being 7.8m wide over walls 1.1m thick. The entrance lies in a square tower containing a scale-and-platt stair in the re-entrant angle. The stair was heated by means of a central well used as the flue for a fireplace at the bottom. Over the doorway is the motto "Haec Corp Sidera Mentum (This House Is The Body, Heaven Is The Soul)". There are three vaulted cellars of differing sizes and a kitchen in the NE corner, where the outer wall required the greatest amount of rebuilding in the restoration. The smallest cellar was for wine and has a service stair to the main living room above. A drawing room lies over the kitchen and the wing contains the laird's private room. Above are two storeys of bedrooms, the uppermost mainly in the roof.

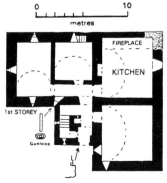

Plan of Leslie Castle

Back view of Leslie Castle as restored

LESMOIR NJ 470280

Not far east of the castle is the farm of Scurdargue from which the celebrated early 15th century Gordon chief Jock o' Scurdargue took his name. There is no evidence of a castle there so presumably he lived at Lesmoir, although he had other residences as well. Previously Lesmoir was owned by the Aberchirders, who obtained it in the late 13th century from the Frendraughts. A wooden building stood on the site in the 12th century but there is no evidence of stone buildings until the early 16th century. In 1537 George, 4th Earl of Huntly granted to James Gordon "the lands of Essie with the croft of Auchleke, with the place and house of Lesmoir, and the lands of Balhene in the barony of Strathbogie". At Druminnor is a heraldic stone removed from Lesmoir but it is uncertain whether this indicated building work at Lesmoir before the grant or that a building constructed by James Gordon bore the arms of his feudal superior. The latter is more likely. A yett at Druminnor may also have come from Lesmoir.

Alexander Gordon, 3rd of this new line rebuilt Lesmoir Castle in the 1590s, it being in 1600 described as built "more sumptuouslie by farr than it was befor". In 1625 James Gordon, 4th laird, was created a baronet of Nova Scotia. Lesmoir Castle was held against General Leslie in 1647. Although described by Leslie as "a place of considerable strength" those within the main building surrendered within two days after the moat was drained and the courtyard was stormed. Leslie hung 27 "Irish" (actually probably western Highlanders) of the garrison. John Leith of Harthill was subsequently confined at Lesmoir for two years. The destruction of the castle to prevent the necessity of garrisoning it was contemplated by the Covenant authorities but there is nothing to suggest that it was demolished. The site was occupied for another century and there is evidence of the house being remodelled or rebuilt (so perhaps it was just unroofed) in the 1660s. Nine years after Sir William Gordon, 9th baronet, died at Lesmoir in 1750, it was sold to John Grant of Rothiemaise. Demolition for materials was commenced but much of the house still stood in 1779 when he went bankrupt and the place was again put up for sale.

The castle was low lying and derived its strength from a moat filled by the Burn of Essie on the south side, the Burn of Newerdrum on the west and south, and the leat from the Milton on the east. The site has a much lowered mound lying in the middle of the NW side of a roughly triangular bailey with its apex at the SE. The court measured about 42m from mound to apex and about 51m from north to west across the mound. The site is now overgrown with trees and shrubs. A few fragments remain of courtyard walls 0.9m thick but nothing stands of the main house. A few battered architectural fragments from it lie in the garden of the farm of Mains of Lesmoir.

LICKLEYHEAD NJ 627237

Lickleyhead belonged to the Leslies of that Ilk until sold c1500 to William Leith of Barnes. It was probably has grandson William, who died c1598, who built a modest tower house to replace an earlier structure perhaps of wood. The Leiths were involved in various feuds and quarrels and Patrick Leith was at loggerheads with John Forbes of Leslie over shooting rights on the Muir of Bennachie. The latter purchased Lickleyhead in 1625 and added a square stair tower at one corner. Over the entrance into this tower are his initials and those of his second wife Margaret Skene. His first wife had been Ann Leslie, through who he obtained Leslie. Lickleyhead passed to another branch of the Forbes family later and in 1700 was sold to William Hay. He sold it in 1723 to Patrick Duff of Craigston. His son, another Patrick, is thought to have added the east wing in the 1730s or 40s. The property then passed through various hands and is now the home of the granddaughter of Don Guillermo de Landa Y Escandon, who purchased it in 1922. See pages 15 and 83.

The original tower house at Lickleyhead measured 10.5m by 7.5m. It had a pair of vaulted cellars linked by a passage on the south side, a hall above which is thought to have had its own entrance in addition to one below, and at least one upper storey. A staircase in the SE corner linked the hall with the bedrooms, whilst a service stair went down to the cellars in the NW corner. The later staircase tower is 5.1m square and has three upper bedrooms reached by a stair in the NW re-entrant angle. The turret containing this has lost its caphouse. Conical roofed bartizans with closets at two levels were added to the north corners. They have small lozenge shaped windows at the upper level like those at Castle Fraser. The upper closets open off a gallery, now subdivided, in the roof. The 18th century east wing provided a kitchen and a drawing room and bedroom now thrown together to made a dining room. Added to the middle of this range to make a T-plan is a wing added by Henry Lunsden of Auchindoir in 1820. It contains two extra rooms and another staircase with straight flights.

LOCH KINORD   NO 441996

Of two islands in Loch Kinord the eastern one is a Dark Age crannog and the larger and probably natural western one once had a castle upon it. There was a residence of some sort here in 1335 when Sir Robert Menzies fled there after the nearby battle of Culblean. Eventually he surrendered to Regent Moray and pledged fidelity to the cause of David II. The castle was visited by James IV in 1505, and in 1646 was repaired and garrisoned by the Marquis of Huntly. A Covenant garrison installed after Leslie besieged and captured the castle in 1647 made itself so unpopular that in 1648 the Marquis of Argyll got an Act of Parliament passed for the destruction of the castle.

LOGIE ELPHINSTONE   NJ 705258   A

This house, now an hotel, takes part of its name from the Elphinstones of Glack who acquired the property c1670. One of them was created a baronet in 1701 and it was he who added the Georgian front. The house then went by marriage to the Dalrymples of North Berwick. They were Jacobite sympathizers and hid Lord Pitsligo after the 1745 rebellion. They sold the house in 1903. Much of the building is of the 18th century but at the back within a courtyard is a 17th century frontage with a round stair turret. Both that front and the courtyard gateway bear ancient coats of arms.

The Peel Ring of Lumphanan

LUMPHANAN   NJ 576037   HS

The Peel Ring dates from c1200 and is unconnected with Macbeth, killed by Malcolm Canmore in this vicinity in 1057. Lumphanan belonged to the Durwards in the middle two quarters of the 13th century and was superseded by Coull Castle, although it remained occupied and was visited by Edward I in 1296. The buildings were then of wood, the word peel referring to the stockade around the edge of the egg-shaped summit 56m by 39m. The mound rises 4m above the bottom of a moat once with water 1m deep held in by an outer bank. At the NE end are foundations of a block 19m long by 6.5m wide, probably a late 17th century "ha' hoose", still intact in use in 1782. Of the same era is the thin section of perimeter walling including a gateway.

LYNTURK   NJ 598122

Near the farm of Castleknowe are traces of a ditch around an area 38m in diameter. A fragment of masonry is said to survive behind the farmhouse with a fragment of a 16th century gunport lying loose. This was the stronghold of John Strachan, a notorious freebooter who stormed Kildrummy Castle in 1530 and was involved in the murders of Alexander Seton of Meldrum and William King of Bourtie. He managed to get his former accomplice the Master of Forbes executed on a false charge of an attempt to shoot James V at Aberdeen. He exiled himself in France in the 1550s.

MIDMAR   NJ 701059 & 704053

The motte by the old ruined kirk rises 6m to a dished summit 23m across. Alexander, 4th Gordon laird of Midmar, built a Z-plan castle (then called Ballogy) on a hill to the SE after being restored to his estates in 1564. It is thought to have been damaged in the 1594 rebellion, hence the remodelling and heightening of the upper parts c1603-9 by the Bell family of masons for the 5th laird. The sale of the castle by the 6th laird c1640 to Alexander Forbes was the first of a sequence of sales by which it passed to Captain Alexander Grant c1728, to William Davidson c1760, to James Mansfield in 1765 and to Colonel John Gordon of Cluny in 1842. The Grants changed the name to Grantfield but it was later changed back to the original name Midmar. In 1977 the then empty castle was sold to the Whartons, who have restored and re-harled the building.

   Midmar is unusual for a Z-plan castle in that the main block is a square of about 8m instead of the usual rectangle. The round tower at the SE corner is 7.2m in diameter and the staircase tower at the NW corner is a square of 5.7m. Both project very boldly, only just touching the main block. The entrance lies at the foot of a scale-and-platt staircase up to the hall. From it leads a passage along the north side of what was originally a kitchen with a fireplace in the main block west wall. In the 18th century a wall was inserted to divide off the room, then a servants' hall from what then became another passage to the wine cellar in the base of the round tower. A stair in a round turret in the southern re-entrant angle between the main block and round tower serves the laird's suite and all the other rooms plus the flat roof of the embattled six storey tower, ending under an ogival cap. At fourth storey level the tower and stair turret are united by an arch. Another stair in a turret with an ordinary conical roof over the entrance leads from the hall to two upper rooms in the main block and three upper rooms in the square tower. All the external corners of the castle are chamfered off to just below the decorative corbelling supporting the gabled square bartizans on the main block and the round bartizans on the stair tower. A dining room range was added east of the main block in the late 17th century. In the 18th century a wing with a new kitchen and other service rooms was added northward of the stair tower, a shorter wing was added north of the dining room, and a terrace created between these two wings, which are of two storeys with plain dormer windows.

Monymusk House

MIGVIE NJ 437068 F

On a hillock rising from level ground to the east and south, with the Burn of Migvie on the west, and the road and church to the north, are a parish hall and slight traces of a polygonal curtain wall 1.8m thick. The castle is mentioned in 1268 in a charter of William, Earl of Mar. It was the seat of the lordship of Cromar, and, although probably destroyed by the Bruces c1308 and not rebuilt, continued to be the convening place of the courts of the lordship until the 16th century. Migvie was held by the Rutherfords of Tarland in the 1440s but by 1452 had passed to the Earl of Huntly.

Midmar Castle

MONYMUSK NJ 688155

Lands here belonged to a priory beside the church until obtained in 1549 by Duncan Forbes. William Forbes in 1587 began a tower of usual plan being a near square of 12m by 11m with shallow wings projecting east and south from the NE and SE corners respectively. The tower is entered by a doorway in the southern re-entrant angle with a stair corbelled out high above it. The basement contains a kitchen and various cellars, one of which has a well and a service stair up to the hall. The interior is much altered and the hall is now panelled throughout. The building was originally of three storeys and attics with a parapet on the east side and bartizans on the west. Only the corbelling of these remains, two more storeys having been added later. A three storey later wing extends south from the tower towards a four storey round SE tower. Another wing extending west from this contains a cross-loop with a bottom roundel, possibly reset. A two storey wing continues the line of the east projection of the main block. Hidden behind this, facing towards the river, are modern service and stable courts. Monymusk is still occupied by descendants of Sir Francis Grant, Lord Cullen, who in 1712 purchased it from Sir William Forbes for £116,000 Scots.

MOUNIE NJ 766287

This long, low domestic-looking building was probably built at the end of the 16th century by John Seton, a younger son of Seton of Meldrum, who had acquired extensive lands in the vicinity. The round stair turret with a square caphouse may be an addition of after 1637 when Mounie was purchased by Sir Robert Farquhar, Provost of Aberdeen, for whom it was made a barony. Farquhar was a wealthy merchant who was paid for supplying the Covenant army by the fines imposed by the Scottish Parliament on all "delinquents" (Royalists) north of the Tay. In the 18th century Mounie returned to the Setons, who in 1970 sold the house to the Martin family. Minor alterations were made under the direction of Sir Robert Lorimer in 1897 when the grounds were landscaped. The house has a kitchen and cellars in a vaulted basement, a hall and chamber above, and bedrooms partly in the roof.

OLD SLAINS NK 052301

Robert Bruce gave Slains to Sir Gilbert Hay who after the fall of his father-in-law William Comyn, Earl of Buchan, was created High Constable of Scotland in his place. In 1452 Sir William Hay was created Earl of Erroll and Lord Slains, and in 1513 the 4th Earl and 87 of his clan were killed along with James IV at Flodden. The 9th Earl was converted to Catholicism by his Jesuit kinsman Peter Hay of Delgatie and took part in the rebellion of 1594 which resulted in his exile and the blowing up of his castle of Slains by James VI's engineers. The castle was never restored for when the Earl returned he extended the tower of Bowness further along the coast and named it New Slains. However Old Slains is still a Hay possession and in 1950 Diana, 23rd Countess of Errol, High Constable of Scotland, built a holiday home on the end of the sheer sided coastal promontory once occupied by the castle. By the neck of the promontory there still stands one high fragment of a 15th century tower which had vaults over the three lowest of four levels. Part of one side wall survives to a length of 9m and contains a second storey entrance with a stair rising from it, while there is 8m of the adjoining end wall, both being 2.3m thick.

Monymusk House

PETERHEAD   NK 138458 (approx)

A lofty T-plan house built by George Keith, 5th Earl Marischal in the 1580s was later surrounded by a gun battery. It was forfeited after the 1715 rebellion and went to Thomas Arbuthnott, who built a new house. The old house was demolished c1860-80.

PHILORTH   NK 004631

Philorth was developed as a seat by Lord Saltoun after he lost nearby Cairnbulg Castle to his kinsman Lord Fraser in the 1630s. Philorth was destroyed by fire in 1915 and nothing now remains of it, Lord Saltoun having transferred back to Cairnbulg. An old picture shows the older part of the house, which was dated 1666, as having two round turrets with sharply pointed roofs placed close together on one side. Substantial additions were made in 1874.

PITCAPLE   NJ 726261

The main block of the present castle may incorporate a tower built by David Leslie of Balquhain shortly after he was granted the estate by James II in 1457. However the building as it now stands with round towers at diagonally opposite corners containing the main stair and the laird's suite respectively and with bartizans on the main block dates from the close of the 16th century. Rooms over the stair are reached by a turret stair, there being five storeys in the towers and four in the main block. Queen Mary was at Pitcaple in 1562 and is associated with a thorn tree which survived until 1923 when the then Queen Mary planted a red maple in its place. In 1645 the castle was seized from its Royalist laird by a party of Covenanters led by Alexander Jaffray. In 1650 Montrose spent a night at Pitcaple as a prisoner on his way to Edinburgh for trial. Lady Pitcaple was his cousin and she showed him a way of escape which appears to have been via a latrine shute. The doomed Marquis is alleged to have commented that "rather than go down to be smothered in that hole I'll take my chance in Edinburgh". Just two months later Charles II was at Pitcaple after landing from Holland. The Lumsdens obtained the castle by marrying the Leslie heiress in 1757 and still own it. The castle was allowed to decay but was restored from a ruinous state in 1830 and given the present continental style of conical roofs to its towers and turrets. Further extensions were carried out later.

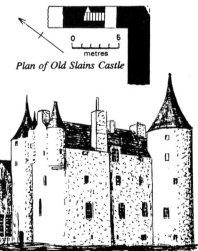

0   5
metres
Plan of Old Slains Castle

Old Slains Castle

Pitcaple Castle

PITFICHIE NJ 677168

Pitfichie was long a possession of the Urrie or Hurry family. It was probably begun by William Hurry, who along with Gordon of Knockespoch and others, was outlawed for a raid on Duncan Forbes' lands of Forneidlie made in January 1590. The house was sold in 1597 to John Cheyne of Fortrie for whom work, probably embellishment, alteration, or completion of an existing structure rather than a new building, was in progress in 1607 with David Bell as mason. In 1658 Pitfichie was sold to the Forbes's of Monymusk and the last recorded inhabitants, noted in 1696, were William Forbes, eldest son of Forbes of Monymusk, and his wife Lady Jean Keith, eldest daughter of the Earl of Kintore. The building was perhaps used as a farmhouse for a while but was roofless by 1796. Some repairs were executed in the late 19th century but in 1936 most of the NE and SE walls fell down. In the late 1980s the castle was purchased and restored by Colin Wood and is now a residence again.

A round tower 6.9m in diameter projects from the south corner of a main block 10.6m long by 8.4m wide. There are three storeys and an attic connected together by a stair corbelled out just above ground level in the eastern re-entrant angle. The stair is surmounted by a small gabled caphouse with the label corbelling characteristic of other work by the Bells. The entrance in the western re-entrant angle has holes for a draw-bar. It leads into an irregularly shaped lobby within the round tower, there being a redented gunport set below the stair turret to cover the SE wall. The remainder of the tower at this level has an irregularly shaped cellar with two more such gunports. From the lobby there lead off the stair and a passage to a cellar and a small kitchen, the fireplace and flue of which have had to be entirely rebuilt. The passage has another gunloop in a recess covering the entrance. The recess also has a draw-bar hole and was evidently designed originally to be the entrance. Perhaps a smaller stair tower was originally intended instead of the existing tower which is big enough to contain a comfortable private room with a latrine at hall level. There are three bedrooms on the third storey and other rooms in the roof. There is at attic level a square gabled bartizan with shot-holes upon the west corner.

Pitfichie Castle as restored

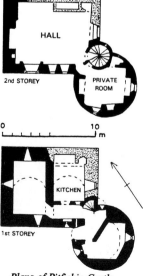

Plans of Pitfichie Castle

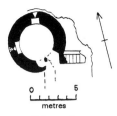

Pitlurg: plan

Pitsligo Castle from the west.

Pitfichie before restoration

PITLURG   NJ 436455

Pitlurg passed in 1539 from the church to the Gordon descendants of Jock o' Scurdargue and was held by them until 1724. All that remains of their castle is one round 16th century tower 6.4m in diameter standing on a rock at the NW corner. It is built of stones with fossil trees. There are two dome vaulted rooms, the lower furnished with gunports and the other converted into a dovecot. The adjoining walls were 1.3m thick, and the stub of one of them has a more recent set of steps to the upper room.

The old tower at Pitsligo

Pitlurg Castle

PITSLIGO NJ 938669 V

Sir William Forbes, younger son of Sir John Forbes of that Ilk, obtained Pitsligo as part of the dowry of Mary Fraser of Philorth, whom he married in 1423. The tower house was probably built soon after confirmatory charters were issued by James I in 1428 and 1430. The courtyard buildings were begun by Sir Alexander Forbes, who succeeded in 1566. On a stair tower in the NE corner is a shield with the Royal Arms and the dates 1577 and 1603, the latter year being most likely the date when the tower was added. His grandson Alexander was created Lord Pitsligo by Charles I in 1633. His initials and those of his wife Joanna Keith appear with the date 1656 lie over the gateway on an outer court to the west, whilst over the inner gateway are initials of Alexander, 2nd Lord Pitsligo and his wife Lady Mary Erskine with the year 1663. The castle was plundered by Hanovarian troops in 1746 and the 4th Lord Pitsligo became a fugitive. His estates were forfeited in 1748 and Pitsligo ended up in the hands of Alexander Garden of Troup who began dismantling the buildings for materials. The process was continued by the banker Sir William Forbes in the 1770s, although a section of the north wing remained in use as a farmhouse until the early 19th century. In recent years the Forbes family have carried out some consolidation although at the time of writing the ruins are not yet in a good safe condition.

The tower house is very irregularly laid out. It measures about 16m by 11.4m over walls 3.2m thick at ground level. There are now just two rooms, a vaulted cellar and a lofty vaulted hall, a third storey which contained the original laird's private room having been dismantled c1705. The cellar has just one loop at the west end, from the embrasure of which a service stair rises up around the NW corner. In the east wall, was the main stair leading up to the hall from an entrance at ground level. A spiral stair in the SE corner then led to the private room and battlements. The hall has been much altered and its only surviving feature is the fireplace in the west wall. One or two south windows and access to a latrine in the SW corner have been obscured by modern patching while another window and perhaps another entrance have been lost with the destruction of the upper part of the east wall.

The palace at Pitsligo

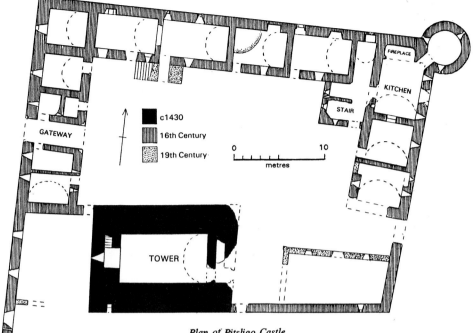

Plan of Pitsligo Castle

It is likely that the first addition to the old tower was a block of c1550 east of it but there is now only a 19th century building in the SE corner of the court. The northern two thirds of the east side of the court contains a block having two storeys of apartments with regular fenestration of later date over a pair of cellars and a kitchen. On the NW corner is a round tower containing gunports in a cellar reached from the kitchen. Above was a suite of three private apartments. The north range contained a gallery over a series of four cellars with vaults aligned longitudinally, a weak form of construction as the weight of the vaults is tending to spread the outer and inner walls rather than bond them as transverse vaults would have done. The external stair towards the west end is associated with the later farmhouse. In the angle between the north and east ranges is the tower containing what was once a very fine staircase with transverse ribs carrying a plastered vault. The tower has two external offsets with mouldings. It may originally have risen to an ashlar-faced top stage surmounted by a flat roof and balcony. The west range contained private rooms for household officials over an entrance passage with guard or porters rooms on one side and four cellars. The wing wall extending further south was part of a low two storey range.

PITTODRIE   NJ 697241   A

Pittodrie was obtained in 1525 by Sir Thomas Erskine of Halton, secretary to James V. His descendant John Erskine was secretary to the Earl of Mar in 1635. Although long held by the Erskines the house is now in other hands and is used as an hotel. The core of it is a much altered L-plan building said to be of 1605. It has a square tower, now rather truncated, in the re-entrant angle and a round turret on one of the long sides. The other parts of the building are modern except for a vaulted chamber on the north side with two gunloops.

Pittullie Castle

PITTULLIE NJ 945671

Pittullie was held by the Frasers from the 14th century originally with the Douglases as overlords until their fall from power in 1455. Alexander Fraser of Philorth gave Pittullie in 1596 to his son Alexander and his wife Margaret Abernethy of Saltoun, but the present house was begun in 1631 by an Ogilvy of Boyne who was married to Mary, sister of the Forbes laird of neighbouring Pitsligo. Pittullie was dismantled in the 1770s by Sir William Forbes after being partly burnt in 1746 by Hanovarian troops. The house is L-planned with main block 20.6m long by 7.2m wide which originally had bartizans on the southern corners. This part contained a hall with a private room beyond over low unvaulted basement rooms with a bedroom above in the roof. The hall was reached by a wide stair in the wing from an entrance in the north end wall of the wing. The hall seems to have been divided with a timber partition at some time, and may always have been so. The private room has a separate entrance and has a service stair leading down. A stair turret in the NW corner of the hall led to the upper rooms. The wing rises high above the main block, ending in a study with two square diagonally placed oriels on the northern corners. There are later outbuildings to the north some of which may have remained in use until the 19th century.

Pittullie Castle

Plans of Pittullie Castle

RAVENSCRAIG NK 095488 F

This castle on a rock beside the Ugie just 0.8km NW of Inverugie was the seat of the barony of Torthorston held by the Cheynes until it passed to the Keiths in the mid 14th century. The existing building assumed to be that licensed in 1491 lies in the NW corner of a triangular moated enclosure which could be somewhat older and has traces of an enclosing wall. The place was originally called Craig of Inverugie although it is called Ravenscraig in a charter of 1589 in which George, 5th Earl Marischal, gave it to John Keith, eldest son of Andrew Keith of Ravenscraig. James VI visited the castle in that year on the occasion of the marriage of the laird's daughter.

The castle has one of the largest tower houses in Europe, the main block being 25.5m long by 13.8m wide over walls 3.2m thick with a wing 10.9m wide projecting 8.5m to the south. An entrance, possibly not original, leads into a passage between two cellars (once vaulted) through to the north wall in which are remains of a wide straight stair up to a round lobby at the NE corner of the hall. This end of the hall is very damaged but seems to have had a passage leading through a window embrasure (or possibly the main entrance passage) to a spiral stair in the SE corner. A fireplace survives in the hall west wall and there were large window embrasures at this end in each side wall. One had access into a private room in the west end of the main block. This room has a latrine and a staircase leading up in the west wall to two other private rooms above it. The other embrasure had access onto a wide main stair leading up in the re-entrant angle. From this stair there was access to another private room in the wing. From one of the window embrasures of this room a service stair led down to a third cellar in the main block and to another cellar (the only one still vaulted) in the wing. Above the room in the wing were two bedrooms. The hall was probably vaulted over at a high level with a flagged roof directly on top. i.e. no third storey.

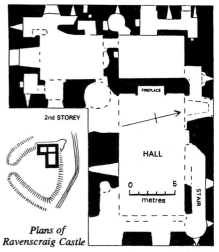

Plans of Ravenscraig Castle

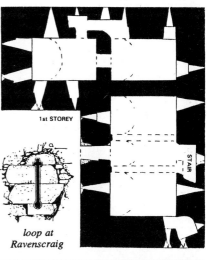

loop at Ravenscraig

Ravenscraig Castle

HALL

0   10
metres

Plans of Terpersie Castle

0   20
metres

Block plan of Skene House

Slains Castle

SHIVAS NJ 898368

Originally there was a Shivas family here. In 1467 the estate went to the Earl of Huntly and was granted to a younger son, the last of whose line was Sir George Gordon, who died in 1568, when Shivas went to the Greys. In the 1570s they commission Thomas Leiper to built them an L-plan house similar in layout with the main rooms at Tolquhon, a later design by Leiper. The Greys were staunch Catholics and a little oratory recess in the hall has the monogram I.H.S. for Jesus surmounted by a cross. NE and SW wings were added to the House of Shivas c1750, and a north wing is of c1830, whilst after a fire in 1900 the house was rebuilt in the "Balmoral Baronial" style. In 1930 Shivas was acquired by Lord Catto and was restored to its original appearance. The building has a long main block with a main stair in the wing leading up to a hall which has a private room at the far end. At the junction of the hall and private room is a round stair turret and their is a stair turret corbelled out above the entrance in the re-entrant angle. There are numerous ornamental triple shot-holes.

SKENE NJ 768097

Skene House is a large house of many periods built around a 14th or 15th century tower house, now Gothicised externally, and altered to the point of having little interest as an ancient building. The Skenes were here at an early date, the estate being made a barony by Robert I in 1318 for his servant Robert Skene. The last of them was the 28th, who died in 1827. Skene has been occupied by the Hamiltons since 1880.

SLAINS NK 102362 F

When Francis Hay, 9th Earl of Erroll returned from exile in 1597 he began rebuilding and extending the tower of Bowness and renamed it Slains to replace the strong but cramped castle at Old Slains blown up by James VI in 1594. Over the years the Earls of Erroll developed a huge palace on this spacious cliff-top site, a corridor being added in 1664, a new front in 1707, and large extensions being made in 1836 and later. Johnston and Boswell were entertained here in 1773. The Earls maintained semi-regal state at Slains until 1916 when the estate was sold to the ship-owner Sir John Ellerman, by whom in 1925 it was dismantled. In the 1980s there were proposals for the pink granite ruins and their attractive surroundings to be restored and developed as a holiday centre but nothing has actually happened. Rising directly from a narrow chasm at the SE is a tower incorporating a vaulted cellar and two upper rooms of what was perhaps a Z-plan building of c1600. One other original cellar also remains.

STRICHEN NJ 944549

Strichen House is a 19th century mansion replacing an castle of the Frasers called Mormond. This branch of the Frasers became Lords Strichan and moved to Inverness-shire after succeeding to the Lovat peerage. A dormer pediment from the castle with the year 1580 and the initials of Thomas Fraser lies in the garden of the Anderson and Woodman Library in the village of Strichen laid out to the NE in 1764.

TERPERSIE NJ 547202

This castle was built by William Gordon, son of Gordon of Lesmoir. He fought at Corrichie in 1562 and in 1572 killed the Forbes' champion Black Arthur. The castle was burnt by the Covenanters under General Baillie just before the battle of Alford in 1645 but was restored. George, 5th laird, and his sons were involved in the murder of Alexander Clerihew of Dubston, a tenant of Lord Forbes, in 1707. In 1746 the then laird concealed himself in the castle after Culloden but was accidentally revealed to the Hanovarian troops searching for him by his children. He was forfeited and Terpersie then went to the York Buildings Company and then to the Gordons of Knockespoch. It was occupied as a farmhouse until 1885 but was later unroofed and a 17th century wing was destroyed to provide materials for a new byre. The building was restored in the 1980s for use as a residence by Captain Lachlan Rhodes.

Terpersie was dated 1561 and is one of the smallest Scottish Z-plan castles having round towers 5m in diameter at opposite corners of a main block 8.8m long by 5.5m wide. The lowest room in each tower is a dome-vaulted cellar with three shot-holes. The entrance in the much rebuilt east wall leads directly into an unvaulted cellar in the main block. A stair opening off the entrance to the SW tower then leads up in the thick south wall to the hall. Access to the bedrooms is by a spiral stair corbelled out in the southern re-entrant angle of the SW tower. The towers have hexagonal upper rooms and conical roofs the same height as the main roof. There are no bartizans. The now destroyed east wing enclosed the original entrance. It contained a new entrance with a wide circular stair and had two rooms over a kitchen at ground level.

TILLYCAIRN NJ 644114 V

Tillycairn was granted by Alexander, Lord Gordon, to James Forbes in 1444. The L-plan tower is thought to have been begun in 1538 when William Forbes married Elizabeth Keith. Work continued for David Lumsden to whom it passed in 1542, and in 1548 the Queen Regent granted him lands formerly belonging to John Strachan of Lynturk in recompense for damage done during a raid by the latter in 1544. Evidence of a change of plan at the top suggests it was still incomplete when Matthew Lumsden, author of "A Genealogical History Of The House Of Forbes", an early example of such a work, died in 1580, and that the upper parts only took their present form after the heir attained his majority in the 1590s. After the last Lumsden died in 1672 Tillycairn passed to Thomas Burnett of Sauchen and then to the Forbes of Midmar. According to Macfarland, Tillycairn was ruinous as early as 1722 (charred beam ends suggest it was destroyed by fire), and it remained so until purchased and restored in the 1970s by David Lumsden, a descendant of the Cushnie branch of the family. It now has brightly painted modern stones bearing the initials of both Davids and their wives with the dates 1550 and 1980.

The tower has a main block 11m long by 7.5m wide from which a wing 5.3m wide projects 4.5m. The re-entrant angle contains a round turret containing a spiral stair connecting all four storeys. The entrance is in the main block immediately south of this stair and leads into a lobby off which lead the stair, a cellar with a service stair at the south end, and a kitchen with its fireplace in the north end wall. From the kitchen opens another cellar in the wing. Above is the hall with a private room in the wing from the vault of which came a pendant discovered in the south cellar in 1916. Above are various bedrooms and attics with round bartizans which seem to have been designed to be of two storeys but not completed as such. The top of the stair turret is increased in girth and covered with a sloping roof and there were sections of open wall-walks (not restored) on the sides facing the re-entrant angle. There are double splayed gunloops in the basement and also several cross-loops with bottom roundels.

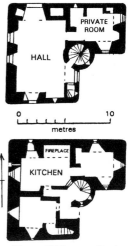

Plans of Tillycairn Castle

Tillycairn Castle

TILLYFOUR   NJ 659195

The Earls of Mar had a hunting seat here which passed to the Leslies in 1508. Sir John Leslie of Tillyfour was made a baronet in 1628. The oldest part of The Place of Tillyfour is a late 16th century squat L-plan building with a short stair turret in the re-entrant angle supported on an unusual squinch arch. The date 1626 appears over the entrance. There is a court with a round arched entrance to the south. Most of the many outbuildings are of 1884 when the house was restored from advanced decay.

TOLQUHON   NJ 873286   HS

In 1420 Tolquhon passed to Sir John Forbes on his marriage with Marjorie, younger daughter of Sir Henry Preston. The Preston Tower was probably built soon afterwards by this couple. The 7th laird replaced whatever outbuildings then accompanied the tower by a fine new mansion designed by Thomas Leiper, whose initials appear on a skew-putt. A panel near the entrance records" Al This Warke Excep The Avld Tovr Was Begvn Be William Forbes 15 Aprile 1584 And Endit Be Him 20 October 1589". In the latter year Tolquhon was visited by James VI. Alexander, 10th laird, was knighted for saving the life of Charles II at the battle of Worcester in 1651 when the King's horse was killed and he was shielded by Forbes' cavalry, eventually escaping on the laird's mount. In his old age Alexander went bankrupt through unfortunate speculation and in 1716 the estate was sold. William, the new 11th laird, refused to leave the castle and had to be dislodged by a party of redcoats in 1718. Tolquhon was later bought by the Earl of Aberdeen and was occupied until the mid 19th century. In 1929 the Marquis of Aberdeen placed the ruins in state guardianship.

Tolquhon Castle

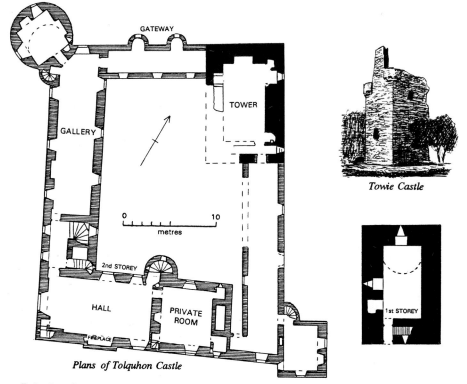

Towie Castle

Plans of Tolquhon Castle

Tolquhon is approached from the north through a large outer court with a gateway having ornate triple gunloops found throughout the main building. The inner court is cobbled with drainage gutters and has ranges on all four sides. The Preston Tower in the NE corner and the L-planned main building in the SW corner are flush with the outer walls but some sort of flanking fire along all four sides was possible from a boldly projecting round tower at the NW corner and a square tower at the SE corner. The courtyard gateway in the north range lies between two small round turrets. Over the entrance are the arms of William Forbes and James VI and the much worn year 1586. Flanking the passage are rooms for guards or porters. The windows in the fronts of the turrets at second storey level retain their iron grilles. The northern part of the east range contained a gallery over a cellar and two brewhouses. The round tower contained a square vaulted cellar, a square vaulted bedroom, and at least one upper room of which little remains reached by a stair in a corbelled out turret.

The Preston Tower measures 12.8m long by 9m wide externally. Part of the north wall stands in a broken state about 15m high and has a couple of corbels from a row supporting the parapet, but the rest is mostly ruined above the cellar vault. The entrance in the south end wall leads to the cellar with two loops and to a straight stair leading up. The Hall has a fireplace in the north end wall and remains of windows with seats on either side at this end. The recess in the SE corner was a latrine. Access to the bedrooms was presumably by a spiral stair in the SW corner. South of the tower is the very ruined east range with a gallery or servants mess-room over unvaulted service rooms. The square tower at its southern end has a dark L-shaped prison reached only by a hatch in the floor of the lower of two private rooms above. A stair connecting these rooms is corbelled out in the NE re-entrant angle.

The main house in the SW corner has a hall and laird's room set end-to-end in the south range, access from the court being via a wide staircase in the west wing. Below the stair is a guard room, and below the hall are three cellars, one having a service stair. Below the private room and connected with it by a service stair is the kitchen. These lower rooms are connected by a passage which has a servery recess in the base of a round turret facing the court on the north side. From the hall this turret contains a stair leading up to the bedrooms which were partly within the roof. A shot-hole off this stair commands the entrance to this part of the house. Above the top of the stair the turret is corbelled out into a square gabled caphouse. From the lobby at the top of the main stair a smaller stair is provided in the angle over the entrance to give access to a bedroom over the west end of the hall and another over the main stair, this part of the west range being carried up higher than the rest.

TOWIE NJ 440129

The last remains of Towie Castle were cleared away c1970. It belonged to a branch of the Forbes family and was supposedly the scene of the burning of Lady Forbes and her household by the Gordons in 1571, but there is good evidence that this happened at Corgarff and that Towie Castle was not built until the early 17th century. The capital messuage of the barony of Towie was at Nether Towie until 1618. The house was a thinly walled building with a cellar in the wing and several others in the main block all linked by a passage along the west side. The wing was the only part which remained standing. It was 4.7m wide and projected 4m from a main block 19m long by 7.8m wide. The wing had three upper storeys and on the west corners were round bartizans supported by label mouldings. A turret stair in the re-entrant angle gave access from the third to the fourth storey but the position of the main stair and entrance is not known.

Towie Barclay Castle

Udny Castle

TOWIE BARCLAY NJ 744439

On the castle are inscriptions referring to Sir Alexander Berkeley who died in 1136, a son of the lord of Berkeley Castle in Gloucestershire. He was the first of a long line of Berkeleys or Barclays in Aberdeenshire. Presumably there was a motte here at that time. The existing castle was built for Patrick Barclay between 1587 and 1593, the latter date appearing on it with the year 1136. Patrick was a Catholic and his castle has similarities to others built by Catholic lords at Gight, Craig, and Delgatie, being the last of the series. Patrick died in 1627 and was succeeded by his grandson Walter who was of a very different religious persuasion, being an ardent Covenanter. On May 10th 1639 the first shot of the Civil Wars was fired from the castle battlements when Walter Barclay and his wife's kinsmen Lord Forbes and the Master of Forbes defended themselves against a group of Royalist lairds. One shot killed David Pratt, servant of Gordon of Gight, the first casualty of the conflict. In 1792 the castle was dismantled and its upper portions taken down. It was in a bad state of decay by 1970 when it was purchased by the Ellington family and restored as a residence.

The main block measures 13.2m by 10.2m and the wing is 8m wide. The original length of the wing is uncertain for its end wall has been rebuilt thinner than before. The entrance leads into a rib-vaulted lobby in a side wall of the main block. The initials of Patrick Barclay appear on the vault boss. In the adjacent corner is a room for a guard or porter, ahead lies one of the two cellars in the main block, while a passage leads off to the main stair in the south wall. A second stair is formed in the SW corner to provide a service stair from one cellar to the hall. It then rises to serve a rib-vaulted oratory high up at the south or service end of the hall. The hall is a very fine apartment with a rib-vault and a fireplace at the north end. Off a window on the east side is a doorway to a room set within the re-entrant angle masonry thickness. No ancient features remain in the wing but analogy with the other castles suggests it contained the laird's room over a kitchen. The restorers have added a new third storey on the main block plus a high attic within a parapet with conical roofed bartizans.

Towie Barclay Castle

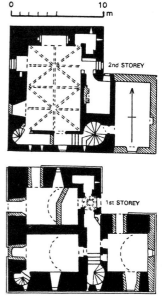

Plans of Towie Barclay Castle

UDNY   NJ 882268

The Udny family were descended from Ranald of Udny who was given a charter of the estate by David II. It was the 12th laird of this line who was saved by his fool at a fire at Knockhall in 1734. The direct male line failed in the earl 20th century and Udny went to Lord Belhaven. In the 1960s his daughter the Hon Margaret Udny-Hamilton tastefully restored the old tower and stripped away a pair of three storey wings added in 1875. The tower was begun in the 1560s and as the four bartizans and the length of open parapet on the south side are reckoned to be early 17th century the tradition that the building was only completed after the successive work of three lairds may be basically true. It is a four storey structure measuring 13m by 10.4m and rising 21m to the top of the roof. The round corners and offset at the level of the hall ceiling recall Fedderate Castle of about the same period. The round arched entrance is flanked by two gunloops and leads into a lobby communicating with the larger of two cellars, a small kitchen, and the stair in the SW corner. A service stair rises from the main cellar to the NW corner of the hall. The hall is a lofty room with a fireplace on the east and windows on the other three sides. In the SE corner a secondary stair rises up to a bedroom at that end for the third storey had two rooms each served separately from below. The main stair then continues up to an attic room in the roof. See p101.

WARDHOUSE   NJ 593289

An oval platform about 48m long by 37m wide with a ravine to the north and a ditch and outer bank on the other sides marks the site of a timber hall of Bartholomew The Fleming in the 13th century. The Gordons later built a stone castle on the site which was captured in 1647 by General Leslie and has now vanished.

WARTHILL   NJ 710315

Warthill was long held by the Leslies and is still owned by their descendants. The old castle was replaced by a large baronial mansion in 1845, part of which has now itself been demolished. On the south side is a reset panel from the castle with the Leslie arms and the date 1686. There is another defaced panel at the back.

WATERTON   NJ 972305

On a mound east of the premises of the Buchan Poultry Products Company are three vaulted cellars of a rectangular building of late date. The lands belonged to Kinloss Abbey which had a grange 1.4km to the east. They then passed to the Knights Templar and then the Bannermans. However the castle was bought by the Forbes family and an heraldic panel on the ruin with the dates 1630 and 1770 refers to them.

WESTHALL   NJ 673266

After the Reformation Westhall passed from the Bishops of Aberdeen to the Gordons, who built the oldest part of the present building. James Horn, Vicar of Elgin, bought the property in 1681 on his marriage to a daughter of the 7th Leslie laird of Pitcaple. Westhall later passed by an heiress to the Dalrymple Elphinstones of nearby Logie Elphinstone and they then added Horn to their name. The small old part lies at the SW corner of the modern house, facing the approach. It has a three storey main block with a square wing engaging the SW corner and a conical roofed round tower on the SE corner. The square tower has an attic within an open parapet with roundels carried on label mouldings. Another label moulding supports a stair in a turret in the re-entrant angle between this tower and the south side of the main block.

OTHER CASTLES AND HOUSES IN ABERDEENSHIRE

BRACKLEY NO 366948 Sir Adam Mackenzie of Glenmuick's house of 1898 lies on site of castle. Gordon laird killed by Farquharson of Inverey in 1666.

BYTH NJ 614565 Heraldry and walling and modern farm on site of a Forbes castle built in 1593. It passed to the Urquharts in the 18th century.

CANDACRAIG NJ 339111 Modern mansion on site of an Anderson castle.

COBAIRDY NJ 576437 Mansion on site of castle of Murrays, later held by Burnetts.

CULTER NJ 854004 Motte called Camp Hill above the River Dee.

EASTER CLUNIE NO 614914 Fragment by steading. 18th century house ruin nearby.

EDINGLASSIE NJ 424388 Mansion on site of Gordon castle burnt by Mackay in 1688.

ENDOVIE NJ 583146 Nothing remains of a tower so close to Balfluig that the lairds were able to shoot at each other from their studies. One was eventually killed.

FAICHFIELD NK 065467 Early 17th century building demolished in the 1960s.

FISHERIE NJ 829579 A barony later held by the Duffs with a castle at The Mains.

GAIRNIESTON NJ 748553 Tree south of farm marks site of castle of Delgarno family.

INVERAMSAY NJ 742240 Former name Peelwalls suggests a timber building here. Later stone castle of the Erskines, owners of estate from 1357, has gone.

INVERCAULD NO 174924 The Farquharsons still inhabit this 16th century tower.

INVEREY NO 090893 Fragments of 16.7m long thinly walled house of two storeys and an attic. Built for the Black Colonel, John Farquharson, c1670.

INVERMARKIE NJ 425397 An Innes property from 1486. Castle destroyed in 17th century. A Duff shooting lodge of 1705 lies on the site.

KINACOUL NO 439968 There are no remains of Deecastle or Kinacoul Castle.

KINBATTOCK NJ 429114 Slight traces of dry ditch around a platform 40m by 28m. It was a 13th century homestead moat and lies elevated at about 300m.

KINTORE NJ 794163 A natural mound bearing a stone circle was heightened in the 12th century to make a motte. It was removed for the railway in 1854.

LOCH GOUL NJ 912143 Bishop de Bernham is said to have been burnt to death in a palace on an islet in the loch in 1282.

LOGIE RUTHVEN NJ 448006 Homestead moat near Loch Davan is site of the Hall of Logie Ruthven where Regent Moray camped before his victory at Culblean (1335).

LONMAY NK 059606 A Fraser castle formerly stood at Netherton of Lonmay.

LUDQUHARN NK 033453 (approx) A long-vanished castle of the Keith family.

OLD MAUD NJ 916471 A castle once stood at Mains of Maud Farm.

PUTATCHIE NJ 622191 19th century mansion now called Castle Forbes being the seat of Lord Forbes replacing Druminnor on site of tower house.

RATTRAY NK 088580 Site of Comyn castle on natural hillock by Old Rattray Farm.

RENATTON NJ 276003 There are slight traces of a castle near the farm.

RUTHVEN NJ 494471 (approx) Vanished seat of "Tam o' Ruthven" (Thomas Gordon).

SHETHIN NJ 886326 Demolished in 1644 by the Covenanters. Belonged to the Ogston or Hoddeston family, later passing to the Setons.

TILLYDRONE NJ 936089 The mound by the River Don NW of St Machar's Cathedral may be the castle of Aberdeen mentioned in 1214.

TILLYHILT NJ 854318 Footings of a Gordon castle beside a ravine.

TULLOS NJ 702218 17th century house 18.8m by 6.1m with hall and chamber over cellars. Ruin half full of debris and farmyard rubbish.

TYRIE NJ 939630 Carved stone from Fraser castle set above farmhouse door.

TYRIE NJ 930631 Site of motte close to church and manse.

NO REMAINS: Auchmeddan NJ 850645, Badenyon NJ 340190, Brucklay NJ 910502, Doagh NJ 507477, Dorlaithers NJ 702473, Freefield NJ 676313, Glenkindie NJ 423145, Idoch NJ 770490, Kinmuck NJ 989354, Lethenty NJ 769247.

VANISHED MOTTES: Auchleven NJ 623242, Auchterless NJ 714416, Belhelvie NJ 940170 approx, Kenerty NJ 830000, Mondurno NJ 945132, Pitfodels NJ 910029

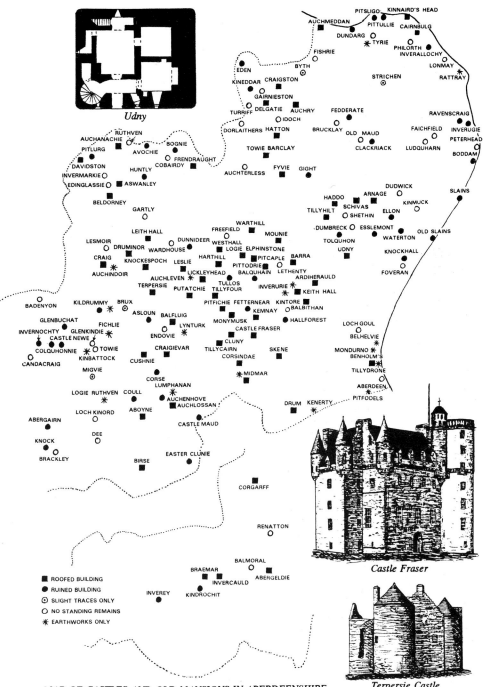

Udny

Castle Fraser

Terpersie Castle

MAP OF CASTLES AND OLD MANSIONS IN ABERDEENSHIRE

CASTLES OF ANGUS & KINCARDINE

AFFLECK NO 493389

This fine tower was built in the late 15th century by the Auchinlecks of that Ilk (the name is now usually corrupted to Affleck). They were here by the late 13th century and were armour-bearers of Earls of Crawford. The last of them disposed of the estate to Robert Reid in the mid 17th century. The Reids of Affleck were forfeited for their part in the 1745 rebellion. In the mid-20th century the tower was taken into state care but was relinquished after a dispute over access. It measures 11.4m by 8.1m over walls 1.6m thick and rises 16m to the top of the parapet. Rising another 2.4m higher are turrets over a SE wing 3.4m wide projecting 1.8m and over a secondary staircase in the SW corner rising from the hall on the third storey to the laird's bedroom above and the battlements. The wing flanks the entrance and contains a main staircase linking the two cellars with the hall plus a vaulted room between them with three windows with seats but no fireplace or latrine. At 4th storey level the wing contains a delightful little oratory with a pointed piscina opening off the laird's room. There is a mural room adjacent to the wing at this level, and two more in the corners flanking the hall fireplace flue. The hall is sufficiently lofty for there to be another room with a latrine in the wing squeezed in between the head of the main stair and the oratory. There is a cusped niche over the entrance. The larger of the two cellars has a dumbbell-shaped loop to the west, and a keyhole loop to the north.

Affleck Castle

Plans of Affleck Castle

Airlie Castle

Airlie Castle

AIRLIE NO 293522

In 1431 James I licensed his Treasurer and Master of the Household, Sir Walter Ogilvy of Lintrathen, to fortify his residence on this strong site on a 30m high promontory formed by the ravines of the Isla and Melgum rivers. The east side, the only one requiring serious defences, still has a curtain wall 3m thick, 11.5m high and 36m long in front of which there was once a ditch 9m wide crossed by a drawbridge. Towards the north end is a shallowly projecting gateway with a machicolation slot and portcullis groove. The two uppermost of three chambers over the gate and the round turret are not ancient. The domestic range of three storeys and an attic on the north side of the court is mostly 18th and 19th century but incorporates remains of a curtain on this side. The original buildings here were looted and burned by the Marquis of Argyll in 1640 following a short siege. The Marquis, a hereditary enemy of the 8th Lord Airlie (then absent at the court of Charles I, by whom he had recently been made an Earl), is said to have personally taken "hammer in hand" and knocked down "the hewed work of the doors and windows till he did sweat for heat at his work". The family then lived at Cortachy, but the 5th Earl of Airlie returned here after living in France in the late 18th century. The castle stood empty at the beginning of the 20th century but the Earls have restored it and again taken up residence.

ALDBAR NO 572577

The Cramonds sold Aldbar in 1575 to Lord Glamis, by whom it was handed over to his brother Sir Thomas Lyon, Treasurer of Scotland. He built a four storey L-plan building with bartizans and a flat-roofed wing with a stair turret in the re-entrant angle by the edge of the ravine called the Den of Albar. There was a large stepped chimney breast at the NW corner and a rounded projection with a gunloop facing the approach on the east. The property reverted to the main line of the family when he died without heirs and in 1670 was sold by Patrick, Earl of Strathmore to Sir James Sinclair. He sold it to Peter and James Young and in 1753 it was sold to William Chalmers of Balnacraig. This family still live on the estate but the house was demolished after a fire in 1964 and only a pile of rubble now remains. It was greatly extended in 1844 and 1854 and a grand new staircase made within the old tower although original window grilles were allowed to remain on the east side. The contents were sold in 1929 but the building was restored in the 1930s and 40s for Robert Chambers. The Court Law to the south may be a motte.

ALLARDYCE   NO 818739

This building on a promontory above the winding Bervie Water has been restored since being purchased in 1969. It was built c1580-1600 by the Allardyce family, the male line of which ended in the late 18th century. The heiress married Barclay of Urie and Captain Barclay-Allardyce, who died in 1854, was the last of their descendants. The building is an L-plan with one wing having an entrance passage with a roll-moulded outer arch leading into a former courtyard. There are two storeys, one partly in the roof, over vaulted cellars. Towards the approach is a shallow round projection carried on a label-moulding, whilst similar mouldings carry a stair over the re-entrant angle itself surmounted by a caphouse reached by a conical-roofed stair turret.

ARBUTHNOTT   NO 795750   G

Arbuthnott House is a cluster of buildings of various periods on a ridge between the Bothenoth Burn on the north and the Bervie Water on the south. In the late 12th century Hugh de Swinton became laird here and his successors took the name Arbuthnott from the place. As Viscounts, a title granted by Charles I, they are still here. Incorporated in a late 15th century outbuilding on the north side is a 7m long section of walling with a triple chamfered plinth similar to that on the chancel of the nearby church consecrated in 1242. Its builder must have been the third laird, Hugh Arbuthnott. It is possible that work of this period may also survive in the much altered hall block built c1420 by Hugh, 9th laird, on the south side. This block is 14.3m long by 7.6m wide and contained a hall over an unvaulted single lower chamber probably used as office space or servants' quarters. The hall had a screens passage at the west end reached from the court by external steps. and three windows on each side. The fireplace at the east end backed onto the flue of a vaulted kitchen in a slightly narrower east extension, over which was the laird's private room.

Allardyce Castle

Allardyce Castle

Arbuthnott House

In the 1470s and 80s much work was carried out at Arbuthnott by Sir Robert, 12th laird. He put a roof on the hall block, added a block of similar dimensions called "The Twin" to the west of it, built two ranges on the north side, and at the west end closed off the approach with a curtain wall with a square gatehouse in the middle. The Twin now forms the south wing of a U-shaped house built in the 1750s for two successive lairds both named John. This has replaced the NW range and the curtain wall and gatehouse. Enough of the NE range survives to suggest it had a kitchen over a pair of vaulted cellars each lighted by a cross-loop with a bottom roundel similar to those at Ravenscraig (see p95). Robert, 14th laird (from 1521 to 1579) extended both the north and south sides by new ranges of which only the outer walls now survive. That on the south probably contained a gallery. Between the two, closing off the east end of the court, is a building of just one storey and an attic bearing the initials of Andrew Arbuthnott, 15th laird, and the date 1588.

The initials of Katherine Lovat, second wife of Robert, 1st Viscount Arbuthnott, survive on The Twin, which seems to have been given a third storey between the time of their marriage in 1653 and his death in 1655. The range was redecorated (vestiges remain) and seems to have had a turret containing a scale-and-platt staircase added on the north side. This was removed and replaced by an infilling between the wings of the U-plan in the 1790s for the 7th Viscount. Of the 1680s, executed for Robert, 3rd Viscount, are the internal stair inserted into the old hall-block and the formation of two drawing rooms with particularly fine ceilings in the south wing.

ARDESTIE NO 505342

The Earls of Penmure had a castle here above the Pitairlie Burn. All that remain are stones dated 1625 and 1688 reset into a farmhouse and some nearby cottages.

AUCHMULL NO 585719

There are no remains of a castle built c1600 by Sir David Lindsay, Lord Edzell as a seat for his son. The latter spent a decade as a fugitive in this district after killing his uncle, Lord Spynie, in a street fight in Edinburgh. The castle was demolished in 1773.

0 _____ 10
metres

Auchterhouse: plan

Old Tower, Auchterhouse

AUCHTERHOUSE   NO 332373   A

This much altered 16th century mansion now serves as an hotel. Some vaults survive and a fine ceiling and mantlepiece in an upper room. Of greater interest, though, is the ruined lower part of a tower house measuring 13m by 10.5m over walls 2.8m thick lying close by. The south wall is reduced to foundations but loops remain to the east and north and in the NW corner are remains of a spiral stair reached from the once-vaulted cellar by a doorway with shouldered lintels suggesting a date close to 1300. The tower is now entered through a breach in the outer wall here but the original entrance must have been at the level of the hall above. The Earl of Buchan resided here in the 16th century. Auchterhouse passed along with the Earldom of Buchan to James, Earl of Moray in 1619, but by 1648 Patrick, Earl of Kinghorne, was in possession. The Earl of Panmure held Auchterhouse in the 1660s.

AUCHTERMEGGITIES   NO 553497

Two shot-holes and three panels dated 1615 (with initials R.B.) and 1657 (with initials M.A.P. and M.M. and a Latin inscription meaning "My foes keep out, O house; to friends and strangers open be; Any may this ever be the will of him that holdeth thee".) are reset in the gateposts and nearby garage of the western approach to the mansion of Balmadies dating from 1820. The estate belonged to the Ochterlony family and was re-purchased by them after passing to the Piersons.

0 _____ 10
metres

HALL

2nd STOREY

Balbegno Castle

Plan of Balbegno Castle

BALBEGNO   NO 639730

A watch chamber at the top of this empty L-plan tower now entered through a later house is dated 1569 with the initials of its builders John Wood and Elizabeth Irvine. In common with a number of Aberdeenshire towers of that period it has a rib vault of two octo-partite bays over the hall which is 9m long by 6m wide, the walls here being 1.6m thick. On the vault were painted armorial bearings of various landed families. The hall fireplace, now mostly blocked, backs onto the private room in the wing reached by a long passage from the hall SE corner. Stairs lead up and down at either end of this passage, and there is a narrow service stair as well. Both hall and private room have original windows and latrines in the wall thickness. One private room window is round headed and has a lady carved at the top. The basement contains a kitchen plus several cellars, whilst the 3rd storey contains four bedrooms, each with latrines. There are two heraldic stones within the re-entrant angle. At the summit are round bartizans with shot-holes. The castle was sold to the Middletons in the late 17th century.

BALFOUR   NO 337497   V

All that survives is a five storey 16th century round tower 6.3m in diameter and stumps of adjoining walls 1.7m thick. The tower basement had three double splayed gunports but one was later opened out into a doorway. A dog-leg passage connected this room with the interior of the castle, which was probably a four storey L-plan building with the tower on the outermost angle. However MacGibbon & Ross suggest that the castle was of the courtyard type and that a NE tower had only recently gone.

BALGAVIES   NO 542513

James VI destroyed a castle of the Lindsays here in 1595. All that remains are two vaulted cellars 3.5m and 3m wide side by side with broken down doorways towards a passage on the south. From the larger cellar a passage leads to a small square cellar in a wing. The outer wall faces are mostly buried under earth and debris.

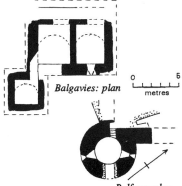

Balgavies: plan

0   5
metres

Balfour: plan

Balfour Castle

Plan of Ballumbie Castle

Ballinshoe Castle

BALLINSHOE NO 417532 V

This ruin beside a lane was built c1600 and measures 8.3m by 6.7m over walls 1m thick. The basement is unvaulted and has two slits to the SW and shotholes on either side of where a destroyed circular stair turret 4m in diameter engaged the north corner. One shothole guarded the entrance of which one jamb survives. Above was a living room with a fireplace in the end wall and window in each side. Above was a bedroom partly in the roof and having a closet in a round bartizan on the south corner. Two of the windows at this level have shot-holes below the sills. The Lindsays acquired the estate in 1559 and it passed to the Fletchers in 1645.

BALLUMBIE NO 445344

A stable block of a later house has been built against the 1m thick outer walls of an L-plan house strongly sited above a ravine. The house measured about 17m along each arm of the L. A tower 5m in diameter with a vaulted basement and a gunport at the top survives on the outer corner. Part of it has been used as a dovecot. Another tower 3.7m in diameter with vaults and gunports lies at the north corner. There is said to have once been a datestone of 1556 with the arms of Henry Lovell, his first wife Janet Scott of Balwearie, and his second wife M. Monorgan (although it seems he only married the latter c1560). Henry was described as a brigand in 1566, James Durham of Pitkerro having complained about his raiding to Queen Mary. The estate was held throughout most of the 17th and 18th centuries by the Moules of Kellie.

BALMAKEWAN NO 666663

Reset over a cottage window by a walled garden, across a lawn from near the existing mansion, is a stone with the year 1674. A thin section of walling probably of that date survives next to it.

Plan of Ballinshoe Castle

BALNAMOON NO 552638

At the NW corner of a mansion of the 1820s lies a tower thought to date c1490. Considerable further work was carried out in 1680. The dormer pediment date 1584 has been brought here from the demolished nearby castle of Findrowie. The property has been a seat of the Carnegy-Arbuthnotts since the early 17th century, but originally belonged to the Collace family. Among the treasures in the house is part of the original National Covenant of 1638 bearing the signature of Montrose.

BANNATYNE   NO 293410

In the late 16th century George Bannatyne of that Ilk lived here. A building of about that era with a bartizan on the NE corner survives in a much altered condition.

BENHOLM   NO 804705

During a storm in 1992, with a planned restoration by new owners still pending, the east half of the badly cracked tower collapsed right down to the ground. Until then the building stood almost complete except for the SE angle round and the adjacent sections of the parapet. It measured 11.5m by 8.7m over walls 1.8m thick and contained two vaulted cellars, a hall over, two more storeys above, and an attic within the parapet. A straight stair from the entrance of the south side led up to the base of a spiral stair in the SW corner. The caphouse still remaining over the stair is a later addition. The hall had three windows, two with seats, a mural chamber on the north side, a latrine in the NW corner, and a fireplace in the east wall beside which was an ogival-headed aumbry. The tower was built c1475 by the Lundie family, but soon passed to the Ogilvys, and then to the Keiths, being used by sons and brothers of the Earls Marischal. The Scotts purchased Benholm in 1659 and in c1760 they added the mansion which fell into ruin after being used as a hospital in World War II.

aumbry

1st STOREY

HALL

2nd STOREY

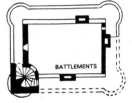

BATTLEMENTS

Plans of Benholm Tower

Benholm after collapse

Benholm before collapse

BRAICKIE NO 628509

The estate of Wester Brackie was given by Robert Bruce to Sir Simon Fraser of Oliver in Peebles-shire. The existing derelict building is dated 1581 with initials of Thomas Fraser. The estate passed to the Grays in the mid 17th century and then to the Ogilvys. The building has a wing 5.4m wide projecting 4.4m from a main block 10m long by 6.9m wide over walls 1.1m thick at ground level. The wing contains two bedrooms and an attic above a wide spiral stair from the entrance up to the hall. A turret stair in the re-entrant angle then serves the wing upper rooms plus two upper storeys in the main block. The third storey contained two private rooms, each with a fireplace and a tiny closet intended to contain a chamber-pot. The hall has a fireplace beside the turret stair and has straight stairs in an end wall, one leading up to the lowest bedroom in the wing, and the other down to the smallest of the two cellars. The cellars have gunloops and there are shot-holes below the upper windows.

Braikie Castle

Braikie: plans

Brechin Castle

BRECHIN NO 597599

The strong promontory site formed by the junction of a tributary with the River Esk was fortified by the Maules in the 13th century. Here, in 1296, John Balliol submitted to Edward I of England. The castle was captured from an English garrison by William Wallace in 1298. Sir Thomas Moule made a heroic defence of the castle against Edward I's army in 1303 until he was killed by a missile from the besiegers catapults. The Barclays acquired Brechin some time afterwards but in 1378 it was given to William Stewart, Earl of Atholl. In 1438 it was forfeited by the then Earl, who had been a party to the murder of James I the previous year, and in 1449 it was given by James II to his consort, Mary. It was later held by the Erskine Earls of Mar, being confiscated by James VI in 1584, but restored to the Earldom in 1585. The vaulted cellars may be of this period. In 1634 Sir Patrick Maule purchased Brechin from the 7th Earl of Mar and in 1646 he was created Earl of Panmure. The 4th Earl built a new show front with a pedimented centrepiece towards the approach from the west c1700 although the round towers at either end may be earlier. He was forfeited for his part in the 1715 rebellion and the castle was taken over by the York Buildings Company. In 1764 a kinsman, William Maule, purchased the estate and was created Earl of Panmure. He enlarged the castle, which now has four ranges around an irregularly shaped courtyard. He was succeeded by George, Earl of Dalhousie, first of the present line of Maule-Ramsays. They once lived at Dalhousie but now live at Brechin.

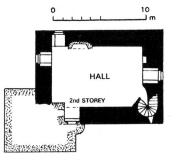

0   10
m

HALL

2nd STOREY

Plan of Broughty Castle

South front of Careston Castle

Broughty Castle

BROUGHTY   NO 465304   HS

In 1454 George Douglas, 4th Earl of Angus was licensed by James II to build a fortalice on a low promontory beside the Tay. It is uncertain what was then built and the present tower and the L-shaped court which protected its east and south sides are known to have been mostly built in the 1490s by Lord Gray. In September 1547 Protector Somerset sent Sir Andrew Dudley to capture Broughty Castle. Lord Grey had already agreed to support the English and the castle was handed over without a fight. Dudley then strengthened the walls and dug a ditch on the landward side. In November the castle was damaged during an unsuccessful attempt to recapture it by the Regent Arran. The castle was only surrendered to the Scots early in 1550 after a combined French and Scottish force based at Dundee stormed an outlying fort newly built on Balgillo hill (now called Forthill). The castle was then returned to the Grays and strengthened by the addition of round towers to the NE and SW corners of the court.

In 1651 the castle was quickly surrendered when attacked by a Covenant army led by General Monck. Lord Leven and other members of the Committee of Estates were subsequently imprisoned in it. In 1666 Patrick, 8th Lord Gray sold the castle to David Fothringham of Powrie. It decayed and took no part in the 1715 and 1745 risings. In the 19th century the tower was used as a coastguard signal station and store for fishing gear whilst the court and outbuildings were robbed of stone for constructing houses in the town, and an ice-house was built in the ditch. The castle was purchased by the War Office in 1854 and in 1860 was renovated at a cost of £7,000. It became the head-quarters of the new 3rd (Broughty Ferry) Forfarshire Artillery Volunteers, and was later (after the 68 pounder guns were removed) used by the Tay Division Submarine Miners Royal Engineers. A new battery (demolished 1967) to landward was built in 1905 and the castle was equipped with 4.7" and 6" guns during the 1914-18 war. The last of these were removed in 1932 and the castle declared an ancient monument, only to be re-armed in 1939. It re-opened as a museum in 1969.

The harled tower house 13.8m long by 10m wide over walls mostly 1.8m thick has keyhole-shaped loops typical of the 1490s. The basement entrance and some windows higher up are original but most of the features above the vaulted cellars are of 1860 and later. At the summit is a caphouse over the stair in the SW corner, a parapet carried on a single row of corbels, and corner rounds. The square wing added on the NW corner with widely splayed gunports is entirely of that period and is left unharled. What remained of the courtyard and outbuildings have been incorporated into outworks suitable for defence by and against 19th century artillery.

CADDAM   NO 658685

The farm of Caldhame or Caddam has three dormer pediments built into the steading wall. They have arms and initials of Andrew and John Barclay, one of their wives, I.S., and the date 1571. The estate later passed to the Middletons of Laurencekirk, one of whom, General John, was made an Earl in the 1660s, and then to the Keiths.

CARESTON   NO 530599

This is a tall Z-plan castle built by the Lindsays in the late 16th century, and later much altered and extended, the stair turret and bartizans now having mock battlements instead of their original conical roofs. The south front now has a symmetrically planned layout with two wings and is dated 1714 with arms of Sir John Stewart of Grandtully, who purchased the estate from the Carnegies in 1707. However, it is said to contain remnants of a 15th century house built by the Dempsters. They took their name from the office of deemster or adjudicator of the Scottish Parliament and were here by the 1290s.

Broughty Castle from the beach

CARNEGIE   NO 535414

Only a walled garden remains on the site of a castle of the Carnegie family descended from a knight called de Balinhard to whom Sir Water Maule granted land here in 1358. The family, later Earls of Southesk, held the estate until the mid 19th century.

CARSEGRAY   NO 464540

On a south facing shelf among woods is a whitewashed 18th century E-plan house. It has been developed from a small early 17th century T-plan house of two storeys and an attic at the east end. A stair turret is corbelled out high up. The doorway in the re-entrant angle is commanded by a shot-hole and has over it an empty panel niche. The barony of Carse was sold by the Rynd family to Charles Grey in 1741.

Claypotts

CLAYPOTTS   NO 452319   HS

Claypotts is one of the best known and well preserved semi-fortified houses in Scotland and lies on the NE outskirts of Dundee not far north of Broughty Ferry. It bears the dates 1569 and 1588 and the arms and initials of John Strachan and is built on the so-called Z-plan with round towers 6.3m in diameter projecting from the SW and NE corners of a main block 10.2m by 7.6m over walls up to 1.6m thick at basement level. Except for the cellar in the NE tower all the tower rooms are quadrangular. Each tower has a staircase in a round turret rising the full height of the building in the re-entrant angle between the tower and the long sides of the main block. The wider western stair was for general use and has the entrance lobby at its foot. The other stair was more private and connected the laird's rooms in the NE tower. There is a blank space for a heraldic panel over the entrance. The cellars are well provided with gunports and one is even provided in the back of the fireplace of the kitchen in the foot of the SW tower. One gunport is given a wider field of fire by means of a groove cut in the eastern stair turret. Beside this is a former latrine outlet.

The hall was entered from the stair through a vestibule screened off at the south end. The hall has windows on either side and a fireplace which has lost its lintel. The comfortable private room in the NE tower beyond the hall has a latrine, fireplace, cupboard and two windows. The third storey contained two living rooms in the main block and bedrooms in the towers. Above are plenty of other sleeping spaces, there being one big room in the main block with access to short sections of wall-walks and angle rounds on the SE and NW corners, and two rooms in each tower, the uppermost being in square caphouses with crow-stepped gables. The SW caphouse is slightly smaller than the tower on which it sits. The existing sash windows are probably late 17th century. Originally there would have been dormers lighting the top storey and the windows lower down would have been glazed in the top half with a pair of small shutters below and grilles for protection.

The Strachans of Claypotts are first noted as tenants of Lindores Abbey in the early 16th century. Whilst John Strachan's namesake grandson was still a minor Claypotts was sold in 1601 to Sir William Graham of Ballunie. He transferred the estate to his son David in 1616 but in 1620 it was sold to Sir William Graham of Claverhouse. His great grandson was the celebrated Viscount Dundee, killed in 1689 fighting for the exiled James VII (who granted him the peerage in 1688). However he lived firstly at Glen Ogilvie and later at Dudhope and can have had little to do with Claypotts. The family were forfeited by William III and in 1694 Claypotts was granted to James, 2nd Marquis of Douglas. Again, it is doubtful whether he or his successors ever used the castle. It passed in the 19th century to the Homes who in 1926 placed it in the guardianship of the Office of Works (now succeeded by Historic Scotland).

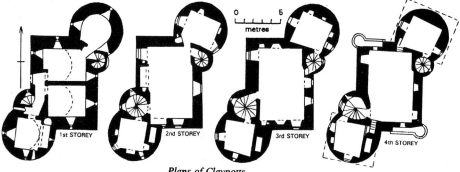

Plans of Claypotts

Cluny Crichton

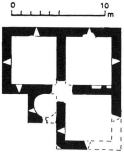

Plan of Cluny Crichton

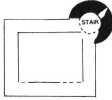

Plan of Clova Castle

Claypotts

CLOVA NO 322734 F

Of an Ogilvy tower of 1600 measuring about 10m by 8m only foundations remain except for a standing section of the 4.7m diameter staircase turret at a corner.

CLUNY CRICHTON NO 686997

This ruined L-plan house with three square unvaulted rooms on each of three storeys was built in 1666 for George Crichton of Cluny. After his grandson died without heirs the estate passed his wife's family, the Douglases of Tillquhillie. It measures about 13m along each of the arms, which are 7m wide over walls 1m thick. The doorway at the foot of a square stair turret in the re-entrant angle is surmounted by two empty panels for heraldic stones and is covered by two shot-holes.

COLLISTON   NO 612464

Over the original entrance at the foot of the main stair of this Z-plan castle is the date 1553. There are initials of John Guthrie and his second wife M. Falconer. Some years beforehand Cardinal Beaton conveyed the estate to John and his first wife Isabella Ogilvy who was probably the Cardinal's illegitimate daughter by his "chief lewd" Marion Ogilvy. The building is 13.6m long by 7.2m wide and has two round towers 4.8m in diameter, one of which contains a wide spiral stair up to the hall. A turret stair corbelled out over the entrance then serves the third storey. The basement contained a passage leading from the stair past two cellars to a kitchen with a fireplace in the far end wall. The nearest cellar has a recess originally used to contain a service stair to the hall. The other cellar became a passage when a new front door was broken into the passage outer wall and an extension containing corridors and a scale-and-platt staircase added on the other side of the building. Over the new doorway (now removed) was the date 1621, the Royal Arms, and the initials H.O and I.L. probably referring to an Ogilvy and a Lindsay. The stair tower has a square caphouse set diagonally to the main block. It is assumed that the other tower was originally similarly finished. In the 19th century it had a sloping roof but since then this tower has been given a flat roof and parapet, the main block has been given parapets, dormer windows and stepped gables, and the stair turret a conical roof. In 1670 Sir Henry Guthrie sold Colliston to Dr Gordon and in 1721 it passed to John Chaplin.

CORTACHY   NO 400594

The round SE and SW towers now lying at either end of an embattled three storey block 24m long above the South Esk are thought to be relics of a courtyard castle built by Sir Walter Ogilvy of Oures who was granted Cortachy by James III in 1473. The present arrangement of this block, with a private room over a kitchen at the east end, and a hall over two cellars and a connecting passage to the west, must be of c1580-16100, the period of the square caphouse on the SW tower. The mock-Elizabethan chimneys on this part and the embattled and conical roofed upper part of the SE tower are Victorian. A third vaulted cellar lies in the NW wing and there is a scale-and-platt staircase in the angle between the two parts. Cortachy passed to Thomas Ogilvy of Clova but was sold in 1625 to the Earl of Airlie, becoming the main seat of the Earldom after the burning of Airlie Castle in 1640. Charles II stayed in what is now a panelled dining room in 1650 and the castle was sacked by Cromwellian troops in 1651.

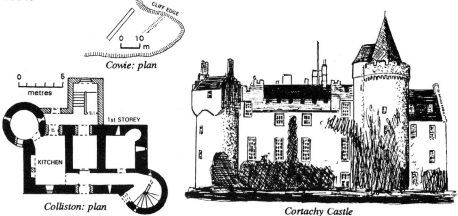

Cowie: plan

1st STOREY

KITCHEN

Colliston: plan

Cortachy Castle

COWIE   NO 887774   F

A path leads southward from the ruined church to a D-shaped headland with a 21m long curtain wall 2m thick rising 1.5m above a ditch on the landward side. Malcolm Canmore is said to have had a castle here but the walling is more likely to be 13th century. Robert Bruce gave Cowie to Sir Alexander Fraser but the castle was probably then in a dismantled state. There is nothing to suggest the site was occupied later.

CRAIG   NO 704563

The castle comprises an inner court with overall dimensions of about 24m by 25m, with to the east and SE an outer court about the same width but twice as long. In the angle between the two there seems to have been a walled garden. The outer court is a 16th century addition and has a gateway at the south end flanked by round towers with gunports on the adjacent corners. A modern range lies in the SE corner of this court. The inner court has small square towers within the south angles. That to the SE now stands isolated except for the south outer wall containing blocked windows of a former range here. Of an east range all that remains is a jamb of the gateway passage through it beside the tower. The tower has a corbelled out parapet with round corners around a gabled attic. Three spouts on each side drain the wall-walk. On the north side of the court is a range 7.5m wide containing a kitchen at the east end, a cellar with a service stair in the outer wall beside it, and two smaller cellars to the west. The 5.8m wide west range has had its vaults removed. The stone dated 1637 over the doorway was reset there after being found buried in the ground near the SW tower. The towers and parts of the court outer walls may go back to the late 15th century when Craig was held by the Wood family. Sir David Wood was Comptroller of Scotland under James V. The domestic ranges were remodelled after the castle was acquired by David Carnegie, 1st Earl of Southesk, and given to a younger son c1620. It later passed to the Scotts of Rossie.

Craig Castle

Crathes Castle

Crathes Castle

CRATHES NO 734968 NTS

The existing castle replaced the original Burnett seat on a crannog in the Loch of Leys. The family were descended from Burnhard, who came to Scotland with David I and were originally settled at Farningdoun in Berwickshire. Alexander, 6th of the line of Kincardineshire Burnetts, was confirmed in the barony of Banchory by James III. The castle was begun in 1553 by Alexander, 9th laird and was completed, or more likely, the upper parts remodelled, in the 1590s by Alexander, 12th laird. His initials and those of his wife Katherine Gordon appear on an original bed and pair of chairs within the building. In 1626 Thomas, 13th laird, was created a baronet of Nova Scotia. Sir Thomas, 15th laird, who died in 1714, added a three storey wing rebuilt only two storeys high after a fire in 1966. The castle has been administered by the National Trust for Scotland since 1952.

The castle is L-planned but with the east wall of the main block thickened to contain chambers and a staircase in the SE corner so that the wing only projects about 3m. The corners are rounded but are corbelled out square about 3m below the corbelling of the bartizans, which are round on the southern corners, but square on the NW. The entrance retains its yett now properly remounted on hinges after being fixed outside for many years. Leading off the lobby are two proper cellars and a small cubby hole, whilst the wing contains a kitchen. The hall above has a splendid plaster ceiling and is the height of two levels in the wing. The wide south window is an 18th century insertion. In this room is the Horn of Leys, given along with an estate here by Robert Bruce to his Forester, Alexander de Burnard. In the SW corner are traces of a former service stair. At the junction of wing and main block on the north side is a secondary stair serving the upper rooms in which are fine painted ceilings discovered under later plaster in 1877. One room has a set of Muses, another Nine Worthies. At the summit a galley occupies the north end of the main block and the wing. See pages 11 and 15.

Dudhope Castle

DUDHOPE NO 394307 V

This recently renovated and re-harled building lies on a shelf of land in a public garden above the centre of Dundee. It is an L-planned mansion dated 1600 with a five storey south wing 8m wide and an east wing 9m wide through which is a gateway passage. The arms of the L measure about 32m and 30m long respectively. On the outer corners are round towers and a smaller pair flank the gateway. Screen walls enclosing the north and west sides of a court survived until the 18th century. The Scrymgeours had their seat here from an early date and there was until the late 17th century a tower house standing in the now unenclosed corner. Alexander Scrymgeour (or Skirmisher) was made Constable of the castle and burgh of Dundee in 1298 by William Wallace and Robert Bruce made them hereditary standard-bearers. They were often in dispute with the Provost and magistrates of the city when not holding these offices themselves. On the building are the arms of Dame Magdalene Livingstone, wife of Sir James Scrymgeour. James I stayed here in 1617 and in 1641 Sir John was made Viscount Dundee by Charles I. The 3rd Viscount was made an Earl in 1660 but this honour died with him in 1669. Graham of Claverhouse purchased the castle and became Viscount Dundee. After he was killed during the 1689 rebellion against William III, Dudhope passed to the Earls of Angus. They never used the castle, which became a barracks and then a woollen mill, being shamefully neglected.

DUN NO 670599 NTS

The House of Dun, now administered by the National Trust for Scotland after having been an hotel, is an Adam mansion of 1758 on the site of a castle of the Erskines. They obtained an estate here in 1348. John Erskine of Dun, d1569, was one of the leaders of the Reformation, being Superintendent of Angus. After the male line failed in 1812, Dun passed to the 12th Earl of Cassillis.

DUNNOTTAR   NO 882839   OP

The large flat-topped rock on which the castle stands is a natural site for a defensible residence and must have been occupied from an early date. There may have been a motte here in the 12th century and a new parish church on the rock, successor to an early chapel apparently dedicated to St Ninian, was consecrated in 1276 by Bishop Wishart. In 1297 William Wallace stormed the rock and the English garrison were burnt alive in the church, which was probably then the only building of mortared stone on the site. Dunnottar is mentioned as a castle in 1336 when the place was garrisoned under Sir Thomas de Roscelyn by the English in support of Edward Balliol. In July of that year the English King, Edward III, was at Dunnottar. Soon afterwards de Roscelyn was killed in an attack on Aberdeen and Dunnottar was recaptured and burnt by Sir Andrew Moray. Most of the buildings and defences were then still probably of wood. In 1346 William, 5th Earl of Sutherland was granted Dunnottar with licence to fortify the site although no remains are attributable to that period.

A new church had been built further inland by 1394 when Sir William Keith, Marischal of Scotland, built an L-planned tower on the highest point of the rock. The church still claimed the site as holy ground and Sir William was excommunicated by the Bishop of St Andrews. Sir William wrote to the Pope that he needed a castle on the rock to protect himself, his goods and his servants from "the malice of the tyrants of the kingdom" and that the church no longer needed the rock. Eventually it was agreed that he would pay compensation to the church. The Keiths subsequently became Earls Marischal and Dunnottar formed their chief seat until George, 10th Earl, was forfeited for his part in the 1715 rebellion and the castle was handed over to the York Buildings Company, being dismantled for its materials in 1718. James V in 1531 issued a charter declaring the castle "is ane of the pricipall strenthis of our realme", and excusing those needed for garrisoning it from service in the royal army.

James IV visited the castle in 1504, Queen Mary came in 1562 and 1564, and James VI in 1580, 1589, and 1594. The castle was captured by Captain Car for the rebel Earl of Huntly in 1592 and was restored to the Keiths a month later. During this period much of the domestic buildings and the entrance defences were built. In 1643 the Marquis of Argyll made his headquarters in the castle in his campaign against Montrose. In 1645 the Earl Marischal shut himself up in the castle whilst Montrose burnt his estates. In 1650 Charles II was at Dunnottar and in 1651 Crown Jewels were deposited in the castle, then commanded by George Ogilvy with a garrison of 69 men with 42 guns. A siege by Cromwellian troops was begun in September that year, although it was not until May 1652 that heavy siege artillery arrived. Seven of the garrison were killed during a bombardment of the tower house and they were forced to surrender. However Charles II's private papers and the Regalia had already been smuggled out of the castle, the latter being taken to Kinneff and hidden under the floor of the church until Charles was restored to power in 1660.

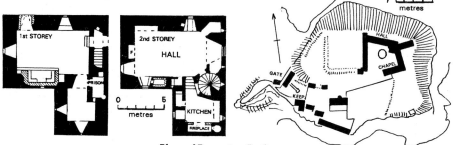

Plans of Dunnottar Castle

The quadrangle, Dunnottar Castle

During the rebellion by Argyll and Monmouth against James VII in 1685 a group of Covenanters comprising 122 men and 45 women were incarcerated in a cellar now known as the "Whigs' Vault" from late May to the end of July. Although the overcrowding was eventually eased by moving some of them to other cellars they were appallingly treated and several tortured after an escape attempt out onto the rock-face. Quite a number of them died.

Entrance to the castle is gained by descending to sea level and them up a few steps to a gateway in a wall 9m high and 2.2m thick. The wall-walk high above gives access to a narrow peninsular called the Fiddlehead which commands the approaches. The gateway arch is flanked by a tall block known as Benholm's lodging. The top storey contained apartments and is still roofed. Below is a vault over another level of apartments and beneath that were three storeys of barrack rooms lighted by gunports and partly carved out of the rock. The entrance pend was closed by a portcullis. On the other side is the vaulted magazine, over which was another barrack room. The pend comes out facing the guardroom, a chamber mostly carved from the rock with a screen of round apertures commanding the passage, which here turns northwards on its ascent up many steps and through two tunnels once closed by gates to the top of the rock. The loops seem too big for actual military use and anyway have glazing slots. It seems that this building was once dated 1575, and most of these works, constituting one of the best defended entrances in Scotland, are of that period.

On the south side of the rock, commanding the entrance arrangements, is the tower house of the 1390s. It measures 12.3m by 7.8m and has a wing 5.7m wide projecting 5m from the south wall. The original cellar was later converted to a kitchen, three of the original four loops being replaced by or altered into a fireplace, sink, and a new doorway respectively. The entrance lies in the east end wall and gives onto a lobby from which a straight stair rises to a spiral stair set over a tiny prison and positioned to serve rooms in both the main block and wing. The hall has windows in each wall, a fireplace at the west end, a latrine in the south wall, and a mural chamber in the NE corner. A kitchen at this level in the wing was later converted into a private chamber. The third storey had a private hall with a trefoil shaped locker in the main block and a bedroom in the wing. The wall-walk 11m above ground has lost its parapet and angle rounds although corbelling for them remains. Within was a gabled roof containing an attic. East of the tower house is a block containing servants quarters over two vaulted cellars. Next to it is the much ruined smithy with a big fireplace and then beyond is a 37m long stable block with two rooms for livery masters at the east end and grooms quarters above reached by external staircases. The upper rooms had dormer windows and there was a timber gallery extending along the south side.

Waterton's Lodging north of the stables is named after Thomas Forbes, Laird of Waterton who was often in attendance on the Earl Marischal in the mid 17th century. The building contained a living room and private room on each of two storeys, access to the upper level being by a spiral stair in a round turret on the north side. Over the stair is a square caphouse containing a room reached by a tiny turret stair on the east. A stone from this building discovered in 1785 was dated 1574 (erroneously given as 1374). Probably the house was built for William, son of the 4th Earl, after his marriage to Elizabeth Hay, daughter of the Earl of Errol. East of the house is an area known as the kirkyard beyond which are remains of an artillery battery looking out to sea.

Most of the buildings around the quadrangle on the NE corner of the rock were built by George, 5th Earl, who succeeded in 1581 and died here in 1623. However, the chapel occupying the east half of the south side (the west half is open) retains some masonry and two small pointed windows on the south side of the building consecrated in 1276. The west range contains seven private rooms for household officials over which is a gallery 34.5m long by 4.5m wide reached by a scale-and-platt staircase in a wing at the SW corner. At the north end of the gallery is a retiring room with a balcony overlooking the sea. The north range blocks one of the west range private room doorways and must be slightly later. It contains on the upper storey a drawing room with a roof dated 1927 with initials of George V, Queen Mary, Lord and Lady Cowdray (the new owners), and George Ogilvy and Elizabeth Douglas, a dining room 16m long by 6m wide, and a retiring room with a latrine. Below are a kitchen with a huge fireplace, three cellars, and a gateway passage to the cliff edge, all being vaulted. The east range contained a suite of two main rooms and a wardrobe for the Countess over a bakery (with an oven in the south end wall), a brewery, and a cellar. In the obtuse angle between the north and east ranges is a square projection containing a scale-and-platt staircase. Projecting eastward at the junction of the ranges is a block added by the 7th Earl containing a suite of two rooms for the himself (one has his arms and the date 1645 on a fireplace) above the cellar known as the "Whigs' Vault". The cellar is not as dark as sometimes described, having five windows, one quite large, and a gunloop. In the middle of the quadrangle is the well, actually a cistern 9m wide fed by pipes from the mainland. To the west of the quadrangle is the bowling green, with a battery to seaward on the north side.

Dunnottar Castle

Durris Castle

Durris Motte

Guardroom windows, Dunnottar

Edzell Castle

DURRIS NO 799968 & 779968

Near the Dee is the motte of a Comyn castle with what may be traces of masonry on the irregularly shaped summit measuring 39m by 32m. The mansion on the hillside some way to the south incorporates a long series of vaults said to be a relic of a 14th or 15th century courtyard castle built by the Frasers to whom were granted the Comyn lands here confiscated by Robert Bruce. At the south end of the mansion lies a modest four storey tower house of c1600 with a tiny bartizan at the SE corner and a staircase wing close to the west end of the north side. The main block is about 8.4m long by 6m wide. The entrance faces west, i.e. the smaller of the re-entrant angles. The larger re-entrant is now filled with three storeys of rooms. The wing has a gabled caphouse, corbelled out on the north side only. The hall has two fireplaces but does not seem to have ever been subdivided. Durris was burnt by Montrose in 1645. The house passed by marriage in the late 17th century to Charles Mordaunt, Earl of Peterborough. It later passed to the 4th Duke of Gordon and was sold in 1834 to Anthony Mactier by whom it was enlarged. It was sold again in 1871.

DYSART NO 694548

Dysart belonged to the Melvilles in the 15th and 16th centuries and then passed to the Guthries and Lyells, hereditary town clerks of Montrose until 1682. There is a worn panel over the doorway of Nether Dysart farm, and in the garden are a dormer pediment dated 1594 with the Melville arms and a gateway lintel dated 1714.

EDZELL   NO 585693 & 583688 HS

Edzell originally belonged to the Stirlings of Glenesk whose seat was the motte with a summit measuring 25m by 60m. In c1357 the estate passed to the Lindsay Earls of Crawford, who at the beginning of the 16th century built a tower house 400m to the north. The existing courtyard buildings are of about the time of James VI's visits of 1580 and 1589, but there must have already been substantial outbuildings by 1562 when Queen Mary held a Privy Council here during her expedition against the Gordons. These chambers were the work of Sir David Lindsay, Lord Edzell, who succeeded in 1558 and died, heavily in debt, in 1610. The castle was occupied by Cromwellian troops during October 1651. John Lindsay was "taken prisoner from his own house" in December 1653 by Royalists during the rising of the Earl of Kinnoul, but was rescued the following day. Lord Panmure was forfeited for his part in the 1715 rebellion not long after purchasing Edzell, which went to the York Buildings Company. The company maltreated the estate and the castle was dismantled for materials in 1764 after it had gone bankrupt, decay having been hastened by an occupation in 1746 by Hanoverian troops. The estate was repurchased by the Earl of Panmure and after his death in 1782 passed to the 8th Earl of Dalhousie. In the 1930s custody of the ruins was handed over by the then Earl to the Office of Works.

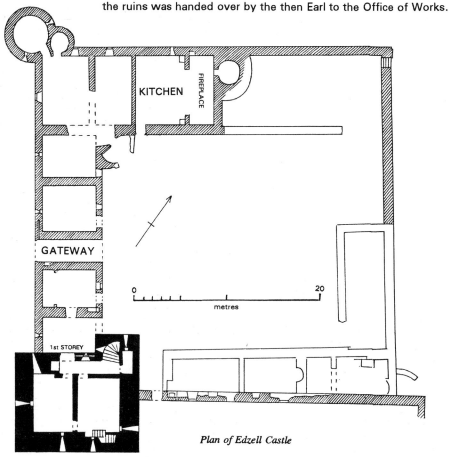

Plan of Edzell Castle

The walled garden, Edzell Castle

The tower house measures 13.4m by 10.4m over walls up to 2.2m thick and has a staircase wing 4.8m wide projecting 2m beyond the NW wall. This wall contains the entrance, which leads onto a passage linking two cellars and the stair. Both cellars contain gunports and another gunport opens off a small room, possibly a prison, tucked under the stair. The hall above has a fireplace in the NW wall and big windows to the SE and SW, whilst the west corner contains a mural bed-chamber. The NE end of the hall was screened off to create a servery with its own fireplace, latrine, and also a service stair down to the cellar at this end. There were two upper storeys of fine private rooms plus an attic within a parapet carried on ornamental chequered corbelling with rounds not only at the corners but in the middles as well. See photo on page 127.

The tower lies in the south corner of a court about 34m square. Ranges on all four sides were intended but only the SW range containing the drawing room and parlour over the gateway and the adjacent part of the wider NW range with a hall over two cellars and a kitchen appear to have been completed. Between the ranges lay a round stair turret entered from the court by a neo-classical style doorway. Over the gateway are empty panels for heraldic stones. South of the passageway is a second kitchen which served the rooms in the adjacent tower house. There are gunloops facing SW which have redented (stepped) outer splays intended to reflect incoming bullets. Further gunloops are contained in a round tower projecting from the west corner. This has its own staircase turret in the north re-entrant angle.

SE of the court lies the celebrated walled garden or pleasance. A doorway near the north corner is dated 1604 with the arms and initials of Sir David Lindsay and his second wife Dame Isobel Forbes and the motte "Dum Spiro Spero (while I breathe I hope)". The wall was divided by pilasters into compartments some of which have a chequer arrangement of recesses representing the Lindsay arms. Alternating with these are single recesses surmounted by sculptured panels depicting the Planetary Deities (Saturn, Jupiter, Mars, Sun, Venus, Mercury, Moon) on the NE side, the Liberal Arts (Grammar, Rhetoric, Dialectic, Arithmetic, Music, Geometry) on the SE side, and the Cardinal Virtues (Faith, Hope, Justice, Charity, Prudence, Fortitude, Temperance) on the SW side. The sculptures are of German inspiration, the Planets being copies from a series on engravings made in Nuremberg by Georg Pencz in 1558-9. The wall is finished with a heavy coping into which are set round headed niches. Only foundations revealed in 1855 remain of a bath-house projecting from the south corner of the garden but the summer house at the east corner stands complete. It has an upper room with a bartizan and shotholes and contains 16th century wood sculpture. Below are two square rooms, one rib vaulted and reached from the garden, the other reached from outside. A round stair turret connects the two levels.

Ethie Castle

ETHIE NO 688468

Cardinal David Beaton is claimed to have lived in the L-plan house at the SW corner of this mansion in 1530 when he was Abbot of Arbroath, and again from 1538 until his murder in 1546. However the comparatively thin walls suggest a construction date after 1549, when Ethie went to Sir Robert Carnegie, and possibly not until after it was given to a younger grandson, Sir John, in 1596. The house is 12.8m long and originally about 7m wide with a stair wing projecting from the west end of the north side. This wing now has a tall modern balconied top, perhaps vaguely like the original arrangement. East of the original house is an irregularly shaped block with projecting staircase turrets probably of early 17th century date. A courtyard to the east and north has 17th century ranges to the west and north with a round tower 3.8m in diameter with gunports on the outer angle. The north range contains a kitchen in the middle of the ground floor and a chapel at the east end of the upper level. This branch of the family were given the title Earl of Ethie in 1647 but in 1662 the title was changed to that of Earl of Northesk. They held Ethie until the early 20th century.

FARNELL NO 624555

Farnell belonged to the Bishops of Brechin until 1566 when Bishop Campbell disposed of it to the Earl of Argyll, a kinsman who had been instrumental in his appointment. An early 16th century three storey house was then doubled in length and a round staircase turret added on the south side. There was a court on this side, a scar of its wall being left on the SE corner of the original house. The stair tower is corbelled out to a square at the top merely to carry a gabled roof, as there is no room there. On the east gable are corbels of a former timber gallery and there are latrine projections at second and third storey level close to the east end of the north side. The north skew-putts have the initials I.M. (Jesus Maria) and the letter M surmounted by a crown. There is an embattled buttress at the SW corner. Farnell later passed to the Carnegies and was used as almshouse for elderly women and then as a farm-workers tenement. Some years ago the house was restored and recovered in pink harling. It is now the home of the Earl of Macduff, heir of the Carnegie chief, the Duke of Fife. See p159.

FETTERESSO   NO 843855

Fetteresso was a Comyn lordship granted by Robert Bruce to Sir Alexander Fraser and carried by his heiress to Sir William Keith. The Keith Earl Marischals replaced the original castle on a mound near the village by present mansion, the oldest part of which is the 17th century south range overlooking a slope to a burn. It is 35.5m long by 7.8m wide and has a passage along the north side linking a kitchen at the east end with six vaulted cellars. A turret contains a service stair leading up from the cellar next to the kitchen. The house was burnt by Montrose in 1645 and rebuilt in 1671. Here at Christmas 1715 the Keiths entertained the Pretender James Stewart. The house was later granted to Admiral Duff. He and his son in 1782 and 1808 built an octagonal bay east of the kitchen, added a range north of this and a large staircase in the angle between the ranges, and also created offices around a court between the ranges. The fittings were dismantled in 1954 after military use of the house during World War II and it was a ruin prior to a recent restoration to create superior apartments.

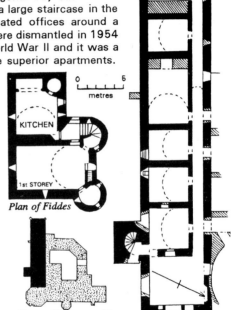

KITCHEN

1st STOREY

Plan of Fiddes

Fiddes

Plans of Fetteresso House

FIDDES   NO 805813

Sir Robert Arbuthnott, a favourite of James III and IV, is said to have recovered Fiddes, a property which his ancestors had owned two hundred years earlier. The family held the estate until it was sold in the late 17th century to James Thomson of Arduthie. The existing castle was probably built by Andrew Arbuthnott, who was given a charter by the young Queen Mary in 1553. It was restored in the 1960s by the Weir family after a long period of neglect. It consists of a four storey main block with a north wing which is not much smaller containing the main private room over a kitchen. There are bartizans on the wing outer corners, whilst the main block has a bartizan to the SW, a turret stair corbelled out at hall level to the NW, and two round turrets rising from ground level on the SE and NE corners. The SE has the head of a straight service stair from the cellar and contains an upper stair to the bedrooms. The other turret contains the main stair to the hall and is joined by a thickening of the north wall to the wing. This extra space is used to contain the entrance and a small room above, plus a larger roof extended over the stair-head on the third storey, whilst the top is a re-instated flat roof and a parapet on ornamental corbelling. On the south side of this turret is a narrow upper stair turret. There are shot-holes in the lowest rooms.

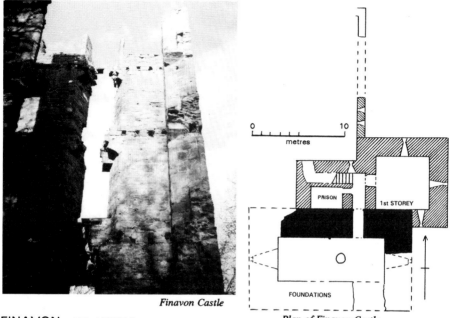

Finavon Castle

Plan of Finavon Castle

FINAVON NO 497566

Close to a stream among shrubs in the estate of the new castle now divided into flats is the base of an early tower house which was once the chief seat of the Earls of Crawford. Here in 1530 the 8th Earl was imprisoned for thirteen weeks by a son known as The Wicked Master who was disinherited and eventually stabbed to death in a drunken brawl by a Dundee cobbler. Lindsay of Edzell took over the estates but the son of the Wicked Master later became 10th Earl and was married at Finavon to an illegitimate daughter of Cardinal Beaton with whom came a huge dowry. The tower measures 17.2m by 10.4m over walls 3m thick and has evidence of a loop at each end and a well in the middle. There was no vault. Only the north wall stands above the foundations and has an entrance passage perhaps inserted later when a tower measuring 9.4m by 9.2m was added to the NE corner, and a wing containing a scale-and-platt staircase rising over a vaulted prison was added in the re-entrant angle. This part is much ruined but the north and east walls of the tower itself, added by Lord Lindsay of The Byres in the 1590s, still stand four storeys high above a vaulted cellar with double splayed gunloops. These rooms have fireplaces and tiers of big windows which had outside grilles. A thin short section of courtyard wall with gunports adjoins the tower and footings can be seen of a thicker wall west of the old tower. Not far to the NW lies a pit about 4m wide. In 1608 Finavon returned to the Earls of Crawford but was alienated by the Lindsays in 1629. It later went to the Carnegies.

FINDROWIE NO 554607

From a vanished castle here demolished in the early 19th century, but shown on a water colour at Balnamoon as an L-plan building with bartizans and dormers, are three dormer pediments re-set in the farmhouse and steading. They are dated 1638 and 1642 with the arms, monograms, and initials of the Arbuthnotts. Another stone of 1584, the likely time of construction, is now at Balnamoon House (see page 112)

FLEMINGTON   NO 527556

A roll-moulded doorway connects two vaulted cellars in the basement of the main block of a late 16th century house measuring 9.4m by 6.9m over walls 1.1m thick. At the north corner is a wing 6m by 4.8m containing the entrance and a wide staircase up to the hall. There are upper stairs over both re-entrant angles, that over the entrance being a rounded turret but the other just a flat projection giving access to a guest bedroom in the wing. There are several shot-holes in the walls. Robert III gave Flemington to Sir William Dishington. The castle was built either by this family or that of Ochterlony, the Reverend John Ochterlony being in residence here and using the house as an episcopal church until he was made Bishop of Brechin in 1742.

FORFAR   NO 455504

Malcolm Canmore held a parliament here in 1057 and there was a castle which was often used by the early kings on the Castle-hill, behind Castle Street, now marked by an octagonal tower and flagpole. The castle was destroyed by Robert Bruce c1308 to prevent it being used by the English and was never rebuilt.

FORTER   NO 183646   V

This castle built for James Ogilvie c1560 was destroyed by order of the Scottish Committee of estates in 1640, fire marks being visible in the hall. The Earl of Argyll carried out the destruction and left the Countess of Airlie to wander on the adjacent hills as recalled in the ballad "The Bonny Hoose o' Airlie". Forter Castle then lay ruinous until restored by the Pooley family who purchased it in 1988. It has a main block 11.8m long by 8m wide containing a hall over what was originally a kitchen at the west end and two small cellars. Engaging the SE corner is a wing 6.2m square containing a wide stair up to the hall and bedrooms above reached by a stair in a turret over the entrance in the western re-entrant angle. The hall has a fireplace in the south wall and has a chamber in the SW corner beside the kitchen fireplace flue. Above are two bedrooms on each of the third and fourth storeys of the main block, plus an attic. There are conical roofed bartizans on the corners of the main block.

Plans of Forter Castle

Forter Castle

FOTHERINGHAM   NO 459441

A huge mansion which replaced the 16th century castle has itself now been removed. The estate was named after the Fotheringhams who are said to have been Hungarians who came to Scotland with Margaret, Queen of Malcolm Canmore. They still live here.

FOWLIS EASTER   NO 321334

The original castle, soon superseded by Castle Huntly as the chief Gray seat, was probably built by Andrew Grey, created Lord Grey after his succession in 1437. The site is defended by steep slopes on two sides and had strong walls on the other sides with a gateway closed by a portcullis. The existing building is called the Lady Tower from its probably one-time use as a dower-house. A tympanum from it now on a later outbuilding is dated 1640 so it is assumed to be the work of Andrew, 8th Lord Grey. The existing dormers on the four storey building are of brick. It measures about 12m by 7m and has on the south side a breast for the basement kitchen fireplace flue and a round stair turret. In the late 17th century Fowlis was sold to the Murrays of Ochtertyre but they never took up residence. At one time the building was used as an ale-house but it is now a private residence again.

GAGIE   NO 448376

Gagie was sold by the Sibbald family to William, a younger son of Alexander Guthrie of that Ilk in 1610. On the gateway and a summer house dated 1614 are arms and initials of John Guthrie. His son eventually succeeded to the Guthrie estate. Another panel bears the arms and initials of his mother Isabella Leslie of Balquhain. The main house has just two storeys and is embellished with conical roofed bartizans at the south end. There are later wings to the NE and NW.

Gardyne Castle

GARDYNE   NO 574488

There is a reset stone with erased arms of the Gardyne family and the date 1568. The west part of the red sandstone building with a new south facing entrance dates from after the property passed to the Lyells of Dysart in 1682, and beyond it is a Victorian extension, but the east end is a tower of the 1560s with a round stair turret at the NW corner. At attic level on the east corners are bartizans which are conical roofed in stone with dormers and mock crenellations. The stair turret has a square caphouse with two upper rooms reached by a tiny stair over the NE re-entrant angle. There are several rectangular gun-ports. The Gardynes had a long-standing feud with their close neighbours the Guthries after a Guthrie son of a marriage between the families was killed in a quarrel by a Gardyne cousin. In 1578 William Guthrie slew Patrick Gardyne and in the 1580s first the Guthrie chief was killed, then the chief of the Gardynes.

2nd STOREY

0   5
m

Plans of Glamis Castle

0   30
m

Fowlis Easter Castle

Gardyne Castle

Glamis Castle

GLAMIS   NO 387481   OP

In 1372 Robert II granted Sir John Lyon of Forteviot the thaneage of Glamis which in 1376 was raised to a feudal barony when Sir John, then Chancellor, married the Princess Joanna. John is said to have been murdered in his own bed by Sir James Lindsay of Crawford in 1382 and the earliest part of the present castle was probably built c1400 soon after the heir, another John, attained his majority. It was a rectangular structure containing a hall over a kitchen and having a round tower at the SE corner. In a much altered state it now forms the SE wing. The much taller and more massive tower house was added by his son Patrick, who was created Lord Glamis in 1445. He served James II as a Privy Councillor and Master of the Household. After John, 6th Lord Glamis died in 1528 his widow, one of the Douglases with whom James V was then at feud, was executed in Edinburgh on a trumped up charge of witchcraft and Glamis Castle was taken over as a royal residence, many charters being dated from it. It was probably at this time that the narrow gap between the old hall and the tower house wing was filled in with rooms. By this time there was also a strong courtyard wall, now vanished, abutting the hall block and surrounding the tower. On the lawn are parts of two corner towers of a later outer court. Surrounding the whole establishment was a moat. The castle was returned to the 7th Earl after James V died in 1542. Queen Mary was entertained here by the 8th Earl in 1562.

Patrick, 9th Lord Glamis, who succeeded at the age of three, accompanied James VI when in 1603 he went south to claim the English throne. There he would have met Shakespeare and thus Glamis became the setting of part of the play Macbeth. There was no real connection and Glamis was probably not a thaneage when the real Macbeth ruled in the 11th century. In 1606 Patrick was created Earl of Kinghorne and in the same year he remodelled the tower house at Glamis, providing the existing skyline with round chimneys, conical roofed bartizans, and balconied gables, plus a wide new staircase in a round turret added in the re-entrant angle. It bears his initials, plus those of his wife Dame Anna Murray. Patrick, 3rd Earl, managed to get his title extended as Earl of Strathmore and Kinghorne. He improved the estate and built a new NW wing to balance the old hall block which was re-roofed by the time he died in 1695. Yet when he and his wife first came to Glamis from Castle Huntly in 1670 hardly any rooms had glazed windows and the estate had been impoverished by his father's support of the Covenant army in the 1640s.

The 9th Earl married the heiress of the English family of Bowes and the 10th Earl adopted the Bowes surname, although name Lyon was later added to give the present family name of Bowes-Lyon. In the 1840s the 12th Earl rebuilt the NW wing devastated by a fire in 1800 and remodelled other parts of the castle. In 1923 Lady Elizabeth Bowes-Lyon, youngest daughter of the 14th Earl, married the Duke of York, who succeeded as King George VI in 1937. Their younger daughter Princess Margaret was born at Glamis, which is still the home of Fergus, 17th Earl, and his family.

The tower house is 21.3m long by 11.4m wide and has a wing 8.8m wide projecting 6.3m. The original entrance, now a window, lies on the south side towards the west end at second storey level and is flanked by a pair of small rooms for guards or porters. It leads into what was probably a retainers mess hall through which the original narrow stair, now replaced by a much wider one, in the re-entrant angle was reached. The lofty vaulted main hall is at third storey level and had a dias at the west end, where there was a fireplace, a window with seats in each side-wall and a private stair in the NW corner. The plaster ceiling has a monograph of the 2nd Earl and his wife Margaret Erskine. Both second and third storeys have latrines in the NE corner now used as access passages to extensions. The room in the wing at second storey level has a mural chamber in the east wall and a latrine in the south wall. On the west wall can be seen corbels of the original parapet. See plans on page 135.

GLENBERVIE NO 769805

The estate belonged to the Melvilles from the 13th century until it passed via an heiress to Sir Alexander Auchinleck. Sir William Douglas of Braidwood obtained Glenbervie by marriage in 1492 and the time of his death in 1513 had built a block 22m long by 9.5m to close off the vulnerable east side of a triangular promontory formed by the junction of the Pilkettie Burn and the Water of Bervie. Facing the approach are conical roofed round towers 5.5m in diameter containing square vaulted cellars having cross loops with bottom roundels found in other buildings of the 1490s. Each cellar also had two double splayed gunloops, now blocked. The main block contained three cellars below a hall and below the private room is a kitchen with a fireplace at the north end. The lower rooms are linked by a passage on the west side.

In 1572 whilst the then laird (who succeeded in 1588 as 9th Earl of Angus) was absent the castle was besieged by Sir Adam Gordon in support of Queen Mary. He left his infantry in trenches in front of the castle whilst he took off his cavalry to surprise and defeat a force which was being assembled at Brechin to raise the siege, the outcome of which is unknown. Sir William Douglas of Glenbervie was created a baronet in 1625, a title which lapsed in 1812 but was revived in 1831. Glenbervie was sold by the 3rd baronet, another William, in 1675 to Robert Burnett of Leys. The Burnetts carried out some alterations but in 1721 sold the estate to William Nicholson of Mergie. It passed in 1831 to the Badenachs, whose descendants the Badenach Nicolsons still live at Glenbervie, their arms appearing over the present entrance into the northern cellar which contains a staircase dating from the remodelling of 1854. Battlements of that period on the SE tower have now been removed.

Glenbervie Castle

GUTHRIE   NO 563505

A modern mansion adjoins a tower containing a hall over two cellars, a bedroom above, plus an attic within a modern parapet with angle rounds. The tower measures 12m by 9.3m over walls mostly 1.6m thick, except for the one side wall containing a straight stair up from the entrance which is thickened to 2.4m. A spiral stair in a projecting turret with cap-house at the top then leads up. The tower is said to have been built in the 1460s by Sir David Guthrie, Lord Treasurer and Lord Justice-General under James III, although it may be of the time of his son, killed at Flodden in 1513. James VI forfeited the Guthries and their neighbours the Gardynes after their feuding harassed the surrounding area for much of the late 16th century, but a junior branch of Guthries managed to obtain Guthrie Castle.

Guthrie Castle

HALKERTON   NO 711719

Only slight earthworks remain of the original chief seat of the Falconers, here by c1150 and created peers in 1647. The 7th Lord adopted the name Keith Falconer after becoming the 5th Earl of Kintore. The family lived at nearby Inglismaldie until c1900.

HALLGREEN   NO 832721

The Dunnett family are thought to have had a castle on this site beside where a burn runs into Bervie Bay in the late 14th century, but the L-planned building recently restored from a derelict state by the Macmillan family was built in the late 16th century by the Raits. It has two vaulted cellars and a passage in a main block 12.6m long by 7.6m wide. The lower room in the wing 5.4m wide projecting 4.2m is unvaulted and probably this space originally contained a wide staircase up to the hall. There are several conical roofed bartizans. The Halls acquired the castle by marriage in 1687 and considerably extended it to the north and west where a small court faces the approach. A buttress strengthens the SE corner rising above a steep slope.

Hallgreen Castle

0   10
metres

Plan of Hallgreen Castle

HATTON   NO 302411

The lands of Newtyle were granted by Robert Bruce to Sir William Olifard (Oliphant) in 1317. On their occasional visits the lairds probably stayed at the vanished castle of Balcraig nearby to the south. In 1575 Laurence, Lord Oliphant, built the existing castle, recently restored from ruin by Roderick Oliphant. In 1617 Newtyle, as the castle was then called, passed to the Hallyburtons of Pitcur. Montrose besieged the castle unsuccessfully in 1645. It consists of a main block 18.3m long by 7.2m wide from which project wings about 6m wide at the NE and SW corners. The latter contained a scale-and-platt stair from the entrance up to the hall. A spiral stair, later removed, then led up in the NW re-entrant angle whilst a service stair led down to the wine cellar. This cellar, plus another, and a kitchen with a fireplace in the east end wall are linked by a passage along the south side of the building. The NE wing contained a private suite of rooms for the laird and his family connected by a spiral stair rising the full height of the building in the NW re-entrant angle. This stair also served bedrooms over a drawing room divided off at the east end of the hall. The drawing room has a closet squeezed in beside the kitchen fireplace flue. The hall has two windows on the north, one facing west, and two more either side of a fireplace on the south side. There are numerous gunports in the cellars and shot-holes below the upper windows.

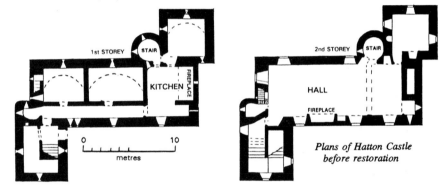

*Plans of Hatton Castle
before restoration*

Hatton Castle as restored (see also page 21)

Inglismaldie Castle

HYND NO 505416

Defaced fragments of an early tower 9.1m square over walls up to 2.7m thick lie on a low wooded mound. The only feature is a damaged double splayed loop to the north.

INGLISMALDIE NO 644669

In 1588 James VI gave former church lands here to John Livingstone of Dunipace who built the existing building of four storeys plus an attic. It passed to John Carnegie, Earl of Ethie in 1635. The property was obtained in 1693 by David Falconer of Newton who later succeeded as the 5th Lord Falconer of Halkerton. The eccentric 8th Lord Falconer succeeded as 5th Earl of Kintore in 1778. Inglismaldie passed to another family c1900 but in 1925 was purchased by Major Keith-Falconer, a cousin of the Earl of Kintore. In 1960 it passed to the Ogilvys. The present entrance on the south side is modern, the original entrance covered by gunloops being now within a west range replacing an older block in this position. The cut down roofs of the bartizans have now been restored. The SW wing and the east wing are late 19th century additions.

INVERGOWRIE NO 365307 & 363304

Nothing remains of the stone castle which Boece claimed King Edgar (d1107) built at Invergowrie. The site lies NE of the present house in the grounds of a hospital which is dated 1601 over the entrance with initials of its builders Patrick Gray and Agnes Napier. It may have been begun some years earlier as Patrick obtained the property in 1568 from Sir John Carnegie, to whom it was transferred from Scone Abbey at the Reformation. Shortly after completion the house passed to David Murray, 1st Viscount Stormont, but in 1615 was sold to Robert Clayhills of Baldovie. It passed to the Hendersons in the 20th century. The building has been altered and extended but retains conical roofed bartizans at the north end, where is the kitchen in the basement, whilst the doorway near the south end of the east wall was covered by a shot-hole in a round staircase turret corbelled out not far above ground beside it.

INVERMARK NO 443804 V

This round cornered tower measuring 11.7m by 8.3m over walls up to 2m thick at ground level reduced to 1.4m thick at hall level was built in the early 16th century by the Lindsays as an outpost controlling this lonely valley. It stood in the NW corner of a small court of which footings survive. The site is said to have been the seat of John de Stirling in the 14th century. The tower originally contained a hall over a vaulted basement, a bedroom above, and a parapet. In c1600 the building was given an extra full storey and an attic for which windows are pieced through the chimney stacks on the north and south sides. The entrance, still closed by a yett made of local Tarfside iron, is in the south wall at hall level. Beside it is a stair in the SW corner down to a vaulted cellar lighted only by double splayed gunloops in each side. Another stair in the NW corner served the upper levels. There is a bartizan on the SE corner.

Inverquarity Castle

HALL

0   5
metres

Invermark Castle

Plan of Inverquarity before restoration

Hynd: plan

STAIR

Invermark: plan

INVERQUHARITY NO 411579

The Ogilvys were seated here from 1420 until the late 18th century, being created baronets in 1626. The licence from James II permitting construction of the L-plan tower specifically allowed the entrance to be fitted with a yett. The main block is 13.4m long by 10m wide over walls 2.2m thick. A wing 8m wide was dismantled to provide materials for a new farm steading and has now been replaced in a restoration of the building in the 1960s for the Grant family by a three storey block making no attempt to imitate the original. The entrance admits into the cellar in the main block over which is a vaulted sleeping or storage loft with three narrow loops. A spiral stair in the re-entrant angle leads up from the entrance. Access from it to the service or north end of the hall is by means of a passage between the hall and the wing. The hall has mural chambers in the north and east walls with a peculiar porch in the angle between, though to have covered the head of a former service stair. The other end has a fireplace in the south end wall and a window with seats in each side wall. The hall vault is 6.3m above the floor and a window high up at the south end suggests there was originally an intermediate floor. The wing contains two rooms corresponding to the height of the hall, probably a kitchen with the laird's private room above. The topmost storey lies partly within a gable roof within the wall-walk. Fireplaces at each end suggest it was subdivided. There is a caphouse containing an upper room reached from the wall-walk over the stair. The finely moulded and corbelled parapet with large angle rounds looks more like early 16th century work than of the 1440s. It has a projection with machicolations protecting the entrance.

KAIM OF MATHERS NO 763649 F

Below the main cliff and almost separated from it by a sea inlet big enough to house a small ship is a platform about 12m wide and 40m long. It slopes from the narrow approach on the north, where there are tumbled fragments of a gateway, to the south where it rises about 12m above the sea. The SW corner of the site, commanding the entrance to the sea inlet, is itself nearly divided off by sheer drops to the sea. On it is a 4m high fragment of the 0.7m thick north end wall and part of the 0.6m thick east wall of a building 4m wide externally and probably once about 6m long. One loop faces north. There are beam holes for an upper floor with a fireplace at the north end.

KELLIE NO 608402 OP

The Mowbrays had a residence here in the 12th century and in 1208 were granted permission by the Abbot of Arbroath to have an oratory within it. They were forfeited in 1309 by Robert I and in the 1320s Kellie went to Walter Stewart. In the mid 15th century the barony of Kellie was renamed Ochterlony after the family of that name then in possession. In the early 17th century Sir William Ochterlony sold most of the lands to Sir William Irvine. The Irvine fortunes were dissipated in the Royalist cause and the barony was sold in 1679 by Sir Alexander Irvine of Drum to the Earl of Panmure for £11,000. In 1681 Kellie was given to a Harry Moule, a younger brother of the then Earl. He was forfeited for his part in the 1715 rebellion and the castle was allowed to decay. It passed to the Ramseys, becoming part of the estates of the Earls of Dalhousie until sold in the 20th century to the Kerr-Boyles.

The castle lies on a rock above the Elliot Water. It consists of an L-planned 16th century tower of four storeys and an attic rising high above low courtyard buildings. The wing rises higher than the main block and contains chambers over the main stair. The main block has a round bartizan with a rectangular appendage beside the end gable like the bartizans of c1600 at Amisfield in Dumfriesshire.

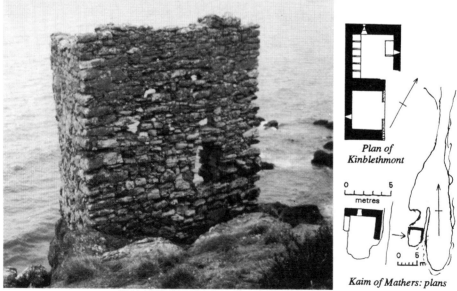

Plan of Kinblethmont

0   5
metres

Kaim of Mathers: plans

Kaim of Mathers Castle

Kellie Castle

KINBLETHMONT   NO 637470

Hidden among shrubs in an estate which has for centuries belonged to the Lindsay-Carnegies is the lower part of a building of c1600 about 12m long by 6m wide containing two vaulted cellars, one of which has been altered later.

Kellie Castle

KINCARDINE   NO 671751

On a tree-clad slight eminence are remains of a 13th century courtyard castle probably built by Alexander II although a castle here is mentioned as early as 1212. The lower parts of walls 2.2m thick above a plinth enclose a court about 34m square. On the east are indications of a range about 7m wide internally which presumably contained a hall either at ground level or over a basement. There was a another range 5.8m wide inside all along the north side. On the south side is the gateway between two towers of now indeterminate size and shape as their outer parts are broken away and the interiors are choked with rubble. On the west side of the western tower are latrine shoots. Within it was drafted John Balliol's abdication document in 1296. The Earl Marischal had the adjoining settlement made the county town in 1532 but the courts were removed to Stonehaven by James VI and the castle allowed to decay. Queen Mary stayed here during the expedition of 1562 against the Gordons. Several generations of the Woods family were custodians in the 15th and 16th centuries.

KINNAIRD   NO 634571

Ancient vaulted cellars and thick walls survive in the mansion greatly enlarged in 1770, and remodelled in the style of a French chateau in 1854-60. Duthac Carnegie married the heiress Mariota de Kinnaird in 1409. In 1616 the then laird, David, was created Lord Carnegie, and in 1633 he was made Earl of Southesk. His daughter married the Marquis of Montrose with whom he did not always agree. The 5th Earl was forfeited after the 1715 rebellion but the estates were bought by a kinsman and the forfeiture reversed in 1855. The family inherited the Dukedom of Fife in 1959.

Kincardine Castle

KINNEFF   NO 855747

A tumbled fragment 3m long, 1m high and about 1.2m thick on a promontory to seaward of Mansefield Cottage is all that remains of a 16th century tower. An earlier castle here was garrisoned by the English for Edward Balliol in the 1330s, coins of that period having been found in the vicinity.

KINNORDY   NO 366545

The Earls of Angus are thought to have had a stronghold on a crannog in the loch which was drained in 1730 but still partly remains as a marsh. The mansion may incorporate remains of a castle of the Ogilvys of Inverquharity. It was sold to Charles Lyell of Gardyne in 1770. Another Charles Lyell was made a baronet in 1848.

LAURISTON   NO 759666

In the 1240s Lauriston, named after a chapel of St Laurence, belonged to the de Strivelyn or Stirling family. In the late 14th century it passed to the Straitons who remained here until the estate passed in 1695 to Sir James Falconer of Phesdo. The castle is strongly sited above a ravine. It seems to have been a 15th century courtyard castle with the main tower at the SE corner. A new house with a bartizan on the SW corner was built on its site c1600. Not much now remains of a curtain wall which joined this building to a tower at the SW corner which has a cellar below courtyard level in the floor of which is a shaft descending to the foot of the ravine. There are three original rooms above, two of them vaulted, and three more levels have been grafted on above the original parapet with angle rounds carried on a single row of corbels in the late 18th or early 19th century.

LINTROSE   NO 225379

Hidden within Lintrose House is a late 16th century house with a round stair turret. It was once a Hallyburton seat and was then called Fodderance.

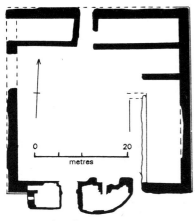

Plan of Kincardine Castle

Lauriston Castle

LOGIE NO 392521

The much altered tower has a NE round staircase turret with one shot-hole high up. The turret now has a sloped roof continuing that of the main tower. Panelling inside and a west extension erroneously dated 1022 are 18th century. Among various worn initials are those of one of the Kinlochs of Kilrie to whom the estate later passed. A dormer pediment now built into the yard wall is dated 1688. The Wisharts long held the estate, which was once called Logie-Wishart.

MAINS OF FINTRY NO 401330 V

The estate was named Fintry by the Grahams after their castle of that name in Stirlingshire. Mains Castle on the south side of the Dichty Burn was built by David Graham. His namesake son was executed in 1593 for involvement in a Catholic plot known as the affair of the "Spanish Blanks". Over the west gate of the court is the date 1562 and over the east range doorway is the year 1582. This range containing a kitchen was probably added slightly later to the north range likely to be of c1560. The exceptionally high top of the stair turret at the SE corner of the house with a projecting caphouse is a 17th century addition perhaps intended to give a view over the higher ground to the south. Only foundations remain of a south range. The courtyard wall on the west has blocked windows of a former range on that side also. Only the corbelling now remains of bartizans on the NW corner of this wall and over the gate, although they were nearly complete earlier this century. That over the gateway had machicolation slots. When the estate was sold to David Erskine it was renamed Linlathen as the Grahams retained the title "of Fintry". The castle and its lands were sold to Sir James Caird in 1913 and handed over to Dundee Corporation for use as a public park. The castle was restored in the 1980s.

Mains Castle

Mains Castle

COURT

0   10

m

Plan of Mains Castle

Melgund Castle

MELGUND   NO 546564

This fine ruin is about to be restored as a private residence for the Gregory family. It looks like a double stepped L-plan tower of c1500 to which a later range has been added but in fact the whole building was erected either c1540 by Cardinal David Beaton or slightly later by his kinsman David Bethune or Beaton. The building is 31m long and is mostly about 9m wide although originally an outer, wall, now missing, on the north side enclosing upper and lower corridors increased the width of most of it to 12.5m. The lower corridor connected the kitchen and cellars; that above was more like a long gallery heated by two fireplaces. It is the west end with walls 1.8m thick surmounted by corbelling for a parapet with roundels that looks like an earlier tower. The second storey room in this part was a comfortable, secure private chamber with roll-moulded window embrasures with seats, a latrine, a service stair, a fireplace in the end wall, and two niches in the western corners with gunports. A wide spiral stair lies in a wing at the NE corner. This projected no further than the missing corridors but was carried up high above them as the west end is four storeys high whilst the remainder had only two and attics. The thick eastern wall of the western part carried the kitchen fireplace flue, now broken down. Beyond was the hall, an apartment 11m long with a wife fireplace on the north side and three big windows facing south, two of them having high sills for placing furniture underneath. The east end contained another fine private room with its own spiral stair in the NE corner. Attached to this corner is a turret 3.4m in diameter containing at second storey level a pentagonal room with a beehive-vault. Melgund passed to the Marquis of Huntly in the 17th century and then to the Elliots of Minto. See photograph and plans on page 148.

Melgund Castle

Plans of Melgund Castle

MERGIE NO 796886

The stair wing in the middle of the south side appears to be an addition and the three storey main block may also be of two periods, probably late 16th and early 17th century. The low basement is not vaulted. A turret stair with blocked shot-holes is corbelled out of the north side. A fortalice is recorded in the document by which the 10th Earl of Angus living at nearby Glenbervie transferred the estate to his youngest son Robert Douglas in 1590. Paul Symmer, a former Cromwellian officer probably related to the Carnegies, was named as "of Mergie" in 1661. In 1672 the house was purchased by Alexander Garrioch, an ardent Jacobite. His estate was transferred to his daughters and thus escaped being forfeited. An ancestor of Burns is said to have been a tenant living in The Stonehouse of Mergie about this time. In 1782 it was sold to Colonel Duff of Fetteresso, who caught the poet Burns poaching on his estate.

MIDDLETON NO 583487

The Gardynes acquired Middleton in the 18th century and built most of the large whitewashed present house. Their descendants, the Bruce-Gardynes, still live here. From an older building there remain a reset dormer pediment and a 16th century roll-moulded fireplace in one of the lower rooms.

Monboddo

MONBODDO   NO 744783

In recent years this building has been restored as the centrepiece of a new rural housing estate. It is a white harled building of three storeys with conical roofed bartizans on the NE and NW corners. The hall lies over cellars and the private room over a kitchen at the west end, the lower level not being vaulted. On the west gable is a heraldic panel with arms and initials of Robert Irvine or Ervine and Jane Douglas with the date 1635. In the 13th century Monboddo was held by the Barclays but in 1593 it was held by James Strachan. It passed to the Irvines and then the Burnetts. Here in 1773 Dr Johnston visited the celebrated judge James Burnett, Lord Monboddo.

MONIFIETH   NO 490329

A country club lies on the site of a grange of Arbroath Abbey where the Durhams, holders of lands here from the early 14th century until c1700, built a castle after the Reformation. Montrose was housed for a night here after his betrayal and capture in 1650. A plot by Lady Grange to effect his escape by getting his guards drunk was only foiled because a sober guard out foraging spotted him trying to get away.

MONTROSE   NO 715576

Castle Place, the town house of the Earls of Montrose and supposed birthplace in 1612 of the famous Marquis, lies close to the site of a castle built by William the Lion but destroyed by William Wallace in 1297 after being used as a base by Edward I.

MUCHALLS   NO 892908   OP

The small court has low screen walls enclosing the south and east sides, the other sides being formed by long low three storey wings with round bartizans on the ends. The north wing has a short SE wing adjoining it with the end wall corbelled out at third storey level, this being the earliest part. Triple shot-holes lie on either side of the segmentally-arched courtyard gateway over which is a panel recording "This work begun on the earth and north be Ar (Alexander) Burnet of Leyis 1619. Ended be Sir Thomas Burnet of Leyis his sonne 1627". The house is renowned for its splendid plaster ceilings thought to have been executed by a craftsman from London. One spans the hall, which also has a magnificent sculptured overmantel dated 1624 with the Royal Arms. In the late 19th century Lord Robertson, Justice General, lived here. He is said to have blocked up a smugglers' secret passage to the so-called Gin Shore.

Muchalls

MURROES NO 461350

This recently restored hall-house of two storeys and an attic appears to be a 16th century later considerably lengthened and lowered c1600. It has a round stair turret on the west side which was re-roofed in 1942 and is carried on two corbels internally, and an entrance on the east side piercing the back of the hall fireplace. Excavations have revealed footings of the barmkin wall. There are a number of shot-holes. Murroes belonged to the Fotheringhams and panelling from their demolished main seat of Fotheringham has been transferred to the house. It lies in a small private garden rather than an estate.

PANMURE NO 544377

Sir Peter de Maule obtained Panmure in 1224. The 14th laird was created Earl of Panmure in 1646 and twenty years later the castle was superseded by a big quadrangular mansion with square corner towers built by the 2nd Earl. This building was remodelled in 1852 but was demolished with explosives in 1955. Foundations of it remain above the east side of the ravine.

PITAIRLIE NO 502367

A stone dated 1631 with initials of Alexander Lindsay is reset in a farm building. The castle passed in the mid 17th century to the Maules.

PITARROW NO 728750

The castle of the Wisharts, here in the late 13th century, was demolished in 1802. Of it there remain a walled garden, a ruined dovecot and three heraldic stones dated 1599 and 1679 built into the farmhouse.

Pitcur Castle

0   10
└─┴─┴─┴─┴─┘ m

HALL

STAIR

Pitcur: plan (see also p159)

Murroes

PITCUR NO 252370

The Halyburtons were lairds here for many centuries, Walter, a younger son of Lord Halyburton of Dirleton, having married a Chisholm heiress in 1432. The ruined tower may date from two periods in the 16th century, the wing containing a private chamber with a dog-leg passage to a latrine above a tiny kitchen and entrance lobby being more thinly walled, although it is difficult to see how access between the rooms could be obtained without it. A staircase in a round turret with stringcourses in the larger of the two re-entrant angles now links all the rooms. There is a recess for a heraldic stone over the entrance. The main block measures 13.5m by 8m over walls mostly 1.4m thick. It contains a hall and several bedrooms over two vaulted cellars. The hall has an old fashioned layout with a fireplace flanked by narrow loops in an end wall although it is possible that the end nearest the stair was divided off as a separate room. The upper parts of the walls have been remodelled, perhaps after abandonment.

PITKERRO NO 453337

In the 19th century a wing was added to the old mansion which was then altered but was restored by Sir Robert Lorimer in 1902. He capped with ogival roofs the rebuilt SW bartizan and a stair turret serving a room in a caphouse over a round tower containing the main stair at the NE corner. At the foot of the main stair is the entrance surmounted by a panel dated 1593 with initials of James Durham and his wife I.F. The property was later sold to the Dick family.

POWRIE NO 421346

In 1412 Thomas Fotheringham acquired Wester Powrie from the Ogilvys who were here c1170. Alexander Fotheringham was captured after fighting on the Jacobite side at Sheriffmuir but managed to escape from confinement in Edinburgh. A castle here was destroyed by the Scrymgeours in 1492. It is uncertain whether the Z-plan building now lacking one of its two round towers was that damaged by the English in 1547. It has a main block 12.5m long by 8.8m wide over walling up to 2m thick in the vaulted cellars, but much thinner at the level of the lofty vaulted hall above. No other Z-plans are known prior to the 1560s and only one other, the destroyed Ferryport-on-Craig had walling as thick as at Powrie. Perhaps the building took its present form c1565 but incorporates lower walling of c1500. The hall has remains of five windows and has a fireplace in the north wall with a salt-box in the east side. A square recess in the SE corner may be associated with a former service stair and this end may have been screened off as at Claypotts, to which Powrie is somewhat similar, if rather larger. The segmental arched entrance on the north admits to a lobby connecting the cellars with a kitchen in the surviving NE tower which is 7.9m in diameter. A spiral stair lies in a round turret in the NW re-entrant angle. Nothing now survives of the bedrooms and the SW corner is missing above basement level.

Not far to the north lies a two storey block 22m long by 6m wide built by Thomas Fotheringham and dated 1604 on one of the windows of the two storey porch. This range has a conical roofed round tower at the NW corner and contains a kitchen at the east end and a bakery at the west end with cellars in between. The chambers above formed two suites each with their own entrances. The kitchen does not communicate with either suite. In 1977 the Fotheringhams sold Powrie to the Clark family, who restored the decayed north range into a fine residence with authentic looking windows having shutters below the glass parts. The property was sold again in the late 1980s.

The restored block at Powrie Castle

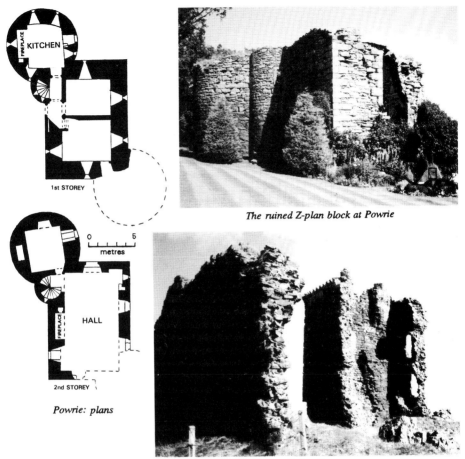

The ruined Z-plan block at Powrie

KITCHEN
FIREPLACE
1st STOREY

0 — 5
metres

FIREPLACE
HALL
2nd STOREY

Powrie: plans

Redcastle

REDCASTLE   NO 689510 & 688511   F

The castle built by William de Berkeley c1165 and used by William The Lion as a hunting seat was probably the motte lying SW of the red sandstone ruin on a promontory above the mouth of the Lunan Water. The northern half of a late 15th century tower house 13.5m long by 10m wide over walls 1.8m thick stands to the height of the wall-walk with corbels for a parapet with angle rounds. This wall has the remains of fireplaces at the level of the hall on the second storey and the fourth storey. Closing off the vulnerable west side of the site 11m from the tower is a curtain wall 1.7m thick, now defaced on its lower parts. It is probably also late 15th century. A stump of the north wall also survives and in the angle between the two is the shell of a house, possibly that occupied by the ousted Episcopal Minister James Rait. Robert Bruce gave the lands here in 1328 to his youngest sister's husband, Hugh, 6th Earl of Ross. Cardinal Beaton obtained it by some means and left it to his illegitimate daughter Elizabeth who married Lord Innermeath. He supported Queen Mary and Redcastle was dismantled by the Protestant party, the south half of the tower then perhaps being destroyed to its foundations. It later passed to the Guthries.

Interior of tower at Redcastle   *Plan of Redcastle*

ROSSIE NO 664534

Only a pile of rubble remains of a house of 1800 on the site of a castle of the Rossie family descended from a knight named Malherbe granted land here by King William the Lion. The estate passed to the Scotts of Logie in 1650.

RUTHVEN NO 302479

The Earls of Crawford had a castle here which was transferred in 1496 to Sir Adam Crichton and in 1744 was sold to Ogilvy of Coul. A new house was then built. Of the older building on a strong site above a ravine there remains a 16th century round tower with three gunloops in the vaulted basement which was long used as an ice-house. It stands at the head of a walled garden NW of the present house.

THORNTON NO 688718

Sir James Strachan obtained the estate by marrying a Thornton heiress in 1309. In 1616 Sir Alexander Strachan was cautioned to the turn of 10,000 merks for carrying on a feud with Sir Robert Arbuthnott. He went into temporary exile abroad in 1618 but in 1625 was honoured with a baronetcy. The last of the direct line became Minister of Keith but was deposed in 1690 for non-conformity. Forbes of Newton married his heiress. The property then passed to the Fullartons, to Lord Gardenstone, and then the Crombies by whom it was much altered. The Thorntons have now returned, Sir Thomas Thornton having purchased the castle in 1893. The L-plan tower house dates from c1500 and has a parapet with angle rounds carried on ornamental corbelling and surrounding a gabled attic. An additional round on the east provides a means of getting round a chimney stack obstructing the wall-walk. A range extends east from the tower and another range extends southward from the east end of that. They contain few features of antiquity but evidently represent a former court on this side for on the NE corner is a round tower bearing a panel with the Strachan arms and the date 1531.

Thornton Castle

TILQUHILLIE NO 722741

This is a recently restored Z-plan castle built in 1576 for John Douglas. At the Reformation the estate went to the Ogstouns, whose heiress was probably John's mother. In the 1640s the castle was occupied by Covenanters. It passed to George Crichton of Cluny in 1665. The entrance lies in a short section of walling cutting off the re-entrant angle between a main block 10.6m long by 7.7m wide containing the hall over two cellars and a kitchen wing 9.3m by 5.9m that engages the SW corner. Another wing 6.1m by 5.8m engages the NE corner. The upper rooms in this wing are served by a narrow stair in the SE re-entrant angle. The western cellar has a service stair to the hall. Numerous bedrooms are provided on the third and fourth storeys. The rounded corners are squared off just below the eaves.

Plan of Tilquhillie Castle

Tilquhillie Castle

VAYNE   NO 493599

This is a Z-plan castle of c1580-1600 with a main block 12.4m long by 7.7m wide over walls 1.3m thick having a round tower 6.4m diameter at the SW corner and a tower 7m square at the NE corner. Both project very boldly and in order to connect the cellar in the tower to what was probably a kitchen in the east half of the main block a round stair turret was provided in the southern re-entrant angle. There is a gunloop in the turret and another in the tower at second storey level. The wine cellar in the western part of the main block had its own service stair in the NW corner to the hall. The round tower contained a wide stair from the entrance up to the hall. Above that level the round tower does not survive but a gable of the main block stands high indicating a third storey of bedrooms plus attics. All the corners are rounded off.

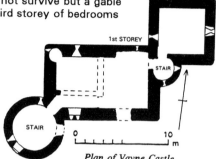

Plan of Vayne Castle

There was probably a court between the main building and the steep drop to the Noran Water about 30m away. Vayne belonged to the Lindsays from the 15th century until sold to the Carnegies in the 17th century. A tympanum over a garden gate by the farmhouse has the date 1678 with initials of Robert, 3rd Earl of Southesk.

Vayne Castle

WHISTLEBERRY   NO 862753

A promontory 56m long with a maximum width of 11.5m has buried footings of a tower about 10m square blocking the neck at the north end. Of a building about 7.5m wide near the middle of the site there remain footings of the south wall and a standing fragment of the NE corner which is cambered below but corbelled out to a square above. There are indications of another wall further south.

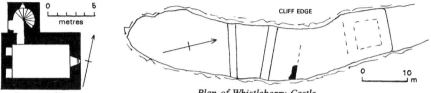

Durris: plan

Plan of Whistleberry Castle

Whistleberry Castle

Vayne Castle

OTHER CASTLES, MOTTES AND HOUSES IN ANGUS & KINCARDINE

AUCHLEUCHRIE NO 442572 Earthworks remain of early castle.
BALLESHAN NO 620520 Gone. "Lord Ogilvy's special residence" in 1612.
BALMOSSIE NO 475331 Mill contains reset parts of roll-moulded doorway and
    gunloop. Lands held by Balmossie family, then Maules of Penmure.
BALNAGASK (NIGG) NO 957051 Motte on southern outskirts of Aberdeen.
BANCHORY DEVENICK NO 910024 Slight traces of Durward motte and bailey castle.

BARRY NO 533347 A motte at the back of the village.

BLACK JACK NO 710535 Cliff-top site of a Gray stronghold.

BRIGTON NO 418467 A moated site.

BROTHERTON NO 803676 Victorian mansion, now Lathallan School, on site of castle of the Brothertons of that Ilk.

CASTLETON NO 333467 Moated site south of house excavated in 1990.

CLAVERHOUSE NO 408338 No remains of the seat of the famous Jacobite leader.

COSSANS NO 384499 A former Lyon seat north of Glamis.

CULTER NO 854008 A motte called Camp Hill above the River Dee.

DENFIND NO 501373 Vanished Lindsay castle. To Maules in mid 17th century.

DRIMMIE NO 515522 Gone. Supposed site of murder of Donald Bane by King Edgar.

DOWNIE NO 519366 Farm on mound. Seat of Duncan de Dunny in 1254.

DRUMTOCHY NO 699800 Remains of uncertain date within mansion now school.

DUNDEE NO 401301 No remains of castle captured by Edward I, nor of Provost Pierson's mansion of c1630 with round corner towers with arcading at bases.

FASQUE NO 648755 Castle replaced by mansion of 1809 bought in 1828 by Gladstones from the Ramseys of Balmain, owners since 1510.

FITHIE NO 633546 No remains of a seat of Fithies of that Ilk. The castle may have been built by the Carnegies, owners after 1549.

FORDOUN NO 736771 Moated platform 75m by wide 40m at one end, 30m wide at the other, close to whitewashed late 17th century house.

FURDSTONE NO 544590 The castle stood where Balnabreich Farm now is.

INSHEWAN NO 448569 Mansion of 1828 on site of Ogilvy castle on a rock.

KILGARY NO 565661 No remains of a castle of the Spaldings.

KINGCAUSIE NO 863000 The granite mansion of the Irvine Fortesques incorporates a tower built by Irvines on former church lands in late 16th century.

KIRKBUDDO NO 502435 Dormer pediment with initials of E.Guthrie is built into steading at rear of Kirkbuddo House.

KIRKSIDE NO 738637 Mostly 18th century but dated 16?? with initials of Andrew Straiton and his wife E.M. on an inner door lintel.

LOCH OF LEYS NO 694978 Original Burnett seat. Traces of crudely built quadrangular court 22m by 15m with hall on one side on island in loch.

LUNDIE NO 309361 Vanished seat of the Duncan family, merchants of Dundee.

MARYCULTER NO 845999 Three storey hall house with scale-and-platt stair in wing on west side probably all late 17th century on older site. Menzies initials.

MORPHIE NO 714642 Former Graham stronghold above the Den of Morphie.

OLD MONTROSE NO 673571 Some moulded stones remain on site of Graham seat.

QUEICH NO 427582 Former Comyn castle on a high rock above Quiech Burn.

PORTLETHEN NO 929967 Three dormer pediments dated 1630 and 1683 with initials R.M.P and M.M. plus others are reset on the farmhouse of 1866.

RESCOBIE NO 506519 Former crannog at west end of loch.

RUTHRIESTON NO 928041 A motte on the south side of Aberdeen.

SHIELHILL NO 428574 Mansion on site of Ogilvy castle on rock above the Esk.

STRACHAN NO 662921 Granted by King William to William Giffard. Motte in loop of Feugh excavated 1981. Ditch found and evidence of occupation until c1310.

WEDDERBURN NO 435346 Site by Fithie Burn of castle of ancient Earls of Angus. Later passed to Ogilvys and then to the Wedderburns of that Ilk.

WEMYSS NO 518532 West Mains of Turin farm lies on site of Lindsay castle.

WOODRAE NO 516566 Only a dovecot remains. When the castle was demolished in the 19th century a Pictish symbol slab was found under the kitchen floor.

VANISHED CASTLES & HOUSES: Baikie NO 319494, Balcraig (south of Hatton), Easter Braikie NO 637514, Kingennie NO 477354, Mondynes NO 771794, Newton NO 287577, Strathmartine NO 372363.

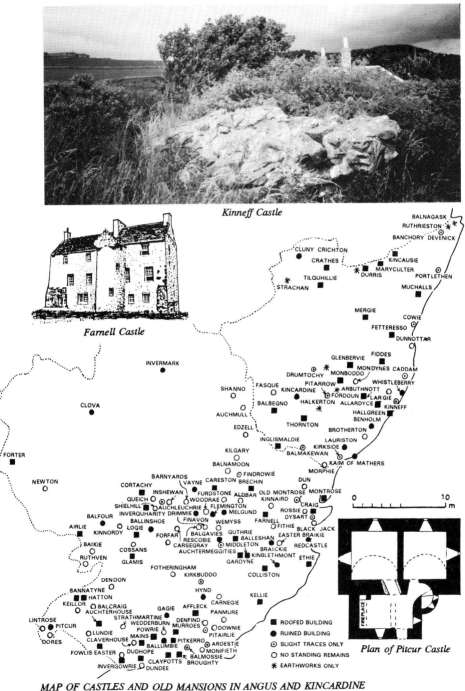

Kinneff Castle

Farnell Castle

BALNAGASK
RUTHRIESTON
BANCHORY DEVENICK
CLUNY CRICHTON
CRATHES   KINCAUSIE
                    MARYCULTER
TILQUHILLIE   DURRIS   PORTLETHEN
STRACHAN   MUCHALLS

MERGIE
                    COWIE
            FETTERESSO
                DUNNOTTAR

                    FIDDES
INVERMARK   GLENBERVIE
            DRUMTOCHY MONBODDO MONDYNES CADDAM
        SHANNO FASQUE PITARROW   WHISTLEBERRY
            KINCARDINE ARBUTHNOTT
CLOVA   FORDOUN LARGIE
        BALBEGNO HALKERTON ALLARDYCE KINNEFF
        AUCHMULL   HALLGREEN
                        BENHOLM
        EDZELL   THORNTON
            INGLISMALDIE BROTHERTON
FORTER   KILGARY   LAURISTON
                    KIRKSIDE
            BALNAMOON BALMAKEWAN
NEWTON   MORPHIE
        BARNYARDS   KAIM OF MATHERS
            VAYNE CARESTON BRECHIN
    CORTACHY   FURDSTONE   DUN   MONTROSE
        INSHEWAN   ALDBAR OLD MONTROSE
    QUEICH   WOODRAE   KINNAIRD
    SHIELHILL AUCHLEUCHRIE FLEMINGTON CRAIG
    INVERQUHARITY DRIMMIE MELGUND ROSSIE
BALFOUR   FINAVON WEMYSS FARNELL DYSART
        BALLINSHOE   FITHIE BLACK JACK
AIRLIE   LOGIE   GUTHRIE   EASTER BRAIKIE
    KINNORDY FORFAR BALGAVIES BALLESHAN
        RESCOBIE   MIDDLETON   REDCASTLE
    BAIKIE   CARSEGRAY   BRAICKIE
    COSSANS   AUCHTERMEGGITIES KINBLETHMONT ETHIE
    RUTHVEN   GARDYNE
    GLAMIS
            FOTHERINGHAM   COLLISTON
        DENOON   KIRKBUDDO
    BANNATYNE   HYND
        HATTON   KELLIE
KEILLOR   CARNEGIE
LINTROSE BALCRAIG   AFFLECK
    AUCHTERHOUSE GAGIE PANMURE
PITCUR STRATHMARTINE DENFIND
    WEDDERBURN MURROES DOWNIE
DORES   POWRIE   PITAIRLIE
    LUNDIE MAINS   ARDESTIE
CLAVERHOUSE PITKERRO MONIFIETH
    BALLUMBIE
FOWLIS EASTER DUDHOPE BALMOSSIE
        CLAYPOTTS BROUGHTY
INVERGOWRIE DUNDEE

0   10
                    m

■ ROOFED BUILDING
● RUINED BUILDING
⊙ SLIGHT TRACES ONLY
○ NO STANDING REMAINS
✳ EARTHWORKS ONLY

FIREPLACE

Plan of Pitcur Castle

MAP OF CASTLES AND OLD MANSIONS IN ANGUS AND KINCARDINE

CASTLES OF BANFF AND MORAY

ASLIESK   NJ 108598

In a field by the farm is the west gable of a wing 6.7m wide which belonged to a late 16th century L-plan building. There are loopholes, a gunloop, and the base of a round bartizan. A small panel with the Innes arms is reset on a gable of the farm buildings. A drawing made by J. Claude Nattes in 1799 shows the castle as then being roofless except for two bartizans with slate roofs with ball finials. The third storey lay partly in the roof and a stair turret was corbelled out above the re-entrant angle.

AUCHENDOUN   NJ 348374

A castle is said to have stood here from early times but the present building is thought to have been built in the reign of James III, probably for John, Earl of Mar, murdered at Craigmillar by his brother the King in 1479. The architect may have been Robert Cochrane, who was then given Auchendoun. He was hanged from Lauder Bridge by jealous nobles in 1482. The castle passed to the Ogilvies and then in 1535 to the Gordons. It was perhaps Adam Gordon, a supporter of Queen Mary's lost cause in the 1570s, who added the courtyard around the L-plan tower. He incurred the hatred of the chief of the Mackintoshes by whom Auchendoun was burnt either during that period or in 1592. It was restored but later abandoned in favour of a residence in a more sheltered site. In 1725 the Duke of Gordon allowed William Duff of Braco to remove stone from the site for construction work elsewhere.

The tower house has a wing 7.4m wide projecting 4.3m from a main block 14.3m long by 10.5m wide over walls 2.5m thick. The entrance lay in the destroyed SW end wall of the main block. It led directly through to a cellar which has a slop drain in a side wall and remains of a segmental-shaped vault. Only one of the loops in the end walls now survives. Leading off the entrance passage was the main staircase in the west corner, whilst there was a service stair in the north corner. Excavations a few years ago revealed a tiny vaulted chamber of uncertain purpose and date below the cellar. The lofty hall had a ribbed vault in two quadripartite bays, possibly a later insertion. Only the springers remain, those in the corners having a false start surmounted by a cap. The hall had a window in the destroyed SW wall, a fireplace in the NE wall, and windows with seats in the side walls near the fire. There was also a mural chamber near the main stair. Off the south corner of the room led a doorway to a square rib-vaulted private room in the wing with a fireplace and latrine. Below this room was a wine cellar reached by a stair leading off the side of the doorway. The wing contained two more storeys of private rooms but the main block had just one more storey which seems to have been a suite of two rooms, an audience chamber or private hall next the main stair and a bedroom beyond it.

Auchendoun Castle

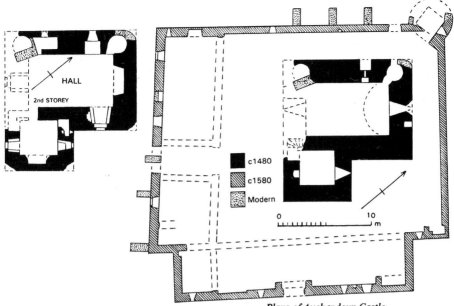

Plans of Auchendoun Castle

Auchendoun Castle

The courtyard measured 30.7m by 20.6m and was entered via a passage through a range, now destroyed, which filled the SW end. This range contained extra sleeping space over offices and service rooms. On the NW side is a postern guarded by a round tower, now mostly destroyed, on the north corner. The buttresses against the NW wall are modern. The range extending from most of the SE side, but rather oddly not quite reaching to the ends, is probably a slightly later addition, perhaps after the burning of the castle by the Mackintoshes. it contained a kitchen, bakehouse, and a brewhouse.

BALLINDALLOCH   NJ 178365

In 1498 James IV granted the lands and mills of Glencarie and Ballindalloch to John Grant for "good and faithful service". John made over Ballindalloch to his son Patrick, who son or grandson built the present castle beside the confluence of the Spey and Avon. In 1829 the castle was flooded and the grounds devastated by the "Muckle Spate" when the Spey overflowed its banks. The castle was besieged and captured in 1590 by James Gordon, a kinsman of the Earl of Huntly. This was the result of a quarrel between John Grant, tutor of the young laird Patrick Grant, and the latter's mother. After Montrose won his victory over the Campbells at Inverlochy in 1645 he devastated this area and burnt Ballindalloch Castle. After the male line of this branch of the Grants failed in the 18th century, the chief of the clan gave Ballindalloch to Colonel William Grant, second son of Grant of Rothiemurchus. His heiress married George Macpherson of Invereshie in Badenoch. After several generations of good military service by this new line a baronetcy was granted in 1838. The 6th and last baronet died in 1982 and the heiress has married a Mr Russell.

The date 1546 appears over a fireplace in an upper room but this is unlikely to refer to the construction of the present building which is more likely to be of c1565-90. It has a main block 12.9m long by 7.3m wide with round towers of 4.8m and 5.2m diameter respectively at the SW and NE corners. There is an additional tower containing the original entrance and main stair near the middle of the north side. A passage runs along this side at ground level to connect two cellars in the main block and a square room probably forming a kitchen in the NE tower. What was originally a round cellar in the SW tower now forms a lobby for an elaborate entrance of 1847 with heraldry. The caphouse on this tower is also of that period. Over the hall on the second storey are two upper storeys, the highest being partly in the roof and having dormer windows. The caphouse with an oriel over the stair tower was added in 1602 soon after Patrick Grant came of age. Two long wings were extended northwards from the north corners in 1718, although one of these was demolished in the 1960s.

Ballindalloch: old plan

Ballindalloch Castle

BALVENIE   NJ 326408   HS

This fine ruin lies on a bluff above the Fiddich north of Dufftown. It is fairly certain that the castle of Mortlach restored in 1304 to John Comyn, Earl of Buchan, is that still standing at Balvenie which is assumed to have been built a few years before then. It comprised a court 33m wide and 40m long enclosed by walls over 2m thick with a range containing a hall over a cellar in the NW corner and another projecting from the southern half of the east side, thus flanking an adjacent gateway. The walls were closely surrounded by a low outer wall rising from the bottom of a dry ditch still surviving on the south and west but filled on the other sides. It is thought that there may have once been round corner towers but that these were removed during a later remodelling, the whole castle having been assumed to have been wrecked by the Bruces in 1308 and to have lain derelict for many decades.

The remodelling is thought to have been executed for James Douglas, Lord Balvenie, a second son of the third Earl of Douglas who himself succeeded as 7th Earl. He was a prudent peaceable man nicknamed "The Gross" because of his size, and died in 1440. It was the killing of his son William by James II that precipitated the downfall of the Black Douglases after an unsuccessful rebellion by James, 9th Earl, and his brothers, one of whom was Earl of Moray. After their forfeiture Lord Glamis was appointed keeper of Balvenie until the castle was given in 1460 to John Stewart, first Earl of Atholl of a new creation. His wife was Margaret, widow of the 8th Earl of Douglas and divorced wife of the 9th Earl. Between 1542 and 1579 John, 4th Earl of Atholl added the northern half of the east front at Balvenie. The four heiresses of the 5th Earl (who died in 1595) surrendered their interest in the estates to James VI in 1610. Balvenie was then granted to James, Lord Innermeath, 2nd Earl of Atholl of another creation, but it then passed through the hands of John, 8th Lord Saltoun, and Sir James Stewart of Killeith before going to Robert Innes of Innermarkie. He was prosecuted in 1623 for carrying firearms and his son Walter was later charged with bragging and brawling. They got into debt and neighbours attacked their lands. Despite this Robert held several posts in local administration, and was made a baronet in 1628, whilst in 1634 he and Walter were commissioned to apprehend rebels. Walter is thought to have been among the many Royalists killed in a battle lost to Leslie's Covenanters nearby in 1649. Montrose rested his men at Balvenie late in 1644.

Balvenie Castle

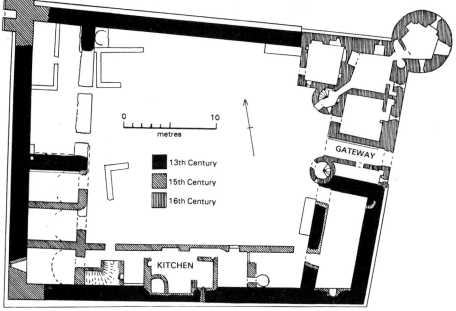

Plan of Balvenie Castle

Because of their losses during the Covenant wars the Innes family had to sell Balvenie in 1658 to Colonel Sutherland of Kinminity. The castle was later claimed by Arthur Forbes and in 1687 was taken over by his creditor Alexander Duff of Braco. A Williamite garrison installed at Balvenie fled after the battle of Killicrankie, leaving the victorious Jacobites to take it over. William Duff strengthened the defences in 1715, installing a garrison of 100 in his determination not to be ousted by the Jacobites. He served in Prince Eugenie's army in Hungary in 1716-7 and committed suicide at Balvenie early in 1718. The castle then went to William Duff of Dipple but he built a new house nearby in 1724 and allowed the older building to decay. Both buildings were occupied by Government troops in 1746. They found that the new house (later abandoned and pulled down in 1929) gave better shelter than the decayed castle.

The 13th century curtain walls have battered plinths and have been much rebuilt in the upper parts and at the corners. There are various curious blocked openings at the SW corner where there was once a round tower. A square latrine turret at the NW corner has replaced a second tower and the present 16th century round tower at the NE corner replaces another original 13th century tower. The irregularly set out block in the SW corner is 9m wide with an average length of 17m. One might expect this to have functioned as a keep but there is no evidence that it originally had more than two storeys or rose above the curtain walls. The existing gabled third storey is of the 15th century. Below the barrel vault forming a solid floor for what was then the lord's private chamber was a dimly lighted hall reached from the court by an external stair. Below this hall was a bakehouse and cellar. The hall range in the NW corner is very ruined. Its walls facing the court were as thick as the outside walls. The three vaulted cellars south of it are 15th century and had above them a chamber of importance reached by a wide stair in the south range. The south range also contained a kitchen and three other service rooms, all very ruined but probably 15th century.

The Atholl Building in the NE corner has been a dignified dwelling. The plinth is here discontinued but there is an external offset on the outer sides and on the two stair turrets facing the court at the level of the floor of the main rooms on the second storey. Also a moulding is carried around the round tower at attic level. The lowest storey, vaulted throughout, comprises the present entrance to the court with a narrow guard room on the south plus three roughly square rooms set in an L-shaped layout with the main staircase set in the re-entrant angle. Two of the rooms were entered directly from the court whilst the other, a kitchen, is reached through the turret. Through it is reached a pentagonal room in the tower. These rooms have widely splayed gunports. The entrance passage has a plain segmental inner arch with traces of an older arch above it. There are roll-mouldings on the outer arch (which retains a two-leaved yett) and around the doorways into the stair turrets. Above these turret doorways are empty niches for heraldic stones. The stair in the re-entrant angle leads up to the private room off which was access to a bedroom in the tower and another to the west. A doorway also leads into the hall to the south which had a more direct approach from the court via the other staircase. The hall has a service stair down to the cellar below it and has three large east windows bearing the marks of former protective grilles. Above were bedrooms with a series of windows with bowed sills set above those below. Above the level of the top windows are the Royal Arms and the arms of Earl John. The west wing was not continued up above second storey level. The hall stair was roofed with a cone of slates but the other turret was carried up a stage higher to end in a square gabled study reached by a narrow turret stair set in the dark NW re-entrant angle.

BANFF NJ 689643 V

The house called The Castle between Castle Street and the shore was built in 1750 for James Ogilvie, 6th Earl of Findlater. The courtyard behind or north of the house is enclosed by walls 1.9m thick and up to 6m high which represent about half of a quadrangular 13th century courtyard castle of the Comyn Earls of Buchan. It replaced an earlier dwelling of the Thanes of Banff, whose heiress one of them married. The court measured just over 40m wide from east to west and was probably 50 to 60m long from north to south. There were no towers or turrets. The north side contains a postern doorway and some recesses, apparently built up window embrasures of uncertain age. Beyond this wall is a length of dry ditch about 10m wide which enclosed the castle at an average distance of 7m from the walls. In Banff Castle was born James Sharpe, Archbishop of St Andrews under Charles II. He was hacked to death here by a group of armed horsemen looking for the local deputy sheriff. The Archbishop's father was Sheriff-Clerk of Banff.

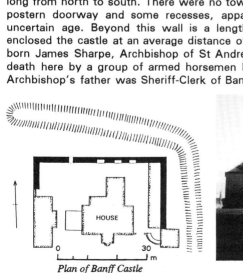

Plan of Banff Castle

Banff Castle

BLAIRFINDY NJ 199286

This ruin lies beside workers' houses for a distillery in Glen Livet. It is said to have been a hunting seat of the Earl of Huntly but it bears a panel with the initials of John and Helen Gordon and the date 1586. The Gordons defeated the Campbells nearby in 1594. A wing 4.8m square contains shot-holes flanking the south and west sides of a main block 10.6m long by 7.3m wide. The entrance, with the panel set above it, lies in the NW re-entrant angle and has over it a turret stair to the upper rooms. Access to the hall was by a now destroyed stair from the entrance lobby. A room occupies the remaining southern half of the wing. The basement cross-walls and vaults have gone but there was evidently a passage on the west side leading past a cellar to a kitchen with its fireplace in the north end wall. The cellar has a service stair to the hall SE corner. The hall has a big NW recess beside the kitchen fireplace flue. There were two bedrooms with fireplaces in the end gables at each of the third and fourth storeys, and further rooms were formed in the wing. Opening off the top level are a machicolation covering the entrance and a bartizan on the NE corner which has shot-holes flanking the two sides not covered by those in the wing.

Blairfindy Castle

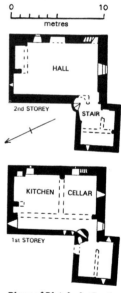

Plans of Blairfindy Castle

Hall fireplace at Blervie

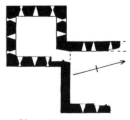

Plan of Blervie Castle

Blervie Castle

Boyne Castle

BLERVIE   NJ 071573

The Exchequer Rolls of Alexander III record the garrisoning of the "royal castle of Blervie or Ulerin" by Alexander Comyn, Earl of Buchan, in anticipation of an invasion by Haakon, King of Norway, which actually took place on the west coast in 1263. Later these lands passed to a branch of the Dunbar family who took their title from Hempriggs, an estate 12km to the NW beyond Forres. They built the existing castle in the late 16th century. In the early 18th century it was purchased by Alexander Mackintosh and then resold to the Earl of Fife. Most of the building was then demolished to provide materials for a new house to the south. The one lofty square tower remaining in a farm steading can be seen from some distance all around, and seven counties are said to be visible from the top. It formed part of a Z-plan building with two towers and contained the laird's suite of rooms. Most of the main block and the other tower containing the entrance and staircase have gone. The main block was 7.7m wide and contained a hall over a vaulted kitchen and cellar, plus two storeys of bedrooms. The hall fireplace survives in the south end wall above the corrugated roof of a lean-to shed. It has joggled voussoirs with the date 1598 and the Dunbar arms on the keystone. The surviving tower is 6.5m square and has five storeys, the first, second, and fifth of which are vaulted. At the summit are decorative mouldings and corbelling for an open parapet with angle rounds. There are numerous double splayed gunports in the basement. The tiered upper windows have inserted wooden mullions.

BOYNE NJ 612657

Boyne Castle is strongly placed above a bend in the ravine of the Boyne Burn not far from where it meets the sea east of Portsoy. The Thanedom of Boyne was granted by David II to Sir John Edmonstone, and in 1486 the estate passed by marriage to Sir John Ogilvie. At some time a castle was built on the other side of the burn nearer the sea and a dovecot still remains on that side. To this older building in 1568 came Mary Beaton, one of Queen Mary's "Four Marys" who married Alexander Ogilvie of Findlater that year. The existing castle was built by Sir George Ogilvie of Dunlugas after he acquired the estate in 1575 from the senior line of the family. His descendants lived there until the castle was sold in 1731 to Earl of Findlater (another Ogilvie) and allowed to decay. The removal of all the dressed stonework has hastened this process.

The castle is built in imitation of the form of buildings three hundred years earlier. Lofty walls up to 1.4m thick enclosed a rectangle of 27m by 24.8m with round towers about 6m in diameter at all four corners. Three sides rise above steep slopes to the burn whilst the fourth side is separated from the higher ground on the south by a dry ditch 17m wide. The ditch is walled in at either end and is crossed by a stone causeway leading to a now-shattered gateway with a passage flanked by round turrets 4m in diameter. Because the court and basement cellars were below the level of the ground beyond the ditch the castle entrance was actually at second storey level with presumably a ramp or steps down into the court. At ground level the castle was well provided with gunports for defence against local raids but the thin walling facing the approach would have made it vulnerable to artillery.

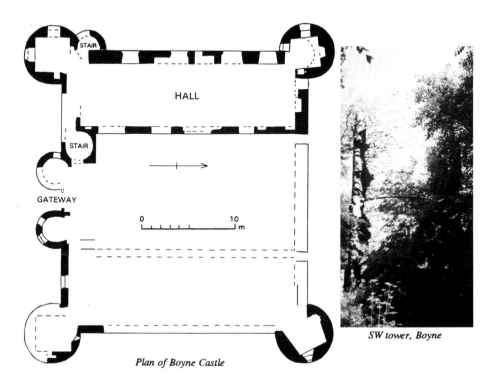

Plan of Boyne Castle

SW tower, Boyne

Interior of hall block at Boyne

It appears that originally there were apartments on both the east and west sides with a south range behind the gateway connecting the two, and a screen wall on the north with two postern doorways. At present only the western range now stands high above the debris and vegetation covering most of the site. This range contained four vaulted cellars each with a separate entrance from the court. Above is a long single room which was divided by timber partitions into a hall with a private room at the north end and probably a service passage at the south end. It is curious that no stair was provided at the north end, but there were two at the south end, set either end of the service passage. The main stair lay in a square turret joining the range to the gatehouse and another lay in an added turret placed against the junction of the SW tower with the west wall. Above would have been numerous bedrooms in a third storey and an attic, whilst the towers contained further rooms. The chamber in the NW tower leading off the private room is vaulted. The destroyed east range contained a kitchen at the south end and a bakehouse and brewhouse with probably just one storey of apartments above.

Brodie Castle

Plan of Brodie Castle

BRODIE   NH 980578   NTS

Malcolm IV is thought to have confirmed the ancient Celtic family of Brodie or Brothie in possession of this estate in 1160 and Michael Brodie had a charter from Robert I in 1311. The family are still here, the present laird being the 35th in line from Malcolm, Thane of Brodie, who died in 1285. The existing castle is dated 1567 on the gable of the SW tower and was built by the 12th laird, Alexander, to whom the lands were returned in 1566 after being briefly forfeited for his opposition to Queen Mary. Also on the building is the name J. Russall with the initials M.M. for master mason. The building is Z-planned, or, more precisely, an L-plan with a stair wing 5.2m wide projecting 4.7m from the north wall of a four storey main block 11.4m long by 7.5m wide over walls 1.2m thick with at the SW tower a tower 6.7m square. The latter tower is likely to represent a slightly later addition and has four main storeys plus an attic within a parapet carried on ornamental corbelling. There are bartizans, one square and the other two round, on the three detached corners. Early in the 17th century a wide new block was added to the NW. This contained a spacious drawing room replacing the modest private room in the SW tower, and a vaulted kitchen below. Above are two storeys of bedrooms, the uppermost have dormer windows.

In 1645 the castle was "brynt and plunderit" by Lord Lewis Gordon in consequence of the 15th laird, Alexander, being a Covenanter. This laird served on the commission which treated with Charles II at the Hague in 1649 and at Breda in 1650. This service caused him nothing but anguish and considerable expenditure and he failed to obtain recompense from Charles when he was restored in 1660. Mary Sleigh, wife of Alexander, 19th laird and Lord Lyon King of Arms, laid out the present ornamental grounds in 1730. Modifications to the castle itself including the filling in of the space between the original stair wing and the 17th century range to contain a spacious new staircase. This laird died in debt and this saved the castle from further alteration as his successors struggled to make ends meet. In 1824 William, 24th laird, commissioned William Burn to enlarge the castle. The substantial additions to the north and east amount to only a portion of what was planned. Even these works were only paid for by a fortunate marriage to the heiress Elizabeth Baillie in 1838. It was just after this that the former cellars in the main block had their vaults removed and were thrown together to make a new entrance hall with a Romanesque arcade on one side. The present laird lives in part of the castle while the main state rooms are open to the public under the administrative care of the National Trust for Scotland.

BURGIE   NJ 094593

Except for its low-lying position among trees Burgie is in almost every respect the twin of Blervie and is in a very similar condition. The main block, except for the stump of the west wall with a hall fireplace dated 1602 with the Dunbar arms, and the staircase tower were demolished in 1802 to provide materials for building a new house. This leaves a six storey tower with a solid flat roof as at Blervie, there being vaults over the first, fifth and sixth storeys. The parapet with angle rounds is carried on decorative corbelling. The tower contained a suite of rooms for the laird reached from the hall by a spiral stair over the NE re-entrant angle. A sketch of the castle made by Claude Nattes in 1799 shows that the main block had two storeys over the hall and there were square bartizans set diagonally on the two free corners, whilst the stair wing had a gabled roof with three conical roofed bartizans. A substantial 17th or 18th century three storey wing extended south from the outer wall of the stair wing. The castle was built by Alexander Dunbar, lay Dean of Moray. He obtained the lands from his brother-in-law Walter Reid, last Abbot of Kinloss Abbey, in 1566.

Yett at Burgie Castle

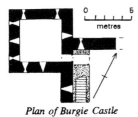

Plan of Burgie Castle

Burgie Castle

CARNOUSIE NJ 670504

Carnousie was a barony created in 1369 for Walter de Leslie, Earl of Ross, the original manor house being on or beside a motte called the Mount of Magy where Castlehill farm now lies at the head of the Maggie Burn. It later passed to various other families and was held by the Dunbars until 1530 when it was granted to Walter Ogilvy of Monycabock. James V licensed Walter to build a new fortified house on the lands but it was actually his second son Walter who

Carnousie Castle

built the present building which is dated 1577 on a stone now reset in its original position as the stair tower SW skewput. It is mentioned as new in a charter of 1583 when Carnousie was sold by Walter to his brother Sir George Ogilvy of Dunlugas. Sir George then handed over the castle and barony to his second son George, who had married Walter's daughter Margaret. They complained to the Privy Council in 1622 about the depredations of Robert Innes and others on the estate. Their son George was created a baronet but got into debt, the wasting of his estates by Royalists in the 1640s not having helped. To settle the debts the lands were finally sold off in 1683 to Sir George Gordon. His grandson Arthur died in exile after taking part in the 1745 rebellion and Carnousie was in 1757 sold to Lord Seafield, by whom it was quickly sold to George Hay, both of them being creditors of Arthur Gordon. George Hay extended the building before selling it to Colonel Patrick Duff. Again there were financial difficulties, forcing his son in 1825 to sell the estate in 1827 to the Stewards of Belladrum. There were further sales of the property in 1827 to Alexander Grant, in 1842 to an Aberdeen advocate named Gordon, and to William Harvey in 1843. The estate was broken up in 1927 and the castle went to the Bisset family. After the war the castle was abandoned and contained only pigs when it was purchased by a restorer and re-roofed, the 18th century wing demolished, and work begun on the interior. After difficulties were encountered the castle was sold to David Williams.

The castle comprises a three storey main block 12.8m by 8.5m with a round tower 7.6m in diameter at the NW corner and a square tower at the SE corner. The square tower contains the entrance and a scale-and-platt stair to the hall with a porter's room tucked under it, plus two upper storeys reached by a turret stair corbelled out over the entrance. The main block contains a kitchen and wine cellar with a service stair under the hall. The passage from the entrance to the kitchen has two ornamental gunloops covering the former and other gunloops are provided in the two towers so as to flank all four sides of the main block. A blackened 18th century window in the back wall of the kitchen fireplace is said to replace another gunloop. The round tower contains a drawing room over a cellar reached from the kitchen and two bedrooms above reached from the hall by a stair in the SW re-entrant angle. The hall has a particularly fine fireplace in the west end wall with a recess beside it. The fireplace had an inscription "My Hovp Is In Ye Lord God" and a frieze of beasts with columns between them. There are three south windows, a north window from which a mural chamber is reached, and an east window in a very wide embrasure onto which lead both the service stair and a passage from the main stair. This last is a similar arrangement to that seen at the service ends of the halls at Gight and Craig, but is here more neatly done as the service access and main approach to the hall from the entrance are kept more separate. The hall was divided into two rooms in the 18th century when the third storey was altered from two rooms in the main block to three, with a consequent rearrangement of fireplaces and windows. The round tower roof once had a finial in the form of a lion with a shield dated 1757 with initials of George Hay and Janet Duff.

CASTLE GRANT NJ 041302

The origins of the Grants are obscure. They either have been Celtic or Norman-French. They came to prominence in the 15th century when a Grant married the heiress of the Lord of Glencharnie, a cadet of the Earls of Strathearn, owner of lands in Strathspey. Their son Duncan Grant of Inverallan is mentioned in 1453 as holder of Glencharnie (about half of the present parish of Duthil) and half the barony of Freuchie. His descendants became increasingly influential and some time during the 16th century built a four storey tower about 18m long by 12m wide over walls 1.8m thick. The more thinly walled SW tower is perhaps slightly later, say of c1600. It contains the principal stair up to the hall and then in a corbelled projection a spiral stair serving two more storeys and an open wall-walk around a two storied caphouse.

Originally known as Freuchie, the castle came to be styled Bellechastle or Castle Grant and by 1600 the laird was styled "of Grant" or "Grant of that Ilk". When John, 5th laird, was offered the title Lord Strathspey by James VI he signified that recognition as chief of the clan was much more important to him by saying "Wha then would be Laird o' Grant". His grandson died in 1663 before Charles II could sign a patent making him Earl of Strathspey. The 8th laird got the lands erected into the Regality of Grant and the name Freuchie was then officially discontinued.

Sir Ludovick Grant lost £20,000 in unpaid expenses incurred through his support of the Government during the 1745 rebellion. It was he who founded the present township of Grantown-on-Spey 2.5km to the SSW in 1766 in order to remove the village of Castleton of Freuchie out of sight of his residence. Additions and alterations of this period gave the castle an appearance that prompted Queen Victoria on a visit in 1860 to record it as looking like a factory. The main block was widened to 8m with a corridor between the old and new rooms and a wing 13.5m long added across the east end. It projects slightly from the south side of the old part and has a spiral stair in the resulting re-entrant angle although this may be a relic of an earlier extension then remodelled. Thus it is likely that in the 17th century the castle resembled Castle Stuart near Inverness with two square wings on the two adjacent corners facing the approach. By 1800 lower wings had been added to these two corners with a raised platform between them. One of these is now roofless. Ludovick married the heiress of the Earl of Findlater and Seafield and in 1816 his grandson succeeded to the latter title, taking the name Ogilvie-Grant. The present Earl has a house on the Cullen estate and Castle Grant has been lying in an empty boarded-up state for many years. Some repairs were begun a while ago but the building is currently far from habitable.

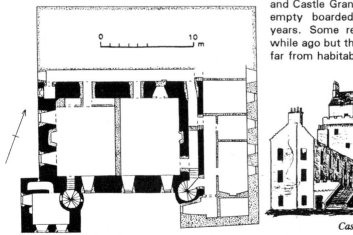

Castle Grant

Plan of Castle Grant

Crombie Castle

Coxton Tower

COXTON NJ 591522

This tower measures just 7m square and was rendered fireproof by having each of its four storeys vaulted with the axes at right angles on alternate floors, a very strong form of construction. The top room has a lofty pointed vault with the roofing slabs laid directly on top of it. This room has closets 2m in diameter in conical roofed bartizans set on diagonally opposite corners. There are shotholes in these and in a square bartizan forming an open look-out point with machicolations on a third corner. There are separate entrances to the two lower storeys and there was no access between them unless there was once a hatch in the bottom vault. The upper doorway is now reached by a stone stair of c1846 replacing wooden steps. The three upper rooms connected by a stair in the NE corner all have small fireplaces, latrines in the wall thickness, and narrow barred windows. Over the upper doorway is a panel with arms of Sir Alexander Innes of Innermarkie and his wife with the year 1644. The family were frequently at loggerheads with each other, Innes of Leuchars and others being in 1635 ordered by the Privy Council to restore the property and pay compensation to his brother John Innes of Coxton, whilst another brother, James, "undeutifully coupled himself in marriage with Marjory Innes, dochter of Alexander Innes of Cotts". Coxton was later sold to the Duffs who built a new house in front of which the tower stands.

CROMBIE NJ 591522

The 9th Innes of Innes obtained Crombie as part of the Thanage of Aberchirder, having married the heiress. Sir Walter Innes, 12th of that Ilk had a charter of the barony of Crombie granted to him in 1453. The existing L-plan building was built either by James Innes, killed at Pinlie in 1547, or Alexander, who brutally murdered a kinsman in 1580. His successor John was outlawed in 1624 for "striking and dinging the kirk officer of Aberchirder". The castle later passed to the Urquharts, Meldrums and Duffs, and in the 20th century returned to the Innes family, going to Sir Thomas Innes of Learney, Lord Lyon King of Arms. It remains roofed but has not been occupied for some years. The castle has a wing 6.3m wide projecting 6.6m from a main block 11m long by 7m wide. The entrance in the re-entrant angle is protected by gunloops and has above it three corbels for a former machicolation. From the entrance there is access to a spiral stair, to a kitchen under the drawing room in the wing and to two cellars in the main block, one of which has a service stair to the hall above. Above were three bedrooms and attics. The southern corners of the main block, obscured for most of their height by an adjoining 19th century farmhouse, have round open bartizans at the summit.

CULLEN NJ 507663

The burgh of Cullen was established in 1822 to replace the original village close to Cullen House on a rock rising 18m above the Cullen Burn 1km to the SW. West of the burgh is the Castlehill, an eminence with remains of a Dark Age vitrified fort and supposedly the site of a medieval castle where Robert Bruce's wife Elizabeth de Burgh died in 1327. The core of Cullen House is an L-plan mansion begun in 1600 by Sir Walter Ogilvie of Deskford and Findlater to replace the strong but inconveniently sited castle of Findlater. The houses of the prebends of the adjacent collegiate church may have furnished the materials. The mansion has much richly decorated stonework and an entrance (now a window) in the re-entrant angle with surmounting heraldry. It is dated 1603 with the arms and initials of Sir William and his wife Mary Douglas. Roll mouldings divide the storeys. To the mansion have been added substantial wings of 1711 and 1861 designed by Robert Adam and David Bryce respectively. Within the building are very fine plaster and tempora painted ceilings. In 1616 Sir Walter Ogilvie was made Lord Deskford and in 1638 he was created Earl of Findlater. In 1645 Cullen House was "pitiably plundered" by the Farquharsons in support of Montrose. The future 4th Earl, then Chancellor of Scotland, inherited in 1701 a second earldom, that of Seafield in Fife. When the 7th Earl died in 1811 his heir was a distant relative Sir Lewis Grant, descended from a daughter of the 5th Earl. Sir Lewis became 5th Earl of Seafield, Viscount Reidhaven, and Lord Ogilvie of Deskford and Cullen, but the Findlater Earldom was not allowed to pass through the female line and became extinct. He took the surname Ogilvie-Grant and his descendants still live at Cullen. However in 1975 the present Lord Cullen sold off the contents of the house, which included many portraits by famous artists and a fine collection of 17th century firearms, and moved into a more modest dwelling in the grounds. In 1984-5 Cullen House was converted into 11 flats.

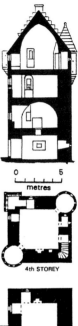

Coxton: plans

Cullen House

DARNAWAY   NH 994550

After Robert Bruce forfeited the Comyns, the lands of Darnaway went to Thomas
Randolph, Earl of Moray, who is said to have had a seat here. The Exchequer accounts
of James II for 1456-8 indicate that he continued work on a new building left
unfinished with the forfeiture in 1455 of Archibald Douglas, Earl of Moray. All that
remains of this is the magnificent oak roof of a great hall 27m long by 10.5m wide.
It has hammer-beams decorated with heads and Gothic arches The rest is all rebuilding
and extensions for the 9th Earl in 1810 and later, but an old print of 1801 (see inside
front cover) shows one end flanked by two tower-like wings probably of c1600 with
square and round bartizans respectively. The castle lies in a clearing in a large forest
and is still the home of the Earls of Moray descended from James Stewart, Lord
Doune. He gained the Earldom by marrying the heiress of Queen Mary's half brother
James, Regent Moray, and was murdered by the Gordons at Donibristle in 1592.

DESKFORD   NJ 509617

The creeper-clad ruin beside the ruined church noted for its fine sacrament house
dated 1551 with the names of Alexander Ogilvie and Elizabeth Gordon may either have
been a transept containing a laird loft over a burial vault or was perhaps part of their
castle. The ruin is 6.9m wide over walls 1.3m thick and lies in the garden of a house
said to incorporate part of a block containing a hall and chamber end to end over
service rooms. A four storey main tower was demolished in the 1830s.

DRUMIN   NJ 184303

On a strong site above the junction of the Avon and Livet, and now in the garden of
a house is the ruin of a tower which formed the seat of the barony of Inveravon. It
was probably built either by Andrew Stewart, the celebrated Wolf of Badenoch,
lawless brother of Robert III or his illegitimate son Sir Andrew Stewart. Andrew's son
Sir William sold the estate to the Gordons who eventually replaced it by Blairfindy
castle to the SE. The tower measures 11.6m wide over walls 2.7m thick at ground
level, and 2.2m thick above the cellar vault. Less than 11m survives of the south wall
but the north wall has a present length of 16.2m. This probably approximates to the

full length. The east wall probably with
separate entrances to the cellar and hall
and staircase is missing and both east
corners now have modern walls
adjoining them. The west wall still
stands four storeys high with corbels
for the former parapet. A large patched
area seems to indicate the former hall
fireplace. The cellar has four loops,
three of them blocked. The third storey
has a round-backed fireplace in the
north wall with a loop east of it and a
latrine in the SW corner. This would
have been the lord's hall or living room.
His bedroom above has an inserted
fireplace with a roll-moulded surround
in the north wall, two west windows,
and a latrine in the NW corner. See plan
on page 181.

Drumin Castle

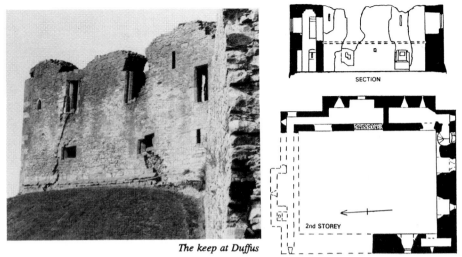

SECTION

2nd STOREY

The keep at Duffus

Duffus: plan and section of the keep

DRUMMUIR   NJ 417448

The present castle is a large Gothic castellated mansion and the original house, now a farmhouse called Mains of Drummuir, lies 3.5km to the ENE above the B9115. It is an early 17th century L-plan house built against a steep slope so that it has three storeys at the front but only two at the back. It is a plain building with crowstepped gables, small windows, and a few shot-holes. There are no vaults. The outside forestair is a modern addition. Alexander Leslie of Kininvie gave Drummuir to his son George c1549. It later passed to the Inverness merchant William Duff who died in 1715. In that year his successor Alexander, Provost of Inverness, seized that town for the Jacobites, unusually reckless behaviour for a family that usually ended up on the winning side. The rather worn dormer pediment on a blocked window on the north side bearing the monogram A.A.D. may refer to Alexander Duff and his wife.

DUFFUS   NJ 189672   HS

David I granted Duffus to Freskin, Lord of Strabock in West Lothian, who erected the motte and bailey earthworks and the original timber buildings c1140. The King was at the castle in 1151 while supervising the construction of his new Cistercian Abbey of Kinloss. In 1286 Sir Regenald Cheyne obtained the castle by marrying Helen, one of the three heiresses of the last of the male line of Freskin. In 1290 the castle sheltered the English Commissioners sent by Edward I to welcome the infant Queen Margaret to Scotland from Norway. Sir Reginald supported Edward I in his campaigns in Scotland and suffered damage to his lands and castle in consequence. In 1305 Edward granted him 200 oaks from the forests of Darnaway and Longhorn for repairing the castle. The fine stone keep is unlikely to have been built during this period of turmoil and is more likely to be of after 1350 when the heiress Mary Cheyne brought Duffus to her husband Nicholas, a son of the 4th Earl of Sutherland and thus himself a descendant of Freskin. Their descendants, surnamed Sutherland, remained at Duffus until it was sold in 1705 to Sir Archibald Dunbar. The castle was burnt by the forces of the rebel Douglas Earl of Moray in 1452 and the lands were plundered by the Royalists in 1645, the then laird being on the Covenant side. For services to Charles II in 1650 he was created Lord Duffus, a title which became extinct in the 19th century. The long-neglected castle is now a ruin in State care.

The keep, Duffus Castle

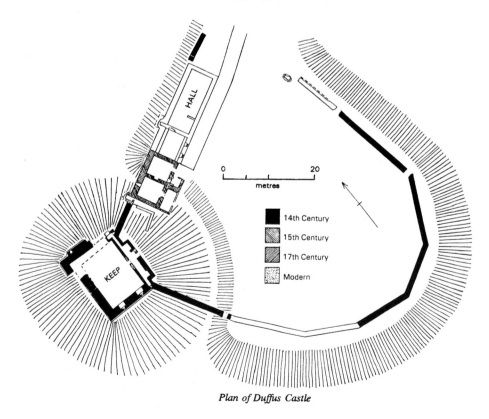

Plan of Duffus Castle

The motte is separated by a ditch from a shovel-shaped bailey platform measuring 80m by 70m. At a distance the entire site is surrounded by a water-filled ditch, more for drainage and to mark a boundary rather than as a serious obstacle to attackers. A cobbled causeway leads into the bailey from a bridge over the ditch and there was perhaps once a gatehouse where there is now just a gap in the curtain wall. This curtain is set back from the platform edge except on the north where a fragment has slipped and lies at a dramatic angle. Much of the wall is reduced to foundations but about half the circuit stands 2.5m high above the courtyard and 3.5m high above the outside. Apart from a missing parapet it does not seem to have stood much higher except where it crosses the motte ditch and ascends to meet the keep. The wall has no towers or turrets and is pierced by no less than three postern doorways. Close to the broken off end of the east wall is an oven, now under glass. On the north side of the bailey is a much ruined domestic range 40m long built after the attack of 1452. Above a series of cellars lay a hall on the east and a private room on the west. An ashlar-faced stair turret was added in front of the western part in the 17th century.

The keep is a classic case of what can happen to a large rectangular building constructed on the summit of an artificial mound. The NW corner has cracked off and slid 2m down the mound slope, and other parts are badly cracked. The keep measures 19m by 15.2m over walls mostly 2.1m thick above a double chamfered ashlar plinth. The east wall was increased to 3.7m thick for much of its length to contain an entrance lobby off which rose a straight stair with a pit prison tucked underneath it. At second storey level there was a mural chamber, possible a chapel, in the remainder of the space not taken by the stair and landing and a passage led from beside it round the NE corner to another mural chamber and latrine contained in a section of the north wall thickened to contain them. The latrine now lies at basement level because of this part having slipped. Another latrine reached from the entrance lobby lies in the NE corner at basement level. From the landing at the top of the main stair there was access onto a spiral stair probably just to the battlements as there is no trace of a third storey. Doorways off the passages in the NE and NW corners led off to the curtain wall-walk, proof that although the curtain makes straight joints with the keep they were designed as one. Each storey of the keep has two window embrasures in the south wall and the upper storey also has a west window and mural chamber. There must have been timber posts or partitions to support the upper floor and roof of a building 11m wide inside. It is likely that the basement was divided into storage on the north and living accommodation on the south as the windows there are not the mere slits to be expected in cellars. The upper storey would have been divided into a private room on the north (with access to the chapel and latrine) and a hall on the south.

DUNPHAIL   NJ 007481

On a bluff above Dunphail House and the Dorback Burn are shattered remains of a 16th century Dunbar castle half buried by its own debris. There are no visible remains of an older Comyn castle on this strong site besieged in 1330 by Thomas Randolph, Earl of Moray. The estate was purchased in the 20th century by Sir Alexander Grant. The castle seems to have been an L-plan with a main block 15m long and at least partly 9.5m wide containing three vaulted cellars linked by a passage on the north side. The wing was 6m wide and projected about 5m but little of it remains. The thinly walled NE wing with an entrance with a draw-bar hole is a 17th century addition probably to contain a stair.

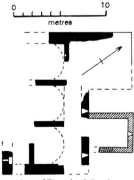

Plan of Dunphail Castle

EASTER ELCHIES   NJ 279444

The first recorded Grant laird of Easter Elchies is Patrick, second son of the 5th laird of Grant. The three storey T-plan house set high above the west bank of the Spey west of Charlestown of Aberlour is attributed to Patrick Grant, Lord Elchies, laird from 1690 to 1754. A turret stair serves a fourth storey room in the wing. A panel on the west wall is dated 1700 with the monogram J.E.S. However the house is thought to be somewhat earlier. It was altered and extended in the 1850s and subsequently neglected. It is now restored to its original form to serve as offices for a distillery.

ELGIN   NJ 212628   F

The Lady Hill (the name may refer to a long lost 15th century chapel) west of the town centre bears the last remains of an early castle and a 24m high Tuscan Column of 1855 to the last Duke of Gordon. The site was probably occupied by the old Mormaers of Moray and a royal castle here existed by 1160. Edward I of England was a visitor in 1296 and 1303 and he described Elgin as a "bon Chastell et bon ville". It is fairly certain that it was then of stone and it is likely that the present remains were built by Alexander III. On the east side of the pear-shaped summit 70m long by 44m wide, facing the approach through a garden, is a 16m long section of the base of a curtain wall 2m thick. At the north end are featureless and defaced 2m high chunks of the formerly 3m thick end walls of what was once probably a three storey keep 20m long with a width of about 12m. It was presumably destroyed by the Bruces c1308 and subsequently plundered of all re-usable material by the townsfolk.

Elgin contains a number of noteworthy 16th and 17th century houses. The last survivor of several around the cathedral is the L-plan building in which the Precentor lived. It has skewputs dated 1557 and a series of heraldic panels referring to Bishops Innes, Stewart, Hepburn, and the Earl of Mar. It had three storeys and a square stair tower rose a level higher to a gabled watch chamber. It was unroofed c1800 and partly demolished in 1851 by the Earl of Seafield, the work being stopped by a storm of protest. NW of the Bishop's Palace is an L-plan building called The College but thought to have been the Deanery. The Dunbars of Thunderton have given their name to a mid 17th century house, now an hotel, in Thunderton Place. Built by Lord Duffus, it was sold to the Dunbars in 1707. A late medieval royal lodging lay on the site. The Tower Hotel in the High Street bears the date 1634 with initials of its builders Andrew Leslie of Glenrothes and Jean Bonyman. It was remodelled in 1860 but preserves a round tower with a crowstepped gabled caphouse.

Keep, Elgin Castle

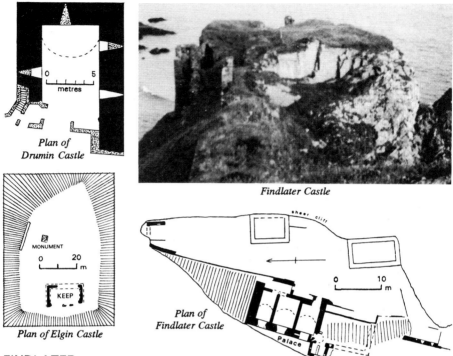

Plan of
Drumin Castle

Findlater Castle

MONUMENT

KEEP

Plan of Elgin Castle

Plan of
Findlater Castle

Palace

FINDLATER NJ 542673

Findlater has the most dramatic site of any of the castles of Banff and Moray. A long narrow promontory projects from the middle of a small bay east of Cullen ringed by cliffs up to 45m high. The promontory is reached by a path to a causeway in which there is a break in front of the former gateway spanned by a moveable wooden bridge. The summit has a sheer drop of about 27m to the sea on the east and a very steep craggy slope on the west. The domestic buildings on the west side date from after James II licensed Sir Walter Ogilvie of Deskford to fortify this site in 1455. The castle was occupied by the Gordons in 1562 but after their defeat at Corrichie was surrendered back to the Ogilvies, who in 1600 transferred to a more conveniently located seat at Cullen. The Earldom that Charles I created for the Ogilvies in 1638 was called Findlater but the castle of that name was by then already falling into ruin.

The castle is approached by a track passed the farm of Barnyards of Findlater near which are two ruined dovecots. The courtyard is irregular in its levels and shape and is 69m long with a maximum width of 17m. A portion of walling survives by the entrance, fragments of a building at the northern tip, and there are foundations of two other buildings on the east side and of retaining walls on the NE. However the principal structure is a ruinous palace block built against the steep western slope. The hall and the chamber to the south of it lay just above courtyard level and have gone, but there remain against the slope two storeys of vaulted rooms below where the hall was. The three upper rooms had quite spacious windows to seaward and were offices or living rooms. Below is a large kitchen and two other vaults, one of which seems to have been a dungeon reached only by a hatch from a window embrasure above. Further vaults below the private room have fallen into the sea although a projecting latrine turret at the junction of the two blocks still remains with traces of a stair behind it.

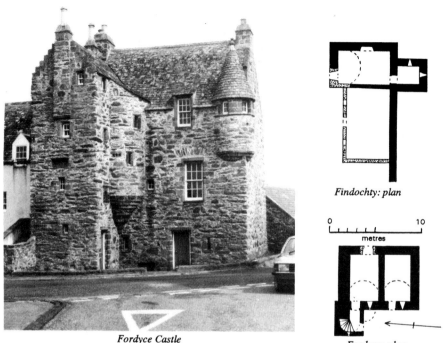

Findochty: plan

Fordyce Castle

Fordyce: plan

FINDOCHTY   NJ 455673

This late 16th or early 17th century building on a low crag looking to seaward about 400m inland was built either by the Gordons or the Ogilvies, successive owners of the property. Of a thinly walled main block 7.4m wide there remain just 5m of the south wall and 14.5m of the north wall. There is a vaulted cellar at the west end, and a ruined cottage occupies most of the rest of the interior. Set 1.7m east of the NW corner on the north side is a turret 3.3m square containing small rooms.

FORDYCE   NJ 556638   V

Fordyce was created a burgh of barony in 1499 by James IV at the request of Bishop Elphinstone of Aberdeen, his Lord Chancellor. The three storey L-plan house by the road junction in the middle of the village bears the date 1562 and the monogram of its builder Thomas Menzies, a burgess of Aberdeen, who, like many of his family, served as Provost of the city. The main block is 8.8m long by 6.7m wide and the wing is 3.2m wide and projects 2.7m. The entrance in the wing leads to the stair to the hall and to the northern cellar, the other being entered directly from the street. A spiral stair in a turret on ornamental corbelling rises from the hall to two bedrooms in the main block and to small third and fourth storey rooms in the wing. There are ornamental shot-holes arranged in threes and fives in the stair turret. In the set of three the middle opening is a lozenge, while in the set of five the three middle ones are false. There are conical roofed bartizans on the NE and SW corners, the latter having Menzies' monogram. In the early 18th century Thomas Ord built an extension to the main block beyond the wing. The new part has a third storey partly in the roof.

FORGLEN NJ 696517

The Abercrombies of Birkenbog obtained Forglen by marriage with one of the Ogilvies of Dunlugas. They still own it although the present baronet lives at Dunlugas. The existing mansion of Forglen above the west bank of the Deveron is mainly of 1842 although it incorporates an older house and has a heraldic stone dated 1577, an inscription, and the cynical motto "Hoip Of Revaird Cavses Gvid Service".

GAULDWELL NJ 311451

This castle, once known as Bucharin of Boharm, is strongly sited on a promontory above a bend of the Fiddich north of Dufftown. It is supposed to have been built in the 13th century by the Freskins of Moravia and the nature of the present ruins suggest an early date. Queen Mary stayed in the castle in 1562. On the west side of a level D-shaped court, now heavily overgrown, is a 42m long section of straight walling 2.5m thick above a plinth which has been ripped away and up to 6m high above the outside. This appears to be the last remaining part of a pentagonal court. Alongside this wall for a length of 21m was a chamber 8.6m wide, presumably the undercroft of a hall. South of it was another undercroft 7.2m wide and 16m long which presumably lay below the great chamber. Each undercroft has two westward looking loops, now mere holes. Probably there was a tower or gateway facing the higher ground rising to the north towards the A95 Keith to Grantown-on-Spey road.

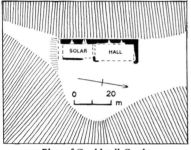

Plan of Gauldwell Castle

Findochty Castle

Gauldwell Castle

Gordon Castle

GORDON   NJ 350596

The lowest 4m of the six storey tower is probably the basement of a tower built in 1498-1502 by George Gordon, 2nd Earl of Huntly. It was called Bog o' Gight, the windy bog, having originally stood alone in marshland crossed by a causeway. It appears from Slezer's engraving that by the early 17th century the tower had been raised to its present height and had become one of several towers grouped around a large main block with blind arcading at second storey level above moulded corbelling on which most of the building was projected out. The towers had bartizans, some of two storeys, and three staircases turrets had respectively an ogival-shaped helm-roof, a lofty conical roof, and a flat roof with a balustrade (the latter stair survives but without the balustade). By this time Huntly Castle had been wrecked during the Covenant Wars and the Marquis of Huntly made this palace his main seat. Montrose and his army were here in 1645, on which occasion his teenage son John Graham died.

Alexander, 4th Duke of Gordon, commissioned John Baxter of Edinburgh to replace all but the old tower with a huge new building with a frontage 170m long. Here Duchess Jane dazzled high society for several decades. Her son George became 5th Duke, but in 1836 this title died with him, when the estates passed to his maternal nephew the 5th Duke of Richmond and Lennox. The title Duke of Gordon was revived for the son of the latter in 1876. Much of the estate was sold to the Crown in 1938 and the mansion itself was used by the army until 1948. By then water damage had so affected the main block and west wing that Sir George Gordon Lennox had them demolished in 1953, the stone being used for the dam of the Glenlatterach Reservoir.

This left the old tower, later restored, the east wing, and the stables, laundry, and other estate buildings which now form a residence of more practical size. The east wing contains a notable octagonal room which has become a shrine hung with the company colours of the Grenadier Guards, with which Sir George and his sons served.

Gordon Castle as it was in the 17th century.

GORDONSTOUN   NJ 184690

Originally called Bog of Plewlands, this was the seat of the barony of Ogston held by the family of that name, the earliest recorded member of which, Simon, died in 1240. The Ogstons sold the estate in 1473 to the Innes family, who were here for seven generations before selling it to the Marquis of Huntly in 1616. Shortly before or after the sale a new house was built and by 1636 the Marquis had added wings with bartizans and unusual hipped roofs. In 1638 the 2nd Marquis sold Plewlands to his cousin Sir Robert Gordon, son of the 11th Earl of Sutherland. The estate then became the barony of Gordonstoun. His son Sir Ludovick drained the marshy Bog o' Plewlands into the small lake in the grounds. The next laird was Sir Robert, known as The Wizard for his scientific experiments and inventions and his tendency to work by night rather than day. It was he who in c1690 added the Round Square, a stable block in the form of a supposed magic circle. His son, known as the "ill Sir Robert", noted for his smuggling activities, remodelled the main block in 1730. There are now balustrades at the top, perhaps of the 1770s. This part was damaged by fire during the Second World War but still retains its original vaults. Gordonstoun passed to the Cummings of Altyre after the "ill Sir Robert" died. In 1934 Dr Kurt Hahn took over the property for a new type of residential educational establishment which both the Duke of Edinburgh and the Prince of Wales attended.

GRANGEHILL   NJ 003585

The estate of Dalvey between Brodie and Forres was originally the barony of Grangehill. All that remains of a Dunbar castle are a walled garden and a gabled 17th century dovecot. The Grants of Dalvey on Speyside eventually acquired the estate and changed its name, the mansion of 1750 being built by Sir Alexander, 5th baronet.

INALTRIE   NJ 518631

Above the Deskford Burn 4km south of Cullen is a D-shaped platform measuring about 30m across the straight south side by 45m the other way. Occupying the western part of the straight side was a building about 17m long of which the defaced lower part of the 1.7m thick south wall survives together with stumps of the thinner end walls. There are two recesses on the inner side and on the outer side 2.2m from the SW corner is part of a projecting latrine turret. The castle belonged to the Ogilvies.

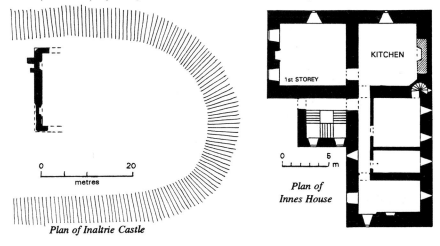

0   20
metres

Plan of Inaltrie Castle

KITCHEN

1st STOREY

0   5
m

Plan of
Innes House

INCHDREWER   NJ 656607

Inchdrewer belonged to the Barclays of Tower and passed to the Lindsay Earl of Crawford in 1414. Later it passed to another family from whom Sir Walter Ogilvie of Deskford or his son purchased it in the late 16th century. The L-plan tower was then built as a seat for the eldest son, the father having his main seat at Boyne. One of this family was created Lord Banff in 1642 and made Inchdrewer his chief residence. On the night of Friday 13th January 1713 George, 3rd Lord Banff, after attending his son's wedding and subsequent festivities for some months in Edinburgh, unexpectedly returned to the castle. Three men, two of them local farmers, were charged with murdering Lord Banff that night and setting the castle on fire to conceal the crime. They were acquitted because the principal witness, the housekeeper Elizabeth Porter, the only other occupant of the castle, had fled to Ireland. The main buildings were still entire when the 8th Lord died in 1803 and it passed to the Abdercrobies of Birkenbog, and there were decayed partial roofs when they were drawn c1880 by MacGibbon & Ross. In the 1960s these parts were re-roofed and the stonework much restored after being purchased by the English Richmond Herald, Robin Mirrlees. His name appears on a stone on an outbuilding with the date 1971. The internal fitting out was never finished or services connected and the castle still lies empty and derelict.

The castle lies amidst flat open fields 4.5km SW of Banff. It consists of an L-plan tower with a wing 6.2m wide projecting 3.4m from the south side of a main block 10.5m long by 6.2m wide. The original entrance lies in the re-entrant angle. The passage seems to have been treated as a sort of internal porch with an inner door and outer yett, being commanded from above by a machicolation slot and from the side by a loop off a passage leading past a cellar to a kitchen with its fireplace in the west end wall. Originally the wing contained a wide staircase rising up over a porter's room or prison to the hall but at a slightly later date a staircase in a round turret rising the full height of the building was added against the east side of the wing. A new roll-moulded entrance doorway was inserted in the south wall of the wing and what was originally a landing at the top of the main stair then became part of the hall. A squinch arch carries a narrow turret stair of the re-entrant angle which originally served all the upper rooms but subsequently only gave access to bedrooms at the west end. In the aborted restoration the third storey was being divided into three bedrooms each with its own bathroom. There is a further suite of three rooms at the top, and from the topmost room in the wing there is access onto a lookout platform formed on the top of the staircase turret and the adjoining part of the wing. There is a conical roofed bartizan on the NE corner and on the NW corner is a round turret rising the full height of the building and containing small round closets off the three upper storeys.

Inchdrewer Castle

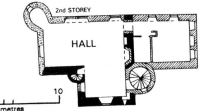

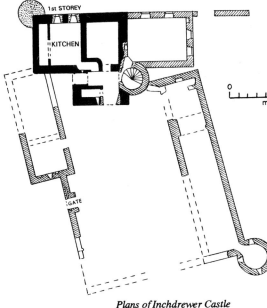

In the 18th century the tower was extended eastward by a two storey block. A court about 16m wide extends 18m southwards from the wing of the tower. The wall on the south side probably containing the main gate has gone except for a SE corner tower 3.8m in diameter with triple shot-holes. There are remains of an east range which probably contained a gallery over a bakehouse and brewhouse. On the west side of the court is a side gate to a former garden. Between it and the tower was another outbuilding.

Plans of Inchdrewer Castle

INNES   NJ 278649   G

This is a remarkable specimen of a domestic rather than a castellated house of the Covenant period, having been built between 1640 and 1653 by Sir Robert Innes, 20th chief of that Ilk, who in 1650 welcomed (after a fashion) Charles II to Garmouth. In a previous house or castle here the 12th chief entertained James III. The 15th chief was a noted reformer while the 17th resigned the chiefship to a kinsman Innes of Crombie, which led to a disastrous family feud. A descendant of the 20th chief succeeded to the Dukedom of Roxburghe in 1805 although by that time Innes House had been sold to the Duff 2nd Earl of Fife. It now belongs to the Tennant family.

Very complete records of expenditure on building the house survive. They show that the workmen were paid mostly in victuals and that the master mason was William Aytoun, designer of Heriot's Hospital near Edinburgh which also had diagonally placed chimney stacks like those at Innes. The building is similar in plan to Leslie Castle built in 1661 and has a four storey main block 22.5 long by 9m wide with a wing 9m wide projecting 8m. In the re-entrant angle is a five storey square turret containing a scale-and-platt staircase rising the full height of the building and ending in a balustrade. A turret stair leads to rooms at the very top of it and the flat roof. At ground level the main block contains a kitchen, a wine cellar with a service stair, and two other cellars, plus what was probably an office in the wing. Externally the building is distinguished from most Scottish houses of its period by the provision of sloping gables with corner finials, square chimney stacks set diagonally, string courses marking the position of the floors, and triangular and semi-circular pediments over the windows. Considerable additions and alterations have been made inside and at the back but a semi-circular single storey porch later added in front of the entrance has been removed so that this side retains its original aspect. See page 185.

KININVIE NJ 319441

John Stewart, 3rd Earl of Atholl granted Kininvie to Alexander Leslie in 1521. The 7th laird, another Alexander, made over the estate to his brother James in 1718 and then became a Jesuit priest, the Leslies being Catholics. A heraldic panel records repairs carried out by James in 1726. The original 16th century tower has four storeys with the highest partly in the roof and has round corners squared off just below the eaves and a gunloops in the basement. A shot-hole commanding the entrance is square shaped, set

Kininvie House

diagonally. A round staircase turret on the east side with a square caphouse now lies in a re-entrant angle between the tower and a late 18th century three storey wing. This wing was baronialised and a new wing added beyond in 1842.

KINMAICHLIE NJ 181321

This yellow-washed early 17th century T-plan house above the Avon serves as a farmhouse. The barony of Kinmaichlie was retained by the Stewarts when in the 15th century the Wolf of Badenoch's grandson sold most of the Inveravon domain to the Gordons. It is now part of the Ballindalloch estate, having been purchased by the Grants in the 18th century. The long main block has been lowered by the Grants but still has three storeys. On one corner is a base corbel in the shape of a mask which once supported a bartizan. Over the stair a gabled caphouse is corbelled out level with the main roof.

KINNAIRDY NJ 609498

This 15th century tower above the east side of the Burn of Achintoul close to its confluence with the Deveron was the seat of the Thaneage and barony of Aberchirder. The hall in the tower has a fine oak-panelled aumbry dated 1493 with heads representing Sir Alexander Innes, 13th chief of that Ilk (he was given Kinnairdy by his father in 1487), and his wife Dame Christian Dunbar. Described as "an misguided man and prodigious" who "wastit and destroyit his lands and guids without ony reasonable occasion" Sir Alexander was shut up by his relatives in Girnigoe Castle in Caithness. The tower was sold to Crichton of Frendraught in the early 17th century and in 1647 sold again to the Reverend John Gregory. He was succeeded by his brother David, a medic and inventor who produced the first barometer here. He had 29 children, three of whom became professors (the Gregories as a whole produced 12 professors in Scottish and English universities), and died in 1720 aged 95. In the 20th century the tower was restored after being sold to Sir Thomas Innes of Learney, Lord Lyon King of Arms. The tower originally had battlements but in a remodelling c1600 these were replaced by a new gabled roof containing a more spacious attic than before. The original parapet corbels were re-used as crowsteps on the gables. Of the same period is the stair turret at the west end with a typical gabled caphouse of that era. The existing windows are larger than the 15th century originals. The vaulted basement is so lofty that there was probably once an intermediate floor to provide a sleeping loft.

2nd STOREY

1st STOREY

0 ⊢—⊢—⊢—⊢—⊢—⊢—⊢—⊢—⊢—⊢—⊢ 10
metres

Lethendry: plans

Kinnairdy Castle

LETHENDRY   NJ 084274

Behind a farm steading above the Haughs of Cromdale are remains of a round-cornered 16th century tower built by the Grants. Jacobite fugitives fled to the castle after the battle nearby to the east in 1690. A wing 4.1m wide projects 2.7m from the north side of a block 11.4m long by 7.1m wide over walls 1.5m thick. The wing contained the entrance and main stair up to a hall, now very ruined, over two vaulted cellars. At the higher levels, now destroyed, the wing no doubt contained bedrooms. The only remaining feature of the hall is what appears to be a fireplace in the east wall.

LETTERFOURIE   NJ 447625

Letterfourie is still owned by a branch of the Gordons given a baronetcy in 1625 and descended from a younger son of the 2nd Earl of Huntly. The large mansion with ornamental gardens dates mostly from 1776 although older work may survive within it. It lies on the slopes of Aultmore near the Buckie Burn.

LEUCHARS   NJ 260649

Built into the Regency front of Leuchars House above the east side of the Lossie NW of Elgin is a stone with the Innes arms and the date 1583 from a tower on this site. A gabled dovecot corbelled out to a square from a round base was destroyed by vandals c1970. The only other dovecot of this type was at Auchmacoy in Buchan.

LOCHINDORB   NH 974364

This castle lies on an island which is at least partly artificial close to the east shore of a remotely sited loch. It was built by the Comyn lords of Badenoch in the late 13th century and consists of a quadrangular court about 48m by 38m enclosed by a wall 2m thick and 6m high with a wall-walk on top. There is a simple archway 2.7m wide in the east wall and at each corner is a rather more thinly walled round tower 7m in diameter. The western towers are mere half-rounds of shallow projection. There are latrines in the curtain beside the northern towers. There appears to have been a range of domestic buildings, probably of wood, on the south side. Edward I took the castle over from the Comyns in 1303 and stayed in it for nine days of hunting. He is thought to have ordered the construction of the outer court to the SE and south to deny an enemy a footing on the island. The only feature of this court is its gateway with a portcullis groove on the south side. There is no means of access between the courts.

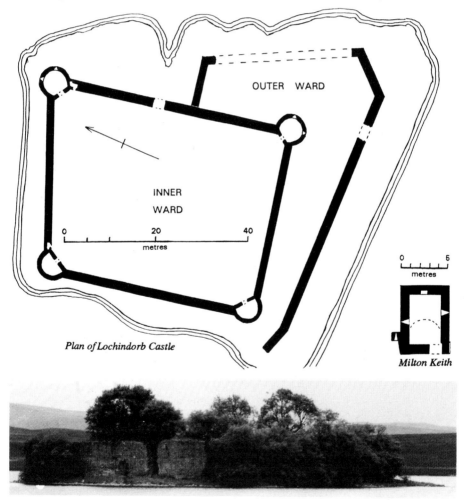

Plan of Lochindorb Castle

OUTER   WARD

INNER WARD

0   20   40
metres

0   5
metres

Milton Keith

Lochindorb Castle

Lochindorb was eventually captured from the English by the Bruces and seems to have been maintained rather that slighted as was his usual policy. During the period of David II's temporary exile in France in the 1330s the castle held an English garrison which successfully held out against attacks by successive regents. After the Earl of Atholl was killed in battle at Culblean by the Regent Sir Andrew de Moravia, the Countess of Atholl took refuge in the castle. A siege was raised when Edward III of England came up to her rescue. Robert II gave the castle to his third son Alexander Stewart, Lord of Badenoch and Earl of Buchan. He had several seats but Lochindorb seems to have been his favourite haunt. From it he swooped down on the settled lands around the Moray Firth, burning, slaying and looting at will. The name Lochindorb indeed means Loch of Trouble. Lochindorb was later held by Archibald Douglas, Earl of Moray, and after his forfeiture in 1455 the Scottish Privy Council instructed the Thane of Cawdor to dismantle the castle. Although its present state and its recorded state in 1793 when all four corner towers were still fairly intact suggests that little damage was done to the stonework, the timbers and other fittings were removed and the yett from the main entrance re-used at Cawdor, where it still remains.

MAYEN   NJ 576477

The existing Mayen House on the north side of a wide southern sweep of the Deveron is only of 1788 but not far away near the B9117 is its predecessor built in 1608 now called Mains of Mayen. Recently restored, it is a block of three compartments on each of two storeys. The upper storey middle compartment has a large fireplace with a salt-box and the southern compartment on the lower storey incorporates what is thought to be the thick west wall of an earlier tower with a latrine within it. The building has a round stair turret, crowstepped gables, and dormer windows. Over the moulded doorway is a coloured heraldic panel with the date 1680 and the arms of the Abernethys and Halketts. In the late 14th century David II gave Mayen to William de Abercromby, whose descendant Laurence Abernethy became Lord Saltoun in 1445. Mayen passed to the Gordons in 1612 and was sold in 1649 to William Halkett, Sheriff Clerk of Banff. It was returned to the Abernethys when one of them married his heiress. Possession of the estate was disputed in the courts in 1683-91 but the Abernethys held onto Mayen until they shot Leith of Leith Hall at an election meeting in the mid 18th century and were forfeited. The property then went to the Duffs, kinsmen of the last laird's wife, who built the new mansion.

MILTON KEITH   NJ 429512   F

In a low lying position beside the Isla on the north side of Keith lies a small four storey building, once part of a much larger house. It measures 7.2m by 5.3m and has a vaulted cellar with two loops. Wall stubs adjoin the western corners and there is a big fireplace which served a second storey room to the south, and smaller fireplaces above. Built into the gable of an entrance lodge of the Strathisla-Glenlivet Distillery are two stones from the house. One has heraldry and the date 1695 and the other a coronet and the intials L.M.O. The present ruin is probably late 16th century but a castle was built here by George Ogilvie c1480 after he obtained the estate of Drumnakeith by marrying a daughter of the Earl of Huntly. From this branch of the family came the Jesuit priest John Ogilvie martyred at Glasgow Cross in 1615, and another John Ogilvie slain fighting for Montrose at Alford in 1645. The house was repaired by Margaret Ogilvie in 1601, and in 1707 it passed by marriage to the 7th Lord Oliphant who was forfeited after the 1715 rebellion. The initials could refer to either of these. Abandoned in 1829, the house became a quarry for the townsfolk. See plan and photograph overleaf.

Milton Keith

Moy House

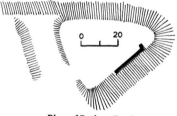

Plan of Rothes Castle

MULBEN NJ 353512

Much of the House of Mulben above the Mulben Burn is of 1696 and the 19th century but the eastern part was once a lofty late 16th or early 17th century house. On the east gable are two former dormer window pediments, one dated 1696 with the Grant arms and the other with the monogram of Ludovick Grant and his wife. Mulben passed by marriage from the Comyns (or Cummings) in 1506 to the Grants of Freuchie. John Grant of Mulben was knighted for his services against the rebel Gordons in 1592, being on the losing side at the fight at Glenlivet. After his succession as the Grant chief, the Mulben estate was erected into a barony in 1616. It was his grandson Ludovick who built much of the present building, possibly to replace another Grant castle nearby at Balnabreich, destroyed by the Jacobites in 1689. Although the Grant Earl of Seafield still owns much of the surrounding land, since 1888 Mulben itself has been owned by the Macphersons, famous as breeders of Aberdeen-Angus cattle.

MOY NJ 016599

The main block with moulded and chamfered window surrounds is partly the work of Sir Ludovick Grant in the 1690s, but vaulted cellars probably of the period 1590-1640 are incorporated. Some of the extensions are of 1762, when Moy was held by Major George Grant. He was cashiered from George III's army for surrendering Inverness too easily to the Jacobites in 1745.

PARK NJ 587571

Park was a Gordon estate from the 15th century until Sir William Gordon was forfeited for his part in the 1745 rebellion. It then went to his wife Jean's family the Duffs. It now serves as holiday flats. Originally a late 16th century Z-plan house with rectangular wings projecting NE and SW from a main block aligned north-south, the building was much extended and altered in 1829. In the SW wing is a moulded and arched entrance doorway, now a window, with a panel above with the Gordon arms. A corbelled out stair turret gives access from the hall over two vaulted cellars to the third storey bedrooms. Originally there must have been a second such stair.

ROTHES NJ 277490 F

In 1390 a younger son of Leslie of Balquhain obtained the barony of Glenrothes by marrying the heiress of the Pollock family. George Leslie was created Earl of Rothes by James II in 1457. A later Earl was killed along with James IV at Flodden in 1513, and the 7th Earl carried the Sword of State at Charles II's coronation at Scone in 1651. This Earl was created a Duke in 1680 but that honour died with him. His daughter's son by the Earl of Haddington became Earl of Rothes. This line owned the site, now a public recreation space, until the 20th century. The castle lies on a spur above the town and has a shallow ditch 23m wide dividing it from higher ground to the west. It comprised a roughly triangular court extending to a point 50m from the 36m long west side. On the SE side is a 20m long section of walling 1.3m thick above a battered plinth and 6m high above the court. At the east end is a fragment of a return wall 2.1m thick above a plinth. Both this part and the other broken end have jambs of windows. That at the east had a pointed head with numerous voussoirs which suggests that the wall may have existed when Edward I was at Rothes in 1296.

Park House

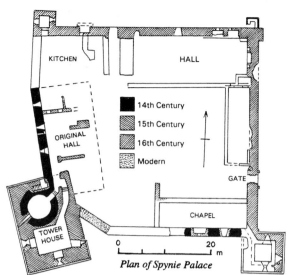

KITCHEN

HALL

■ 14th Century

▨ 15th Century

▧ 16th Century

⬚ Modern

ORIGINAL HALL

GATE

CHAPEL

TOWER HOUSE

0   20
|_____|_____|
        m

Plan of Spynie Palace

Rothes Castle

ROTHIEMAY NJ 554484

Rothiemay was held by the Earl of Atholl at the time of his defeat and death at Culblean in 1335. It the 15th and 16th centuries it was a seat of the Abernethys, one of whom was killed at the battle of Harlaw in 1411. At about the time of a peerage as Lord Saltoun being granted in 1445 they built a palace block with a hall and chamber end to end over a series of vaulted basement rooms. A long south wing was later added and this was later embellished and further extended into an 18th and 19th century mansion. The castle is shown on Hardyng's map of Scotland of c1465 and in documents of the following two centuries it is variously described as a castle, fortalice, tower, tower and fortalice, house and fortalice, place, and finally house.

In 1562 Alexander Abernethy, 6th Lord Saltoun, was host here to Queen Mary for a night during her campaign against the Gordons. His lands were dangerously near the Gordon powerbase at Huntly and in 1568 he and other northern barons reported to the Privy Council of the infant James VI that "thair landos, rowmes and possessionis wer and ar in utter perrell and dangeit to be invaidot and persewit with fyre, swerd, and all uther kynd of hostilities by George, Earl of Huntlie, his assistaris and complices". Ten years later Lord Saltoun had in his charge at Rothiemay the Border reiver Archie Batie, who to his embarrassment managed to escape. In 1612 the 8th Lord Saltoun sold Rothiemay to Sir James Stewart of Killeith, later Lord Ochiltree, who in 1617 sold it to John Gordon of Cairnburrow. The latter made it over to his son William. In 1618 Patrick Livingstone of Inchcorse took refuge at Rothiemay from George Gordon of Gight after a quarrel over the will of Dame Margaret Stewart, Lady Saltoun. Gordon of Gight just failed to capture Livingstone by surprise ourside the house and after a complaint was made to the Privy Council was imprisoned in Edinburgh Castle.

William Gordon of Rothiemay was one of those burnt to death in the mysterious fire at the neighbouring Crichton seat of Frendraught in 1630. His widow engaged a party of wild Highlanders to make "daylie incursions against Frendret, and kill some of his men", although it is clear that they also on occasion maltreated their employer. The Sheriff of Banff drove out the Highlanders from Rothiemay and returned shortly afterwards to displace a party of troublesome Gordons. He garrisoned the house with "powder, bullet, and 24 souldiours" and removed Lady Rothiemay off to Edinburgh for trial by the Privy Council. She was imprisoned there from April 1635 until February 1637 when Charles I ordered the council to terminate her trial and set her free on sufficient sureties.

Rothiemay was captured by Montrose from a Covenant garrison in October 1644. In August 1651 it was taken over and held for some years by Cromwellian troops. The Rothiemay Gordons got into debt and in 1712 sold the estate to Lord Boyne's son Archibald Ogilvie. In 1741 it was acquired by William Duff, Lord Braco, later Earl of Fife. he lived there with his large family for many years and made some of the additions. The Forbes family purchased the estate in 1890 from the Duffs. In 1960 they pulled down the mansion and replaced it with a much more modest house incorporated in which are ancient fragments including a doorway, and an iron grille over a lower window, whilst an heraldic stone lies reside the entrance doorway.

SPYNIE   NJ 231658   HS

The cathedral of Moray stood here until removed to Elgin in 1224. However the Bishops continued to live in a palace by the SW end of the loch with beside it a harbour and a village which was made a burgh of barony in 1451 for Bishop Winchester. The loch was reduced to its present size when drained by Telford's canal of 1808. The palace is assumed to have been burnt along with the town and cathedral of Elgin in 1390 although there is no work obviously of the period immediately afterwards as might be expected. Bishop David Stewart's problems with the Earl of Huntly in the 1460s prompted him to build a huge new tower house at Spynie as a refuge. The tower bears his arms, plus those of William Tulloch, Bishop 1477-82, and Patrick Hepburn, Bishop 1535-73, and the Royal Arms, all added by Bishop Hepburn.
   James II visited his friend Bishop Winchester at Spynie twice, and James IV came in 1493 and 1505. Queen Mary stayed at Spynie shortly before her forces defeated the Gordons at Corrichie. In 1566 Bishop Hepburn had custody of the English agent Ruxby who was involved in a plot by Queen Elizabeth intended to compromise her cousin Queen Mary. In 1567 he briefly sheltered his kinsman, Patrick, Earl of Bothwell, Queen Mary's discredited third husband who was then fleeing from his many enemies. In the early 1570s the Bishop found himself on the same side as the Gordons in their fight against the allies of the Protestant regency and he had custody at Spynie of their prisoner the Master of Forbes. The Bishopric was in this period officially abolished, although Hepburn managed to retain control of the lands and revenues. After he died Spynie became a secular barony eventually granted by James VI to his favourite Alexander Lindsey, created Lord Spynie. However the palace and lands were handed back later so that James could restore the Bishopric.

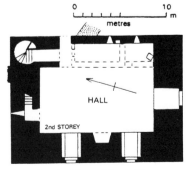

Spynie: Plan of Tower House

Gateway, Spynie Palace

John Gordon, Bishop at the time of the signing of the National Covenant, was declared deposed and excommunicated by the General Assembly. He retired to Spynie Palace and stocked it with provisions and arms ready for a long siege. However in July 1640 General George Munro somehow got hold of the Bishop and his family by easier means than attacking Spynie and they ended up as prisoners in Edinburgh Tolbooth. A Covenant garrison then installed at Spynie was besieged in 1645 by a force 2,000 strong led by the Earl of Huntly, but General Middleton came to its relief and Huntly was forced to retire "steeped in disgrace". Bishops were reinstated under Charles II but after Bishop Colin Falconer died in 1688 the palace was allowed to decay until the present recent schedule of repairs by the Scottish Office, now Historic Scotland.

The palace courtyard measures about 45m from east to west and 40m from north to south within walls up to 2m thick. The south side with traces of a gateway, the west side, and the recently rebuilt SW wall are 14th century work. The original hall lay on the west side where there are fragments of later crosswalls. A large new hall 10m wide by about 26m long raised over an undercroft below courtyard level was provided on the north side c1500, when the outer walls on the east and north of the court were rebuilt. Recent clearance of the undercroft has revealed a well in the NW corner. West of the hall block was a passage to a watergate and beyond that a kitchen and service area. At the west end of the north walls is a small tower and there is a broken down latrine turret at the NE corner. More impressive is the boldly projecting tower 7.5m square above a battered plinth added to the SE corner. The two sides still standing high show that there were four upper storeys over a thickly walled low basement in which Bishop Hepburn inserted two wide splayed gunports. A range of this period against the south wall contained a chapel on the second storey where several fine traceried windows remain and there is thought to have been a gallery on the north side. The gateway was blocked by this range and a new gate was made in the east wall. It has buttresses bearing square bartizans set at forty-five degrees to the main wall with a row of machicolation slots between them.

Tor Castle   *Tower House, Spynie Palace*

Tor Castle: plan

Hall block at Spynie Palace

The tower house at the SW corner measures 18.8m by 13.4m above a double chamfered plinth and rises 22.5m to the wall-walk. Corbels and corbelled courses supported now-destroyed machicolated parapets with angle rounds within which was a gabled attic. The tower basement has a doorway on the north side from which passages lead to a circular dungeon which is actually the basement of a 14th century round tower about 9m in diameter and a rectangular room which Patrick Hepburn later provided with two widely splayed gunports. The hall above communicates with the cellar only by means of a hatch in the floor of a mural room set above the embrasure of a loop flanking the south wall of the court. A stair also leads down to a postern on the north side outside the curtain wall. The hall has two windows with seats in the embrasures and a fireplace between them in the west wall. Above a third window in the south wall are the added heraldic panels already mentioned. A spiral stair in the NE corner rises to the upper storeys, battlements and the wall-walk on the west curtain. The wall-walk on the south curtain was probably reached from a wooden platform at the head of steps up from the court to an entrance into the hall beside the base of the stair. Within the east wall at each upper level were vaulted mural rooms just large enough to take a bed. The inner walls and vaults have collapsed leaving a thin outer wall which although relatively secure from bombardment by an enemy has nevertheless proved insecure in recent years, necessitating considerable repairs and the re-instatement of the vanished adjacent section of the curtain to act as a buttress.

TOR NJ 125530

In a field north of Dallas village is a single fragment of a tower 13m long by 9.6m wide over walls 2.2m thick supposedly built in 1400 by Sir Thomas Comyn or Cumming of Altyre. Originally it was protected by marshland and probably also a water filled moat.

WESTER ELCHIES NJ 256431

This estate above the north side of the Spey west of Charlestown of Aberlour passed in 1565 from the bishopric of Moray to James Grant, a cadet of Freuchie. A domestic looking three storey L-plan house with a few shot-holes was built in the early 17th century incorporating what appears to be a thick west wall of an earlier tower. A further wing and a round stair turret were added later to make a Z-plan. In the 18th century Wester Elchies passed to the Grants of Ballindalloch, one of whom founded the town opposite bearing his name in 1812. The building was extended later. By the 1970s it was empty and very decayed and was entirely pulled down.

OTHER CASTLES AND HOUSES IN BANFF AND MORAY

AIKENWAY NJ 292508 Site only in sharp bend of Spey 2km NE of Rothes. Alternate name Oakenwalls suggests an earthwork with timber defences and buildings.

AUCHAYNANIE NJ 454495 A Gordon tower with bartizans survived until c1910.

AUCHENTOUL NJ 615523 One three storey wing and round tower with shot-holes plus a big walled garden remain of an E-plan house like Haddo & Birkenbog.

BALNABREICH NJ 343502 Vanished Grant castle destroyed by Dundee in 1689.

BIRKENBOG NJ 536651 Timothy Pont's map c1590 shows E-shaped house here.

BUCHRAGIE NJ 657648 Former Ogilvy castle near crossroads of B9121 and B9139.

CULLYKHAN NJ 837662 Slight traces of early castle on Castle Hill. Seat of Hamelin de Troup who complained to Edward I about Roger Cheyne and Duncan Frendraught.

EDINGIGHT NJ 564557 Two storey late 16th century house of John Innes, extended in 1615. Overmantle dated 1681. Restored 1955 for Innes Lord Lyon King of Arms.

FORRES NJ 035587 Castlehill Park marks site of an early royal castle in loop of Mosset Burn. Old drawing suggests a motte with a polygonal shell wall on top.

GRANGE NJ 481515 Church of 1795 on site of moated manor house or castle.

INVERHARROCH NJ 380310 Vanished Gordon castle by upper reaches of Deveron.

INVERUGIE NJ 152685 A castle of the Keiths stood near the present mansion.

KINNEDDAR NJ 223695 Barony and castle of Bishops of Moray. Cairn in field north of graveyard marks the site of the castle.

LOGIE NJ 006508 Whitewashed mansion possibly incorporating 17th century work, supposedly on site of a Comyn castle.

MONTBLAIRY NJ 689584 Vanished Comyn motte above west side of the Deveron.

PITGAIR NJ 764587 Slight tumbled fragments of a tower of uncertain date on spur above a burn 5km SW of Gardenstown.

PORTSOY NJ 585660 Castle Brae marks the approximate site of house of Sir William Ogilvie for whom Portsoy was created a burgh of barony in 1550.

QUARRYWOOD NJ 183642 A 16th century dovecot alone remains.

VANISHED CASTLES: Earnside NJ 110621, Findrassie NJ 195651, Hempriggs NJ 103637, Rathven NJ 444655, Skeith NJ 504603, Tronach NJ 477688

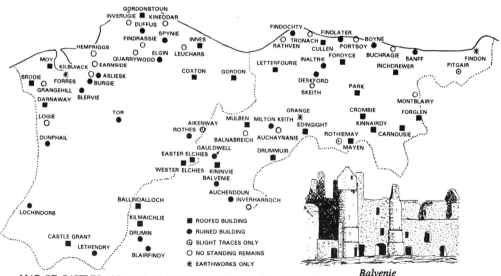

MAP OF CASTLES AND OLD MANSIONS IN BANFF AND MORAY

Balvenie

A GLOSSARY OF TERMS

Angle-Rounds	- Round open bartizans at the corners of a wall-walk.
Ashlar	- Masonry of blocks with even faces and square edges.
Attic	- A top storey used for servants or storage within a gabled roof.
Aumbry	- A recess or cupboard for storage.
Bailey	- A defensible space enclosed by a wall or palisade and a ditch.
Barbican	- A building or enclosure defending a castle entrance.
Bartizan	- A turret corbelled out from a wall, usually at the summit.
Caphouse	- Small square gabled space over a staircase or round projection.
Cateran	- A brigand or marauder living in the Scottish Highlands.
Corbel	- A projecting bracket supporting other stonework or timbers.
Crannog	- A small artificial island occupied as a dwelling.
Crow Steps	- Squared stones forming steps upon a gable.
Curtain Wall	- A high enclosing stone wall around a bailey.
Dormer Window	- A window standing up vertically from the slope of a roof.
Entresol	- A level intermediate between the main floors of a building.
Gunloop	- An opening for firearms with an external splay. See also shot-hole.
Harling	- Or Roughcast. Plaster with gravel or other coarse aggregate.
Hood Mould	- A projecting moulding above an arch or lintel to throw off water.
Jamb	- The side of a doorway, window, or other opening.
Keep	- A citadel or ultimate strongpoint. Originally called a donjon.
Light	- A compartment of a window.
Loop	- A small opening to admit light or for the discharge of missiles.
Machicolation	- A slot for dropping stones or shooting missiles at assailants.
Moat	- A ditch, water filled or dry, around an enclosure.
Motte	- A steeply sided flat topped mound, usually mostly man-made.
Moulding	- An ornament of continuous section.
Mullion	- A vertical member dividing the lights of a window.
Ogival Arch	- An arch of oriental origin with both convex and concave curves.
Oriel	- A bay window projecting out from a wall above ground level.
Palace	- An old Scottish term for a two storey hall block.
Parapet	- A wall for protection at any sudden drop.
Pediment	- A small gable over a doorway or window, especially a dormer.
Pit Prison	- A dark prison only reached by a hatch in a vault.
Plinth	- The projecting base of a wall. It may be battered or stepped.
Portcullis	- A wooden gate designed to rise and fall in vertical grooves.
Postern	- A secondary gateway or doorway. A back entrance.
Quoin	- Dressed (i.e. carefully shaped) stone at a corner of a building.
Ravelin	- An outwork with two embankments meeting at a sharp angle.
Rebate	- Rectangular section cut out of a masonry edge usually for a door.
Redent	- A step in an outer splay of a gunloop to reflect incoming bullets.
Rib Vault	- A vault supported by ribs or decorated with them.
Scale-and-platt Staircase	- Staircase with short straight flights and turns at landings.
Skewputt	- Bottom bracket of a gable upstanding above a roof.
Shot-hole	- A small round hole in an outer wall face for discharging firearms.
Solar	- The lord's private room, doubling as a bed-chamber.
Tower House	- Self contained house with the main rooms stacked vertically.
Wall-walk	- A walkway on top of a wall, protected by a parapet.
Ward	- A stone walled defensive enclosure.
Yett	- A strong hinged gate made of interwoven iron bars.

INDEX